Global Democracy and Exclusion

♨METAPHILOSOPHY

METAPHILOSOPHY SERIES IN PHILOSOPHY

Series Editors Armen T. Marsoobian, Brian J. Huschle,
and Eric Cavallero

The Philosophy of Interpretation, edited by Joseph Margolis and Tom
Rockmore (2000)
Global Justice, edited by Thomas W. Pogge (2001)
Cyberphilosophy: The Intersection of Computing and Philosophy, edited by
James H. Moor and Terrell Ward Bynum (2002)
Moral and Epistemic Virtues, edited by Michael Brady and Duncan
Pritchard (2003)
The Range of Pragmatism and the Limits of Philosophy, edited by Richard
Shusterman (2004)
The Philosophical Challenge of September 11, edited by Tom Rockmore,
Joseph Margolis, and Armen T. Marsoobian (2005)
Global Institutions and Responsibilities: Achieving Global Justice, edited
by Christian Barry and Thomas W. Pogge (2005)
Genocide's Aftermath: Responsibility and Repair, edited by Claudia Card
and Armen T. Marsoobian (2007)
Stem Cell Research: The Ethical Issues, edited by Lori Gruen, Laura
Grabel, and Peter Singer (2007)
Cognitive Disability and Its Challenge to Moral Philosophy, edited by Eva
Feder Kittay and Licia Carlson (2010)
Virtue and Vice, Moral and Epistemic, edited by Heather Battaly (2010)
Global Democracy and Exclusion, edited by Ronald Tinnevelt and Helder
De Schutter (2010)

Global Democracy and Exclusion

Edited by

Ronald Tinnevelt and Helder De Schutter

WILEY-BLACKWELL

A John Wiley & Sons, Ltd., Publication

CONTENTS

NOTES ON CONTRIBUTORS

Eric Cavallero has taught at Yale and the University of Arizona, and is currently assistant professor of philosophy at Southern Connecticut State University and associate editor of *Metaphilosophy*. His research has been supported by the Center for Ethics and Public Affairs at Tulane and by the Harvard Program in Ethics and Health. His articles have appeared in *Legal Theory*, *Philosophy, Politics and Economics*, and the *Journal of Political Philosophy*.

Deen Chatterjee teaches philosophy at the University of Utah and is editor in chief of the forthcoming multivolume *Encyclopedia of Global Justice* and series editor of Studies in Global Justice. His publications include, most recently, *Democracy in a Global World: Human Rights and Political Participation in the 21st Century*.

Campbell Craig is professor of international politics at Aberystwyth University. He is the author or co-author of four books and many other works on the history of American foreign policy during the Cold War; his most recent book, cowritten with Fredrik Logevall, is *America's Cold War: The Politics of Insecurity* (Belknap Press of Harvard University Press). He is currently editing a volume on the nuclear revolution in the post-Cold War world.

Helder De Schutter is assistant professor in social and political philosophy at the Katholieke Universiteit Leuven. He works on the normative foundations of language policy, nationalism, and federalism. He has published in a number of journals, including *Inquiry, Journal of Applied Philosophy, Critical Review of International Social and Political Philosophy, Ethical Perspectives, Language Problems and Language Planning*, and *Algemeen Nederlands Tijdschrift voor Wijsbegeerte*. In 2008–2009 he was a visiting research fellow at Oxford's Centre for Social Justice and Nuffield College.

John Exdell is associate professor of philosophy at Kansas State University. His recent research is on racial justice issues, with a focus on the connection between American racial politics and the principle of justice as desert. He is also writing on the idea of humanitarian military intervention proposed by some liberal philosophers as a needed revision in traditional just-war theory and international law.

Robert Fine is professor of sociology at the University of Warwick, where he is active in the M.A. Programme in Social and Political Thought and the Social Theory Centre. He co-convenes the European Sociological Association Network on Racism and Antisemitism. His most recent books are *Cosmopolitanism* (Routledge, 2007), *Democracy and the Rule of Law: Marx's Critique of the Legal Form* (Blackburn, 2002), and *Political Investigations: Hegel, Marx and Arendt* (Routledge, 2001). His current research is on understanding antisemitism.

Andreas Føllesdal (Ph.D. Harvard 1991) is professor of political philosophy and director of research at the Norwegian Centre for Human Rights, Faculty of Law, University of Oslo. He publishes in the field of political philosophy, with a focus on issues of international political theory and human rights, particularly as they arise in the wake of changes in Europe. He is the founding editor of the Themes in European Governance series at Cambridge University Press.

Carol C. Gould is professor of philosophy, Hunter College, and professor, Doctoral Programs in Philosophy and Political Science and director of the Center for Global Ethics and Politics, the Graduate Center, City University of New York. She is editor of the *Journal of Social Philosophy* and executive director of the Society for Philosophy and Public Affairs. She is the author of *Marx's Social Ontology, Rethinking Democracy,* and *Globalizing Democracy and Human Rights,* is the editor of seven books, and has published numerous articles in social and political philosophy, philosophy of law, feminist theory, and applied ethics.

Hans Lindahl is professor of legal philosophy at Tilburg University in the Netherlands. His research focuses on issues of political representation, sovereignty, and collective identity, particularly in the context of the E.U. legal order. He has published articles in a wide range of journals and is the editor of the volume *A Right to Inclusion and Exclusion? Normative Fault Lines of the EU's Area of Freedom, Security and Justice* (Hart, 2009).

Raffaele Marchetti is lecturer in International Relations at LUISS University and the University of Naples L'Orientale. His research focuses on international political theory and global politics, and his publications include *Global Democracy: For and Against: Ethical Theory, Institutional Design, and Social Struggles* (Routledge, 2008), *European Union and Global Democracy* (co-editor, CPI, 2009), *Global Democracy: Normative and Empirical Perspectives* (co-editor, Cambridge University Press, forthcoming), and *Civil Society, Ethnic Conflicts, and the Politicization of Human Rights* (co-editor, U.N. University Press, forthcoming).

William E. Scheuerman is professor of political science and West European Studies at Indiana University. He is the author of five books, including (most recently) *Liberal Democracy and the Social Acceleration of Time* (Johns Hopkins, 2004), *Frankfurt School Perspectives on Globalization, Democracy and the Law* (Routledge, 2008), and *Hans J. Morgenthau: Realism and Beyond* (Polity, 2009).

Ronald Tinnevelt is associate professor of legal philosophy at Radboud Universiteit Nijmegen. He is coeditor of *Between Cosmopolitan Ideals and State Sovereignty* (Palgrave, 2006), *Does Truth Matter?* (Springer, 2008), and *Nationalism and Global Justice* (Routledge, 2010), and he was recently awarded a Vidi scholarship from the Netherlands Organisation for Scientific Research (NWO).

Daniel Weinstock holds the Canada Research Chair in Ethics and Political Philosophy at the University of Montreal, where he is also director of the Ethics Research Center. He has written extensively on the management of diversity in liberal democracies, on nationalism and federalism, and on global justice. He is completing a book on the moral and political relationships between children, families, and the state, and is embarking upon a new research project on the political philosophy of cities.

INTRODUCTION:
GLOBAL DEMOCRACY AND EXCLUSION

RONALD TINNEVELT AND HELDER DE SCHUTTER

Questions about the ethical and political significance of boundaries are at the center of the current debate on global justice. Can we take boundaries as inherent for ethical discourse? To what extent do we have duties of cosmopolitan justice? Can we justify severe and extensive global poverty if we strongly support the moral equality of all persons? Is cosmopolitanism at odds with rootedness in a particular culture? Do global political institutions provide the best framework for the protection of basic human rights?

These questions gain in relevance and depth in our globalizing era—an era in which we are witnessing a strong growth of transboundary problems and in which social and political space are "no longer wholly mapped in terms of territorial places, territorial distances and territorial borders" (Scholte 2000, 3).

One of the main consequences of this process of deterritorialization is that we need to rethink our concept of *democracy*. The assumption on which most theories of democracy have been based in the past—a symmetrical relationship between political decision-makers and the recipients of political decisions—has turned out to be naïve (Held 1995, 16). Those who shape global and transnational public policies are not (or not always) accountable to those affected by them. Border-crossing issues like migration flows and global warming attest to the untenability of this assumption.

But what, then, *is* the relevant constituency for these issues? Who is responsible for what, and to whom? Several normative theories and policy models have recently been developed to answer democracy's boundary problem. Whereas some theorists deny the possibility of projecting genuine forms of democracy to the transnational and global level, others argue that democratic decision-making need not necessarily be bound to the territorial borders of sovereign nation-states.

Liberal nationalists and statists are probably the best-known proponents of the first group. David Miller, for example, argues that the challenges that the process of globalization poses to our national democracies don't necessarily call for a widening of the demos or for considering "new ways of constituting the demos" (Miller 2009, 202).

Analogous to the debate concerning the scope of justice, however, other positions within this first group could (in principle) be distinguished. One could claim, for example, that democracy requires a Rawlsian basic structure or a context of reciprocity. Although proponents of these alternatives need not deny that a global basic structure or a global reciprocal context may one day arise, they would argue that in the absence of these contexts global democracy makes no sense.

Enthusiasts of the case for transnational democracy, in contrast, often articulate a version of the "all-affected principle" to deal with the boundary problem. This principle states that whoever is affected by a public decision should be included in the democratic process that makes the decision. This leads to a justification for extending democracy beyond national boundaries, because it is no longer the case in the current world that the decisions of one state only affect citizens from that same state. Many decisions (such as on environmental, terrorism-related, or migration-related issues) affect people living in other states, and the all-affected principle stipulates that those people should be included in the democratic process in which the decision is made. So, depending on the scale and nature of political and socioeconomic problems, the required political solution and the proper scope of the relevant democratic community will differ. Local problems demand local responses and constituencies, whereas global political problems require supranational solutions and will affect a global constituency. Democracy should therefore be at least partly transnational in scope.

Interestingly, while the potentially *inclusive* ideal of the all-affected principle might at first sight be thought logically to lead to a cosmopolitan form of democracy instantiated within the bounds of a *global* people, few adherents of this principle are prepared to draw this conclusion. And indeed, virtually all political theorists today still propose to overcome or deal with the many postnational or globalized features of our present condition through *bounded* political communities, which preserve an explicit link between the principle of democracy on the one hand and either the principle of *national* or the principle of *cultural-political* identity on the other.

Jürgen Habermas, for instance, argues that a political community can only understand itself as a democracy if it can "distinguish between members and non-members" (2001, 107). Similar arguments can be found among a variety of politico-philosophical positions—liberalism, communitarianism, agonism, deliberative democracy, poststructuralism, and so on. At the heart of these arguments is the assumption that collective identity and self-determination imply a distinction between insiders and outsiders, or, as Carl Schmitt (1996) argues, between friends and enemies. Without such a distinction, claims Michael Walzer, "we would have no reason to form and maintain political communities" (1983, 64).[1]

---

[1] For an overview of these arguments, see Abizadeh 2005.

But why does every definition of a "we" imply "the delimitation of a 'frontier' and the designation of a 'them'"? (Mouffe 1993, 84.) Habermas explains the need for exclusion or closure on the basis of the fact that self-legislation necessarily presupposes a "clearly defined self" to which one can ascribe collectively binding decisions (2006, 76). Self-legislation, writes Seyla Benhabib, is always also self-constitution: "'We, the people' who agree to bind ourselves by these laws, are also defining ourselves as a 'we' in the very act of self-legislation. It is not only the general laws of self-government that are articulated in this process; the community that binds itself by these laws defines itself by drawing boundaries as well, and these boundaries are both territorial and civic" (2004, 45).

Within this kind of reasoning, however, the political culture of a world society will always lack the common ethical-political dimension—the social boundary between insiders and outsiders—that is essential for a corresponding democratic global community. The all-affected criterion and the principle of democracy will therefore collide at the highest political level.

The focus of this collection of chapters is on this potential conflict and its underlying values. Does democracy or popular sovereignty imply exclusion and drawing borders? And if so, what type of exclusion and borders, and what kind of justification can we give for them? More important, if democracy really requires some kind of exclusion, is global democracy then a paradoxical union of two contradictory ideals? Can we create a demos on the global level?

The Chapters

To answer these questions, one first needs to know more about the relationship between cosmopolitanism and human rights. Proposals for transnational citizenship and forms of global democracy, after all, are mostly grounded in moral cosmopolitanism and a concern for political agency. In his contribution to this book Robert Fine examines the connection between human rights and cosmopolitanism, and tries to determine whether critics like Costas Douzinas are right to claim that cosmopolitanism contains an idealisation of human rights. Fine specifically focuses on three historical "stages" of cosmopolitanism: the development of Enlightenment cosmopolitanism in the eighteenth century, its effect on the rise of the human sciences, and the human rights revolution of our day.

But what "political arrangement of international society" (Walzer 2003, 171) is capable of guarding against human rights atrocities? According to proponents of the idea of world government, the only possible solution is the creation of some form of international authority. Only an authoritative regime can secure peace and really tackle the global problems that our globalizing world faces. In his chapter Campbell Craig discusses the return of this idea to the domains of international relations theory and international political philosophy. Although the idea of world government has a long history, it has been picked up with renewed vigor by theorists like Alexander Wendt, Daniel Deudney, Otfried Höffe, and Luis Cabrera. Craig, however, reserves the term "world government" not only for the traditional idea of a formal world state but also for a looser system of global governance. David Held's and Daniele Archibugi's models of cosmopolitan democracy can, therefore, also be seen as forms of world government.

Given the intensifying dangers of a system of international anarchy, an important question is which of these two forms "world government" is best able to deal with collective action problems. Craig discusses the advantages of both models and examines whether some of the traditional arguments against world government really hold up under close scrutiny. These arguments fall roughly into two broad categories: practical arguments that center on the *feasibility* of a world state—such as its ungovernability or unaccountability—and normative ones that deal with its *desirability*.

Whereas Craig mainly discusses the feasibility and desirability of the idea of world government, Carol Gould, Eric Cavallero, and Raffaele Marchetti all develop a philosophical framework to make sense of democracy and human rights in a globalizing world. Globalization, after all, has transformed the conditions under which our liberal democracies can function (McGrew 1997). Nation-states are no longer able, by themselves, to guarantee the successful realization of their basic principles of justice and democracy. But what model of global democracy is best suited for our political and socioeconomic constellation?

Gould specifically addresses the emergence of cross-border communities and transnational public spheres. Building on her *Globalizing Democracy and Human Rights* (2004), she further develops the two criteria that are needed to determine the scope of democratic communities—common activities and impact on human rights—and examines what guidelines these criteria can offer for a democratization of international and transnational organizations. According to the "common activities" criterion, equal rights of participation are required whenever people—for example, in cross-border associations—engage in common activities. The "impact on human rights" criterion, on the other hand, depends not on organized common activities but on interdependence. People have a right to a substantial input in decision-making whenever the decisions of international organizations or other governments affect the fulfillment of their basic human rights.

In his contribution, Cavallero criticizes these two criteria because they are underinclusive as well as overinclusive. Suppose the United States—after a few nasty incidents with imported toys—decides to alter its consumer safety standards and to reduce drastically the importing of

Chinese toys. Do Chinese factory workers really have a right to substantial input in decision-making because the fulfillment of their basic human rights is affected? According to Cavallero these effects are irrelevant from a democratic perspective. Rather than emphasizing basic human rights, he proposes that we interpret the all-affected principle on the basis of the idea of external costs: individuals are relevantly affected by the exercise of a sovereign competence if (1) its exercise imposes governance norms on them or (2) its exercise could otherwise be reasonably expected to impose external costs on them. This boundary criterion is part of a larger defense of a federative form of global democracy.

Raffaele Marchetti also zooms in on what is required for a claim of democratic participation to make sense. In particular, he analyzes the fact of political exclusion of foreigners as an instance of injustice. Those who bear the effects of political decisions taken abroad often do not have a political voice in the decision-making process. Marchetti locates the rationale for this form of transnational exclusion in an interaction-dependent conception of justice. Duties of justice, according to this conception, are only generated when individuals or collectivities actually interact. Beyond this context no duties of justice apply, and no duty exists to create some kind of interaction.

The central aim of Marchetti's contribution is to analyze how this interaction-dependent conception of justice informs most (including some of the more progressive) stances in contemporary political theory. In particular, Marchetti uses this exclusion critique against realists, statists, nationalists, cosmopolitan democrats, supranational contractarians, and international "no harm" theorists. All these theorists support some form of "transnational exclusion." At the end of his chapter, Marchetti points toward the case for an *all-inclusive* project of global democracy, encompassing every member of the human species. Everyone should be included in the democratic process of making decisions on global affairs.

Rather than focusing on what is required for claims of democracy to kick in, William Scheuerman concentrates in his chapter on the extent to which forms of cosmopolitan democracy as defended by Held and Archibugi require or depend on a cosmopolitan rule of law. He notes that cosmopolitan democrats are often both unfamiliar with and silent about the traditional notion of the rule of law, which states that state action should rest on legal norms and rules that are clear, public, and general, thus making arbitrary ruling impossible. Scheuerman argues that the absence of this notion in the work of cosmopolitan democrats may make it impossible for them to ensure that their democratic proposals can guard themselves both against problematic arbitrary supranational *political* intrusions and against problematic discretionary *court* authority. The result is that cosmopolitan democrats are more vulnerable than they often claim to the specter of a "planetary Leviathan," a despotic world government. Scheuerman concludes that this analysis does not make cosmopolitan democracy an undesirable ideal; global democrats should take the traditional rule-of-law virtues more seriously and should come up with a more robust notion of the rule of law.

Although Scheuerman mainly focuses on the importance of the rule of law for the debate on global democracy, a wider lesson can be drawn from his chapter. Collective self-legislation (both on the national and on the transnational level) is not only an act of self-*constitution* but also an act of self-*ordering*: legal norms regulate human behavior in a specific way. In his chapter, Hans Lindahl critically examines this process of collective self-ordering. The main question he poses is: Are legal boundaries becoming irrelevant in our globalizing era, or are they the necessary condition of every postnational and global legal order?

If we follow Habermas's proposal for a "world domestic polity without a world government," legal boundaries are temporal and defeasible. Although Habermas argues that the "self-referential concept of collective self-determination demarcates a logical space for democratically united citizens who are members of a particular community" (2001, 107), he still accepts that a global legal order could progressively include formerly excluded groups and individuals. "The normative model for a community that exists without any possible exclusions," according to him, "is the universe of moral persons—Kant's 'kingdom of ends.' It is thus no coincidence that 'human rights,' i.e. legal norms with an exclusively moral content, make up the entire normative framework for a cosmopolitan community" (2001, 108). A similar line of thought can be found in the work of other proponents of forms of transnational and global democracy.

Lindahl scrutinizes this assumption in the first part of his chapter. He critically examines the different ways in which legal orders draw the boundary between legality on the one hand and illegality on the other. The distinction between inside and outside, according to Lindahl, is constitutive for all legal orders (national, regional, and global). Every legal order is bounded in a fourfold way: in terms of subject, matter, space, and time (*"who* ought to do *what*, *when* and *where"*). In the second part of his chapter Lindahl examines the implications of this connection between legal orders and their boundaries for the ideas of unity and plurality.

The issue of drawing boundaries has proven to be especially acute in the liberal egalitarian tradition. Liberals have in theory always defended a universal account of right and justice in which a strong notion of human rights predominates. Liberal polity, however, differs from this egalitarian ideal. Liberal democracies are (in certain respects) relatively closed societies, and justice is subordinated to the demands of states. In his contribution, Deen Chatterjee examines this conflict between moral equality and the liberal practice of exclusive membership. He argues that the idea of (democratic) equality need not be limited to the domestic order but can be extended to the international and supranational level. The conflicting loyalties of statism and globalism can be reconciled within a global democracy that is composed of nation-states.

But what kind of common identity can and should support forms of global democracy? Andreas Føllesdal focuses on a specific version of this question: Must citizens of (national or international) democratic societies share an identity that is *unique* to them and that they consequently don't share with others? Liberal nationalists like David Miller and deliberative democrats like Jürgen Habermas argue that a unique identity is a presupposition of democratic self-determination. But why is this question relevant for the discussion on global democracy? What is wrong with the claim that a democratic society needs a unique political identity? The main reason why Føllesdal focuses on this claim is because it is often used to conclude that a global commitment to human rights cannot provide enough trust and solidarity to sustain a global democratic order. International human rights are too broadly shared to unite the members of a transnational or supranational political community. Against Miller and Habermas, Føllesdal argues that a democratic order does not presuppose an exclusionary political identity.

In our contributions, Daniel Weinstock and we, respectively, also discuss the liberal nationalist claim that democratic decision-making can best (and maybe even only) be realized within bounded political communities with a unique national identity. Weinstock and we differ, however, in our focus. Weinstock argues that liberal nationalists are wrong to claim that spontaneous communal feelings are the primary and most common source of feelings of solidarity, reciprocity, and trust. What motivates citizens to act according to political morality—to be responsible and committed members of a democratic society—is often determined by a mix of self-interest and coercion. In fact, the required motivation for democratic citizenship is in many cases the result of institutional design and presenting people with the right incentives. If the empirical conditions for democratic citizenship, however, are the result of political artifice and not the natural effect of a shared national identity, an important objection against transnational citizenship and "global community-building" has been countered. How such a global democratic polity can be constructed is the topic of the last part of Weinstock's chapter.

In our chapter, we develop a different perspective on the relation between liberal nationalism and global democracy. It is not our aim to question liberal nationalism's main claims, but we do explicitly deny that these necessarily lead to a rejection of forms of global democracy. In fact, liberal nationalists can even support certain proposals for global democracy. We specifically focus on three arguments that liberal nationalists use to defend their claim that liberal democratic communities should be national communities: the identity argument, the deliberative democracy argument, and the social justice argument. According to the first argument, sharing a national culture offers us a context of identity. The second, deliberative democracy argument implies that deliberative democracy (or republican citizenship) works best in nationally bounded communities. And the third, social justice argument stipulates that the sacrifices needed to make a welfare system work depend on the existence of a shared national culture. We argue that these liberal nationalist premises are not sufficient to refute global democratic ideals. Endorsing liberal nationalist premises is compatible with endorsing the case for global democracy.

John Exdell focuses on the social justice argument from a different angle in his chapter. He examines the empirical claim made by Walzer and others that unregulated migration has a negative effect on the feelings of solidarity and trust that are necessary to support the welfare system of liberal democratic societies. Restraint of entry serves to protect welfare (Walzer 1983, 39). To refute this claim and argue that claims for relatively open borders are not utopian, Exdell examines an important example that counters the social justice argument—the case of the United States. The United States, after all, combines a strong common identity with a dislike of liberal welfare policies.

Taken together, the chapters collected here present a state-of-the-art analysis of the normative foundations of global democracy. In the current world order, examining the case for global democracy is crucial. If it is indeed the case—as some cosmopolitans argue—that "either democracy is global or it is not democracy" (Marchetti 2008, 1), a more fundamental task for contemporary political theory can hardly be envisioned.

Acknowledgments

Many of the chapters in this collection grew out of a special workshop entitled "Global Democracy and Exclusion," which we jointly convened within the framework of the XIIIth World Conference of Philosophy of Social Philosophy and Law (IVR) in Kraków in early August 2007. We thank the participants and speakers at the workshop for very fruitful discussions. We also wish to extend our sincere thanks for all their help to the editor in chief and the managing editor of *Metaphilosophy*, Armen T. Marsoobian and Otto Bohlmann.

References

Abizadeh, Arash. 2005. "Does Collective Identity Presuppose an Other? On the Alleged Incoherence of Global Solidarity." *American Political Science Review* 99:45–60.
Benhabib, Seyla. 2004. *The Rights of Others: Aliens, Residents and Citizens.* Cambridge: Cambridge University Press.

Habermas, Jürgen. 2001. *The Postnational Constellation: Political Essays.* Cambridge, Mass.: MIT.

———. 2006. *Time of Transitions.* Cambridge: Polity Press.

Held, David. 1995. *Democracy and the Global Order: From the Modern State to Cosmopolitan Governance.* Cambridge: Polity Press.

Kymlicka, Will. 2001. "Territorial Boundaries: A Liberal Egalitarian Perspective." In *Boundaries and Justice: Diverse Ethical Perspectives,* edited by David Miller and Sohail Hashmi, 249–75. Princeton: Princeton University Press.

McGrew, Anthony. 1997. "Democracy Beyond Borders? Globalization and the Reconstruction of Democratic Theory and Practice." In *The Transformation of Democracy: Globalization and Territorial Democracy,* edited by Anthony McGrew, 231–66. Cambridge: Polity Press.

Marchetti, Raffaele. 2008. *Global Democracy: For and Against: Ethical Theory, Institutional Design and Social Struggles.* New York: Routledge.

Miller, David. 2009. "Democracy's Domain." *Philosophy and Public Affairs* 37:201–28.

Mouffe, Chantal. 1993. *The Return of the Political.* London: Verso.

Schmitt, Carl. 1996. *The Concept of the Political.* Chicago: University of Chicago Press.

Scholte, Jan Aart. 2000. *Globalization: A Critical Introduction.* Basingstoke: Macmillan.

Walzer, Michael. 1983. *Spheres of Justice: A Defense of Pluralism and Equality.* New York: Basic Books.

———. 2003. *Arguing About War.* New Haven: Yale University Press.

2

COSMOPOLITANISM AND HUMAN RIGHTS: RADICALISM IN A GLOBAL AGE

ROBERT FINE

Introduction

Let me begin with a rough and ready formulation of how the relationship between cosmopolitanism and human rights is normally conceived from a cosmopolitan point of view. Cosmopolitanism imagines a global order in which the idea of human rights is an operative principle of justice, with mechanisms of global governance established specifically for their protection. However, the cosmopolitan imagination is not restricted to this agenda. It incorporates wider issues concerning peace among states, social solidarity across borders, the efficacy of international law, and the activism of global civil society. It envisages the reformation of political community at the national level to render it compatible with cosmopolitan values and new forms of political community at the transnational level. It would still be implausible to think of the cosmopolitan imagination apart from some notion of human rights, that is, rights which belong to all people by virtue of their human status.

Cosmopolitan thought has come under attack for all manner of alleged deficiencies. It is criticised as naive for thinking that the real world actually operates on human rights principles, or as chauvinistic for associating the idea of human rights exclusively with Western civilisation and defining its defence in terms of a clash of civilisations. It is viewed by some of its critics as an *ideology* of human rights, a point made forcibly by Costas Douzinas when he associates it closely with the moral mission of combating evil once advanced by George W. Bush (Douzinas 2007, 3–7). The normative significance of the relationship between cosmopolitanism and human rights is contested on democratic grounds for the failure of supra-national institutions and legal systems to match the co-existence of rights and democracy attained at the national level. In general, cosmopolitanism is criticised for not recognising the unpleasant realities behind the facade of human rights or, indeed, for evading reality altogether (Zolo 1997 and 2002). Within the cosmopolitan literature much effort has gone into confronting such legitimacy problems (e.g., Habermas 2006; Bohman

2007). The suspicion remains, however, that cosmopolitanism may justifiably be criticised for its idealisation of human rights.

In this chapter I review the relationship between cosmopolitanism and human rights with the aim of addressing the charge of idealisation. I do it through a number of brief encounters. I begin with the development of Enlightenment cosmopolitanism in the eighteenth century and its reconstruction of the rights of man and citizen. I argue that Enlightenment cosmopolitanism radicalised the rights of man from the perspective of the rights of man, that is, from within the framework of natural law theory. In the second section I address the legacy of Enlightenment cosmopolitanism that carried over into the rise of the human sciences. I maintain that this legacy was not drowned in a sea of methodological nationalism, as is now argued within the existing cosmopolitan literature (Beck 2006), but rather that the human sciences sought to preserve the universality of the cosmopolitan conception of humanity whilst overcoming the limitations of a natural law framework (Chernilo 2007a). In the third section I consider the "human rights revolution" of our own time and argue that we should resist the temptation to treat this development positivistically as the realisation of the cosmopolitan vision. I conclude with a brief reference to the current crisis of cosmopolitanism and how we might respond to it from a cosmopolitan point of view.

I suggest that a problem of legitimacy is latent in cosmopolitanism's claim to carry out a break with the tradition of social theory, that is, in overstating its own novelty, whilst at the same time drawing unreflectively on the tradition of natural law. This problem is reinforced by a self-conscious casting of history in terms of epochs that is grounded in an unsustainable realism about epochs—humanistic universalism in the eighteenth century, national particularism in the nineteenth and twentieth centuries, the reconciliation of universalism and particularism in the current "age of cosmopolitanism." I wish to defend the legitimacy of cosmopolitanism by addressing a weakness internal to cosmopolitanism: that of giving itself criteria of legitimacy that it cannot live up to.

Cosmopolitanism and the Rights of Man: The Radicalisation of Natural Law

We know that cosmopolitanism goes back to the ancient Stoics and that it played a pivotal role in the natural law theorising of early modernity (Toulmin 1992). As a modern political way of thinking, however, cosmopolitanism started life as a universalistic commitment of eighteenth-century Enlightenment thought. It was from the start a philosophy of right committed to realising the universalistic potential inherent in the rights of man.

The declarations of the rights of man and citizen that accompanied eighteenth-century revolutions announced that every "man" should be conceived as a bearer of rights simply by virtue of the fact that he is a man. They marked the difference between the principle of the modern political state and traditional societies in which the possession of rights, "personality" in the language of Roman law, either was absent altogether or was a privileged status distinct from the servile condition of the majority of the people. To be sure, the rights of man presupposed all manner of exclusions and silences, but they also provided the universalistic framework within which struggles for inclusion could take place: whether for women, slaves, servants, wage labourers, foreigners, the colonised, the racialised, the criminalised, the infantilised, the pathologised, the disabled, Protestants, or Jews.

Cosmopolitanism was in effect a critique of the rights of man from the perspective of the rights of man. It was an international movement whose aim was to expand the rights of man beyond the national limitations of their protagonists and defend them against those who would restrict fellow feeling to members of the same nation, class, or religion. The cosmopolitan obstinacy was to insist, as Hegel put it, that "a human being counts as such because he is a human being, not because he is a Jew, Catholic, Protestant, German, Italian, etc." (Hegel 1991, § 209R).

It was Kant above all who gave the name "cosmopolitanism" to the movement for the extension of the rights of man beyond the nation. He recognised that no sooner were the rights of man articulated than they entered into conflict with the national organisation of political community that underwrote their existence (see Kant 1991 and Arendt 1979, 267–302). The revolutions that declared the rights of man also designated that it is the nation that grants these rights and in its more radical versions declared there could be no rights but those declared by the nation. Kant explored the contradiction between the universalism of the concept and its particular national existence and revealed the various ways in which this contradiction was played out. He referred to the lawlessness of international relations, the perpetual wars that governed relations between European states, the exclusion and stigmatisation of foreigners within states, and the subjection of colonised peoples in the non-European world.

The treatment of foreigners in the unfolding of the French Revolution illustrates the kind of problem Kant addressed under the cosmopolitan register: that of institutionalising the rights of man through the prism of the nation. At the dawn of the revolution a cosmopolitan spirit prevailed. Decrees were passed offering French citizenship to resident foreigners. Foreign societies and newspapers were encouraged. Support was given to foreign revolutionaries. Foreign "benefactors of humankind" (including Tom Paine, William Wilberforce, and Mary Wollstonecraft) were awarded honorary French citizenship. The glorious new dawn was not to last, however. Terror, suspicion, xenophobia, and war suppressed the spirit of universality, and the idea of universality itself was translated into a power that denied the free personality of individuals. The fate of Tom Paine, the man who signed himself "humanus," was symbolic: he was impoverished, imprisoned, and finally expelled (Kristeva 1991). This example of the treatment of foreigners indicates how readily the rights of man can be subordinated to emergent forces of nationalism.

The relation of the revolution to slavery is equally indicative. In Enlightenment thought slavery was a common metaphor for illegitimacy and tyranny, but the *philosophes* were more equivocal over the realities of the *Code Noir*, which legalised slavery in the French Empire (Muthu 2003). The plurality of Enlightenment thought cannot be reduced to one univocal movement. Rousseau declared the words "slavery" and "right" mutually exclusive, but he apparently wrote not a word about the *Code Noir* (Buck-Morss 2000, 830). His conception of the simplicity of the "noble savage," epitomised by the Amerindians of the New World, was philo-native, but he tended also to portray "noble savages" as incapable of lifting themselves above the level of beasts. By contrast, Diderot portrayed Amerindians as cultural agents from the beginning, dismissed the very idea of "inferior" and "superior" peoples, repudiated the European pretence to "civilise" non-Europeans, and affirmed a strong notion of common humanity (Muthu 2003). After 1789, protests against the slave trade were stirred in the Society of the Friends of Blacks and supported by amongst others Mirabeau and Talleyrand. The rights of man were also invoked by slaves themselves—notably, the revolution-aries of Saint Domingue (Haiti) who under the name of the Black Jacobins declared freedom from slavery in 1793, sent a delegation to Paris to secure the abolition of slavery in the Declaration of the Rights of Man of 1794, declared a black republic when the French state re-instated slavery in 1803, and then eliminated the white population on the island (Bhambra 2007, 110–11). Both the treatment and the response of slaves show how readily the claim to rights can be associated with the denial of rights to others.

Under the heading of the "cosmopolitan point of view" Kant sought to give concrete realisation to the universality of the rights of man. His argument contained four key elements: (1) the generalisation of repub-licanism within all societies; (2) the establishment of legal authority at the international level; (3) the extension of rights to foreigners; and (4) putting an end to the barbarities associated with colonialism. These elements together constituted a whole. If the rights of man were to belong to all, then the benefits of republican government could not remain a preserve of French or American superiority but had to be made available to all nations. If international law was to become more than mere words, a Federation of Nations had to be established, with the same kind of authority to enforce law between societies as the state had to enforce law within societies. If the rights of man were to become universal, then civil and political rights had to be supplemented with cosmopolitan rights that guaranteed "hospitality" to strangers landing on foreign shores.[1] If the barbarities associated with colonialism were to be ended, then the fiction that colonial territories were lands empty of people had to be dispelled.[2]

Kant's visionary agenda was the result of a sustained intellectual effort on the part of an ageing and sedentary philosopher to translate the universality intrinsic to the rights of man into something substantial. It was a response to the darkening of the glorious new dawn the French Revolution had ushered in. Kant was well aware that cosmopolitanism might be considered "fantastical" because European states continued to relate to one another more like atomised individuals in a Hobbesian state of nature than legal subjects under international law. His obstinacy, however, was to hold that the idea of a cosmopolitan condition was nonetheless right and that it was necessary to look beyond immediate circumstances to longer-term historical tendencies to see the justification of the cosmopolitan point of view: to the inter-connections of peoples around the world, to the consequence of travel and movement across borders, to the expansion of commodity exchange between nations, to the risks and costs associated with war, and not least to the education of modern republican citizens.

And yet the chasm between cosmopolitan principles and the actuality of the emerging world order gave a sense of unreality to Kant's political writings. In his own *Philosophy of Right* Hegel, who was Kant's most astute critic, tried to tease out the internal weaknesses within Kant's conception of a cosmopolitan order. The rights of man could readily be subverted into a duty of unconditional obedience to the nation that grants these rights, predisposing states towards legal authoritarianism and citizens towards militant nationalism. The extension of the rights of man through the republicanisation of other nations was fine in theory, but in practice Napoleon's armies revealed that "wars of liberation" are bitterly resisted by invaded peoples and can involve the kinds of cruelty and rightlessness Goya memorably depicted in his "disasters of war." Kant's conception of a Federation of Nations could not provide the alchemy Kant envisaged—that of turning perpetual war into perpetual peace. States soon learn how to defend themselves militarily in the knowledge that legal arguments cannot win wars and they are quick to appreciate that wars can be useful to bolster internal unity, encourage self-sacrifice, impose discipline, expand territories, and designate enemies.

---

[1] Kant's article 3 in *Perpetual Peace* confers the right to hospitality when an alien cannot be turned away without putting his or her life at risk. It is not for Kant a generalised right, although he does write of a right to travel, visit, and associate.

[2] Kant rejected, for example, Lockean views of property that allowed Europeans to declare colonised territories *res nullius* (no-man's land) and on this basis to justify seizure of the lands of indigenous hunting and pastoral peoples. As Kant put it, pastoralists and hunters have a legitimate right to live "the way they want to live" in their own way and defend their land by force if necessary against attempts to dispossess them.

The idea of "cosmopolitan rights" was indeed a harbinger of "human rights" to come, but there was no guarantee to prevent the "right of hospitality" from playing the traditional role it had in the old European division of the world, that of serving as a pretext for European states to subdue "uncivilised" peoples who decline to provide the required hospitality to European visitors.

Hegel acknowledged the visionary character of Kant's cosmopolitan thought—and berated Kant's critics for their failure to understand the concept of cosmopolitanism—but Kant's own observation that every right is a right of coercion was a reminder to Hegel that every *expansion* of rights is also a *re-invention* of new forms of coercion. Hegel was more sympathetic to Kant's cosmopolitanism than most commentators recognise, but he had a keen awareness of the chasm between the concept and its realisation. The limits of Kant's natural law indicate that the "dialectic of universality," as Raymond Aron once put it, was still in its infancy (Aron 1969, 191–221), but his critical insight remains: the solution to exclusion is not just inclusion but restructuring that which gives rise to exclusion in the first place (Bhambra and Shilliam 2009, introduction).

Cosmopolitanism and Social Theory: The Preservation and Transcendence of Natural Law

It is a common trope in current cosmopolitan writing that eighteenth-century cosmopolitanism failed to generate a legacy for nineteenth-century thinkers, that it was philosophically marginalised by the time of Hegel, and that it was largely absent from the subsequent development of the human sciences. Ulrich Beck, for example, has described the sociological tradition as steeped in what he calls "methodological nationalism" (Beck 2006), and Jürgen Habermas has argued that we have to jump over two hundred years of history in order to pick up the threads of the cosmopolitan tradition (Habermas 1996). This account of the history of cosmopolitan thought seems to me misleading. The rise of the human sciences represented not a break from cosmopolitanism but rather its *Aufhebung*, that is, its preservation and transcendence (Chernilo 2007a). Classical social theory sought to denature cosmopolitan thought, to extract it from the frame of natural law theorising, but at the same time it adopted as its own premise the universalistic concept of humanity characteristic of Enlightenment cosmopolitanism (Löwith 1993, 42–43). Perhaps nowhere was this more evident than in the opposition to antisemitic ways of thinking about the problems of modern capitalist society displayed by the founding fathers of classical sociology; think, for instance, of Marx's defence of the rights of Jews to full civil and political equality or Durkheim's defence of the Dreyfusards (Fine 2008). Beck was not wrong to criticise "methodological nationalism," if we mean by this a critique of the reification of society, but it does seem to me that his critique is aimed at the wrong target (Beck 2006; Chernilo 2007b; Fine 2007). Classical sociology was at its core a critique of methodological nationalism.

The ghost of Kant has continued to haunt not only the human sciences but also the hopes and expectation of peace that prevailed in liberal and socialist traditions. In the aftermath of the First World War Friedrich Meinecke in Germany, Emile Durkheim in France, and George Herbert Mead and John Dewey in the United States, though at one time or another tempted into more or less bellicose nationalisms, were united in recognising the co-existence of nationalism and cosmopolitanism in the modern world and in seeking to reconcile patriotism with cosmopolitan values. Even the conservative Meinecke wrote that "the true, the best German national feeling includes the cosmopolitan ideal of a humanity beyond nationality" and that it is "un-German to be merely German" (Meinecke 1970, 21). The more socialistic Durkheim wrote of the need to divert the energies of societies "from the disputes that bring a clash between cosmopolitanism . . . and patriotism." Societies, he wrote, "can have their pride not in being the greatest or the wealthiest, but in being the most just, the best organised and in possessing the best moral constitution" (Durkheim 1992, 74–75). Dewey and Mead warned against the "fool's paradise" of the pre-war age, the idea that "cosmic forces were working inevitably to improve the whole state of human affairs," but looked to reconcile national- and international-mindedness through the establishment of the League of Nations and the right of national self-determination (Joas 2003, 72–73).

This is not to deny the equivocal nature of these attempts to rescue cosmopolitan ideals from the gore of war. The transformation of the rights of man into the right of nations to self-determination carried the risk of *substituting* the rights of nations for the rights of man and creating a class of aliens for whom membership of the nation was denied (Arendt 1979, 295). The reconciliation of nationalism and cosmopolitanism ran the risk of feeding the hubris of a "universal nation"—that is, a nation which claims that its particular values and interests correspond with the values and interests of humanity as a whole and that its enemies are enemies of humanity (Habermas 1998, 188–201).

After 1945 the spirit of Kant was again visible amongst those who sought to revive cosmopolitan ideas in the aftermath of totalitarian terror and address the equivocations of the earlier generation (Fine 2006). In *The Origins of Totalitarianism* Hannah Arendt argued precisely along such lines when she wrote that the experience of antisemitism, imperialism, and totalitarianism had demonstrated that "human dignity needs a *new guarantee* which can be found only in a *new political principle*, a *new law on earth*, whose validity this time must comprehend the whole of humanity, while its power must remain strictly limited, rooted in and controlled by newly defined territorial entities" (Arendt 1979, ix). Arendt argued for a philosophy of right based no longer on "the essentially barbaric idea that 'right' is what is good for the whole" (whether the whole is the German people, or the proletariat, or humanity itself) but on the principle that "the right to have rights, or the right of every individual to belong to humanity, should be guaranteed by humanity itself" (1979, 298). She maintained that the appeal to nature and to natural law could no longer be convincing and that human beings now have no place to turn but to humanity itself.

From Hegel to the classical sociologists to Arendt we see not only the continuance of a cosmopolitan legacy but also a collective endeavour to understand the divisions of the modern world on the basis of universal conceptions of humanity. Cosmopolitan and nationalist ways of thinking are not consecutive properties of particular epochs but coeval presences in the modern world. There is a cost incurred in returning to the Enlightenment as the source of the cosmopolitan imagination if it means viewing the human sciences as the loss of cosmopolitan imagination. The rendering of the present age in terms of the long-awaited realisation of the cosmopolitan ideal is precisely the kind of over-extension of enlightenment ambition that has to be avoided if the legitimacy of cosmopolitan existence is to be upheld.

Cosmopolitanism and Human Rights: The Dialectics of Progress

At the time of Hannah Arendt's writing, international law still operated largely in terms of treaties and agreements between sovereign states; the idea of sovereign statehood was largely restricted to Europe, America, and Russia; the rest of the world was either under their imperial control or outside world society; and in Europe itself the division of the world into power blocs made a mockery of national sovereignty. Today it might appear, by contrast, that many of the elements of the cosmopolitan condition are all firmly in place and that we can now speak of our age as an age of cosmopolitanism, though not yet as a cosmopolitan age.

In the sixty-four years since the end of the Second World War much has changed. Old colonial forms of rule have been dismantled and delegitimised. Eurocentrism has been severely fractured. Regional and global institutions have been constructed from the European Union to the World Trade Organisation, from Amnesty International to the International Chamber of Commerce. Social inequalities, though larger than ever at the global level, are no longer perceived exclusively as "our own" problem, not only because we need each other more in a world risk society (Beck 2006) but also because we have a sense of binding obligations in relation to others beyond our own borders (Brunkhorst 2005). Legal textbooks now refer to international law as a higher and compelling law (*ius cogens*). The idea of exclusive state sovereignty has been replaced by sovereign equality under international law. Individual human beings are now subjects of international law. Human rights have been transformed from a set of moral declarations to elements of an enforceable legal system. And even the most hegemonically inclined of states, such as the United States, cannot simply ignore their long-term rational interest in "binding emerging major powers to the rules of a politically constituted international community" (Habermas 2006, 150). In political argument appeal is now regularly made to the idea of human rights either to justify state actions or denounce them (Krisch 2004). Today it is commonplace within the public sphere to hear certain state actions described as "wars of aggression," "disproportionate responses," "collective punishment," "crimes against humanity" or even "genocide"—as if we are now all experts in international humanitarian law and appeal to it as to the absolute and universal standards of natural law.[3]

It no longer sounds hyperbolic to speak of a "human rights revolution" since 1945 and of its consolidation since the fall of the Berlin Wall in 1989. And yet the idea of a human rights revolution has suffered and has been seen to suffer major reversals after the September 11th attack on the World Trade Centre and the Anglo-American declaration of a "war on terror" in 2001 (Bowring 2008; Harvey 2005; Miéville 2005). The result, it seems to me, is a world increasingly bifurcated between the idealism of human rights and the realism of justified and unjustified violence. On the one hand, we hear the voice of cosmopolitanism declaring that positive laws are becoming in our own age congruent with the natural laws of the cosmopolis. On the other, we hear the voice of realism devaluing the whole business as a global hypocrisy and in its most active mode calling for the destruction of this false facade.

Can this division be overcome? I am neither optimistic nor pessimistic, but I would make the sociological observation that human rights are a social form of right that has arisen in our own times and is an achievement of our age—albeit an achievement that can be rolled back and never simply taken for granted. The existence of human rights is for better or worse now part of the social world we inhabit. Human rights exist not just in the mind but as a determinate social form external to our

---

[3] To grasp the expansion of human rights law we need only think of the formation of the Nuremberg Tribunal (1945), the International Court of Justice (1946), the Universal Declaration of Human Rights (1948), the Convention on the Prevention and Punishment of the Crime of Genocide (1948), the European Convention on Human Rights (1950), the International Covenant on Civil and Political Rights and the International Covenant on Economic, Social and Cultural Rights (from 1966), the Vienna convention on the Law of Treaties (1969), the United Nations Convention Against Torture and Other Cruel, Inhuman or Degrading Treatment (1987), the ad hoc tribunals for war crimes committed in the former Yugoslavia (1993) and Rwanda (1994), and the International Criminal Court (2002). To be sure, all the norms contained in these treaties, conventions, and declarations are frequently broken, but what is new is that they exist.

own subjective feelings and opinions of it. It has a legal status within international law and has percolated into other areas of international and domestic law (including criminal, humanitarian, civil, welfare, immigration, and family law). It is the product of struggles from below and legislation from above. It can be instrumentalised in the service of state power and reclaimed as a promise of "civil repair" for the wrongs committed by the state (Alexander 2006).

All this is to say is that the idea of human rights is no longer a "mere idea" in the heads of philosophers but has an external existence in the world. In this sense it is more like what Hegel called "objective spirit": both spirit and objective, both a concept and something existent in the world (Fine 2001, ch. 2). Like body and soul, they form a unity. Both the concept and its existence in the world are equally one-sided when viewed in isolation from one another. In seeking to understand human rights we are like a tightrope walker: we fall one way into formalism, mere conceptual thinking; the other into realism.

Conceptual thinking comes in two versions: conservative and critical. In a conservative mode it offers a more or less accurate empirical description of how human rights law currently functions, but its aim is simply to rediscover the concept in every sphere of human rights it finds—to fasten on what lies nearest at hand and prove that it is an actual moment of the concept. In its critical mode conceptual thinking wishes to transform existing laws and institutions and elevate them to the level of the concept. It looks to the construction of an ideal cosmopolitan condition in which human rights are for the first time legislated through a global parliament, adjudicated through a network of world courts, and enforced through a U.N. army and police. Its vision is of a wholly legalised international order in which human rights finally trump the exercise of power. These two faces of conceptual thinking give to cosmopolitanism an ambiguous appearance: either of endorsing the age in which we live as a cosmopolitan age or of striving for a radical and perhaps utopian transition—in the words of Habermas, from a world in which law is in the service of power to one in which power is in the service of right (Habermas 1996). In either event, the politics of human rights is conceived as an anticipation of a world in which human rights are fully embedded within an international legal framework and violations are prosecuted as criminal acts within a legal order (Smith 2007).

Realist thinking presents itself as the antithesis of cosmopolitanism. It discounts the concept of human rights as froth on the surface of what is real. It addresses laws, institutions, and practices from an exclusively non-conceptual point of view. It focuses on the political and economic interests concealed behind human rights. It attends to the rhetorical uses and ideological appropriations of the concept but not to the concept itself. It constructs a hermeneutics of suspicion in which human rights are devalued as a category of understanding and as a standard of judgment. It treats the idea of human rights essentially as a fraud designed to stigmatise enemies and elevate friends. In its eyes cosmopolitanism either idealises the existing international order (as is claimed, for instance, of Rawls's *Law of Peoples*) or idealises the potentiality of the present epoch to reconstruct itself according to cosmopolitan principles (Zolo 2002).

Realism and conceptualism appear in this scenario as mutually dependent discourses defined by their hostility to one another and the caricatures they construct of one another. They do not, however, exhaust our universe. There is more to life than is contained in this conceptualist-realist divide.

The idea of human rights is the product of a certain stage in the development of capitalist society (Brunkhorst 2008). T. H. Marshall wrote of a movement from civil rights to political rights to social rights that has characterised modern constitutional states (Marshall 1950). Employing these insights we may view the idea of *human* rights as a stage in the development of the idea of right itself—one that Marshall prefigured, even if it remained at the margins of his thinking. Its emergence should not be understood as making obsolete less developed legal forms. It does not *supplant* the civil, political, and social rights associated with the nation-state, it supplements them. When Marshall analysed the development of citizenship as a development of civil, then political, then social rights, he assigned them broadly to the evolution of constitutional states in the eighteenth, nineteenth, and twentieth centuries. His distinctive contribution, however, was to argue that modern citizens are only full citizens if they possess all three kinds of right. Similarly, we might say that human rights do not substitute for civil, political, and social rights but are capable of co-existing with them. Citizens become world citizens when they possess all four kinds of right.

A more appropriate model perhaps is to be found in Hegel's *Philosophy of Right* (Fine 2001). Hegel wrote of a complex movement from rights of personality to rights of property, moral conscience, civil association, political participation, and national self-determination and finally rights of world citizenship (Hegel 1991). Many commentators see the state as the apex of this movement, but for Hegel the state is only one sphere among many in the system of right. It is not the "last" sphere, for inter-state relations and world history come after the state, and in any event the state retains the contradiction between formal equality and informal inequality inherent in the simplest forms of right. So too the fact that the human rights revolution has occurred in a radically asymmetrical political-economic order suggests that it should not be viewed as the final culmination of the system of right as a whole but as a contradictory social form. Its legitimacy lies in *supplementing* the functional capacities of nation-states and tempering their temptation to imagine themselves, as Hobbes once put it in *Leviathan*, as an "earthly God." However, it suffers its own legitimacy problems.

In the nineteenth century, international law largely served imperialism as the "gentle civilizer" of nations (Koskenniemi 2001; Anghie 2004). In the twentieth century, its support for national self-determination underwrote the displacement of stateless peoples unable to enjoy this right. Even the laws guaranteeing the rights of minorities confirmed that the minorities were not full participants in the nation-state. Today the legitimacy problems of international law are visible in the diminished capacity of supra-national institutions to address social inequalities (Pogge 2002), regulate the aggression of big powers (Sands 2006), interpret human rights without gross political prejudice (Habibi 2007), or, as I mentioned at the start of this chapter, match the co-originality of rights and democracy possible at the national level (Chung 2003).

Within the cosmopolitan literature much effort has gone into confronting such legitimacy problems.[4] And yet the vast chasm between "the global co-existence of the abstract idea of human rights and concrete norms of social and political exclusion" have led one keen observer, sympathetic to cosmopolitanism, to comment on the "latent legitimation crisis of world society" (Brunkhorst 2008).

Cosmopolitanism and the Crisis of Human Rights: The Turn to Judgment

If a crisis of human rights is in the air, it poses a difficult challenge for cosmopolitan thought. Today criticism or even hatred of the idea of human rights has become commonplace across disparate political lines. The sheer negativity of much of this criticism opens the way to all manner of popular hostility. The gap between the idea of universal human rights and the specific political rights enjoyed by members of a particular community is leading a generation of radical scholars to revisit cosmopolitanism, as it were, through a lens, darkly. Human rights, we are told, only have value when they are an expression of resistance from below and cease to have value as soon as they become objectified in positive laws (Douzinas 2007). Human rights, we are also told, are the property only of *homo sacer*, that is, a human being reduced to "bare life" (Agamben 1998). At the moment individuals are reduced to the status of a human being in general, their own rights are usurped by the right of others to intervene on their behalf. Since those who suffer inhuman repression are unable to enact the human rights that are their last recourse, somebody else has to inherit their rights in order to enact them in their place (Rancière 2006; also Zizek 2005). Human rights in these accounts appear

---

[4] For example, Jürgen Habermas justifies the restricted democratic legitimacy of international institutions by reference to the limited functions they perform compared with nation-states (Habermas 2006). He also argues that the normative substance of human rights, though admittedly not resting on democratic procedures of legislation, rests on legal principles tried and tested within democratic constitutions and is granted a supplementary level of democratic legitimacy through the activism of global civil society.

as an abstract universal that masks a concrete politics of Western military intervention. That they be better than nothing for those reduced to bare life is made invisible. This negative "dialectic" is symptomatic of the current legitimacy crisis of human rights. Hostility to human rights is the shibboleth by which we recognise, as Hegel put it, "the false friends of the people" (Hegel 1991, 17).

From a cosmopolitan point of view we do not defend human rights as a natural law substitute for a post-traditional age, nor do we reify the legality of human rights in the juridical sense of the term. But because we do not turn the idea of human rights into an absolute, we also do not suffer the disillusionment that may arise when it becomes apparent that it is not absolute. Our endeavour is to create what I would call a "human rights culture"—one that allows us to understand human rights as one element in a larger system of right, an emergent form of subjectivity in a global age, and to make political judgments in a way that neither over-values nor de-values its subject matter (Fine 2008). Learning to understand the world and make reflective judgments from this point of view is a crucial part, as Hannah Arendt put it, of our "cosmopolitan existence" (Arendt 1992, 75–76).

Acknowledgments

I should like to pay special tribute to Daniel Chernilo for the collaborative work we are doing in this area. I also wish to offer my thanks to Gurminder Bhambra, Alison Diduck, Glynis Cousin, Lydia Morris, David Seymour, and Ronald Tinnevelt for their generous and helpful comments, as well as to all those involved in the production of this chapter.

References

Agamben, Giorgio. 1998. *Homo Sacer: Sovereign Power and Bare Life*. Stanford: Stanford University Press.

Alexander, Jeffrey. 2006. *The Civil Sphere*. Oxford: Oxford University Press.

Anghie, Antony. 2004. *Imperialism, Sovereignty, and the Making of International Law*. Cambridge, Mass.: Harvard University Press.

Arendt, Hannah. 1979. *The Origins of Totalitarianism*. New York: Harcourt Brace.

———. 1992. *Lectures on Kant's Political Philosophy*. Edited and with an interpretive essay by Ronald Beiner. Chicago: University of Chicago Press.

Aron, Raymond. 1969. *Les désillusions du progrès: Essai sur la dialectique du progrès*. Paris: Gallimard.

Balibar, Étienne. 2004. "Is a Philosophy of Human Civic Rights Possible?" *South Atlantic Quarterly* 103, nos. 2–3:311–22.

Beck, Ulrich. 2006. *Cosmopolitan Vision*. Cambridge: Polity.

Bhambra, Gurminder. 2007. *Rethinking Modernity: Postcolonialism and the Sociological Imagination*. Basingstoke: Palgrave.

Bhambra, Gurminder K., and Robbie Shilliam, eds. 2009. *Silencing Human Rights: Critical Engagements with a Contested Project*. Basingstoke: Palgrave Macmillan.

Bohman, J. 2007. *Democracy Across Borders: From Demos to Demoi*. Cambridge, Mass.: MIT Press.

Bowring, Bill. 2008. *The Degradation of the International Legal Order: The Rehabilitation of Law and the Possibility of Politics*. London: Glasshouse.

Brunkhorst, Hauke. 2005. *Solidarity: From Civic Friendship to a Global Legal Community*. Cambridge, Mass.: MIT Press.

———. 2008. "Cosmopolitanism and Democratic Freedom." Paper presented at Onati Institute for Sociology of Law conference "Normative and Sociological Approaches to Legality and Legitimacy," 24–25 April.

Buck-Morss, Susan. 2000. "Hegel and Haiti." *Critical Inquiry* 26:821–65.

Chernilo, Daniel. 2007a. "A Quest for Universalism: Re-assessing the Nature of Classical Social Theory's Cosmopolitanism." *European Journal of Social Theory* 10, no. 1:17–35.

———. 2007b. *A Social Theory of the Nation State: Beyond Methodological Nationalism*. London: Routledge.

Chung, R. 2003. "The Cosmopolitan Scope of Republican Citizenship." *Critical Review of International Social and Political Philosophy* 6, no. 1:134–47.

Douzinas, Costas. 2007. *Human Rights and Empire: The Political Philosophy of Cosmopolitanism*. London: Routledge-Cavendish.

Durkheim, Emile. 1992. *Professional Ethics and Civic Morals*. Translated by Cornelia Brookfield. London: Routledge.

Fine, Robert. 2001. *Political Investigations: Hegel, Marx, Arendt*. London: Routledge.

———. 2006. "Cosmopolitanism and Violence." *British Journal of Sociology* 57, no. 1:49–67.

———. 2007. *Cosmopolitanism*. London: Routledge.

———. 2008. "Judgment and the Reification of the Faculties: A Reconstructive Reading of Arendt's *Life of the Mind*." *Philosophy and Social Criticism* 34, nos. 1–2:157–76.

Habermas, Jürgen. 1998. *The Inclusion of the Other: Studies in Political Theory*. Cambridge, Mass.: MIT Press.

———. 2006. *The Divided West*. Edited and translated by Ciaran Cronin. Cambridge: Polity.

Habibi, Don. 2007. "Human Rights and Politicised Human Rights: A Utilitarian Critique." *Journal of Human Rights* 6:3–35.

Harvey, David. 2005. *The New Imperialism*. Oxford: Oxford University Press.

Hegel, Georg. 1991. *Elements of the Philosophy of Right*. Edited by Allen W. Wood and translated by H. B. Nisbet. Cambridge: Cambridge University Press.

Joas, Hans. 2003. *War and Modernity: Studies in the History of Violence*. Cambridge: Polity.

Kant, Immanuel. 1991. *Kant: Political Writings* Edited by Hans Reiss. Cambridge: Cambridge University Press.

Koskenniemi, Martti. 2001. *The Gentle Civilizer of Nations: The Rise and Fall of International Law, 1870–1960*. Hersch Lauterpacht Memorial Lectures. Cambridge: Cambridge University Press.

Krisch, Nico. 2004. "Imperial International Law." Hauser Global Law School Program, Global Law Working Paper 01.

Kristeva, Julia. 1991. *Strangers to Ourselves*. New York: Columbia University Press.

Löwith, Karl. 1993. *Max Weber and Karl Marx*. Preface by Bryan Turner. London: Routledge.

Marshall, T. H. 1950. *Citizenship and Social Class and Other Essays*. Cambridge: Cambridge University Press.

Meinecke, Friedrich. 1970. *Cosmopolitanism and the National State*. Princeton: Princeton University Press.

Miéville, China. 2005. *Between Equal Rights: A Marxist Theory of International Law*. Leiden: Brill.

Muthu, Sankar. 2003. *Enlightenment Against Empire*. Princeton: Princeton University Press.

Pogge, Thomas. 2002. *World Poverty and Human Rights: Cosmopolitan Responsibilities and Reforms*. Cambridge: Polity.

Rancière, Jacques. 2006. "Who Is the Subject of the Rights of Man?" *South Atlantic Quarterly* 103, nos. 2–3:307–9.

Sands, Philippe. 2006. *Lawless World: Making and Breaking Global Rules*. Harmondsworth: Penguin.

Smith, William. 2007. "Anticipating a Cosmopolitan Future: The Case of Humanitarian Military Intervention." *International Politics* 44, no. 1:72–89.

Toulmin, Stephen. 1992. *Cosmopolis: The Hidden Agenda of Modernity*. Chicago: University of Chicago Press.

Zizek, Slavoj. 2005. "Against Human Rights." *New Left Review* 34 (July–August). Available at http://libcom.org/library/against-human-rights-zizek

Zolo, Danilo. 1997. *Cosmopolis: Prospects for World Government*. Cambridge: Polity.

———. 2002. "A Cosmopolitan Philosophy of International Law? A Realist Approach." *Ratio Juris* 12, no. 4:429–44.

3

THE RESURGENT IDEA OF WORLD GOVERNMENT

CAMPBELL CRAIG

The idea of world government is returning to the mainstream of scholarly thinking about international relations. Universities in North America and Europe now routinely advertise for positions in "global governance," a term that few would have heard of a decade ago. Chapters on cosmopolitanism and governance appear in many current international relations (IR) textbooks. Leading scholars are wrestling with the topic, including Alexander Wendt, perhaps now America's most influential IR theorist, who has suggested that a world government is simply "inevitable" (Wendt 2003).[1] While some scholars envision a more formal world state, and others argue for a much looser system of "global governance," it is probably safe to say that the growing number of works on this topic can be grouped together into the broader category of "world government"—a school of thought that supports the creation of international authority (or authorities) that can tackle the global problems that nation-states currently cannot.

It is not, of course, a new idea. Dreaming of a world without war, or of government without tyranny, idealists have advocated some kind of world or universal state since the classical period. The Italian poet Dante viewed world government as a kind of utopia. The Dutch scholar Hugo Grotius, often regarded as the founder of international law, believed in the eventual formation of a world government to enforce it. The notion interested many visionary thinkers in the late nineteenth and early twentieth centuries, including H. G. Wells and Aldous Huxley. In 1942 the onetime Republican presidential candidate Wendell Willkie published a famous book, *One World*. And after the Second World War, the specter of atomic war moved many prominent American scholars and activists, including Albert Einstein, the University of Chicago president Robert Hutchins, and the columnist Dorothy Thompson, to advocate an immediate world state—not so much out of idealistic dreams but because only such a state, they believed, could prevent a third world war fought

---

[1] For a more extensive discussion of new scholarship on world government, see especially Catherine Lu, "World Government," in Edward N. Zalta, ed., *The Stanford Encyclopedia of Philosophy* (Winter 2006); available at plato.stanford.edu/entries/world-government/

with the weapons that had just obliterated Hiroshima and Nagasaki.[2] By the 1950s, however, serious talk of world government had largely disappeared. The failure of the Baruch Plan to establish international control over atomic weaponry in late 1946 signaled the demise of world government, for it cleared the way (as the plan's authors quietly intended) for the United States and the Soviet Union to continue apace with their respective atomic projects. What state would place its trust in a world government when there were sovereign nations that possessed, or could soon possess, atomic bombs?[3]

Certainly, neither the United States nor the Soviet Union was willing to do so, and once the two states committed themselves to the international rivalry that became known as the Cold War, the impossibility of true global government became obvious, and the campaign in favor of it diminished. Even after the invention of thermonuclear weaponry and intercontinental missiles in the late 1950s—a technological development that threatened to destroy all of humanity—few voices in the West (it was never an issue in the Soviet bloc, at least until Gorbachev) were raised to demand a new kind of government that could somehow eliminate this danger. There were some exceptions: a surprising one was the common conclusion reached by the two American realists Reinhold Niebuhr and Hans Morgenthau, who deduced around 1960 that the "nuclear revolution" had made a world state logically necessary. But how to achieve one when the United States and the Soviet Union would never agree to it? Niebuhr and Morgenthau had no answer to this question. The British philosopher Bertrand Russell, however, did: the antinuclear activist once argued that, since his preferred solution of total disarmament was not going to occur, the nuclear revolution had made global government immediately necessary, and thus the only way to achieve it was to wage war on the USSR. There was a perverse logic to this, but we can be thankful that his demands were not heeded.

The end of the Cold War, together with the emergence of various intractable global problems, spurred the resurgence of writing about world government. In this chapter I introduce three themes that appear frequently in this writing: how the "collective action problem" lies behind many of the current global crises; the debate between those who support a softer form of "governance" and those who look toward a full-fledged world state; and the fundamental question of whether world government is possible, and whether it is even desirable.

[2] See Paul Boyer, *By the Bomb's Early Light: American Thought and Culture at the Dawn of the Atomic Age* (New York: Pantheon, 1985); and Luis Cabrera, "Introduction," in Cabrera, ed., *Global Government/Global Governance*, forthcoming.
[3] See Campbell Craig and Sergey Radchenko, *The Atomic Bomb and the Origins of the Cold War* (New Haven: Yale University Press, 2008).

The Intensifying Dangers of International Anarchy

Certainly one of the most evident failures of the nation-state system in recent years has been its inability to deal successfully with problems that endanger much or most of the world's population. As the world has become more economically integrated and culturally interconnected, individual countries have become increasingly averse to dealing with international problems that are not caused by any single state and cannot be fixed even by the focused efforts of individual governments. Political scientists refer to this quandary as the "collective action problem," by which they mean the dilemma that emerges when several actors have an interest in eradicating a problem that harms all of them, but when each would prefer that someone else do the dirty work of solving it. If everyone benefits more or less equally from the problem's solution, but only the actor that addresses it pays the costs, then all are likely to want to "free ride" on the other's efforts. The result is that no one tackles the problem, and everyone suffers.

Several such collective action problems dominate much of international politics today, most notably the imminent danger of climate change, the difficulty of addressing terrorism, and the complex task of humanitarian intervention. All of these are commonly (though not universally) regarded as serious problems in need of urgent solutions, and in each case powerful states have repeatedly demonstrated that they would prefer that somebody else solve them. The recent environmental summit at Copenhagen represents only a particularly vivid example of this process at work.

The solution to the collective action problem has long been known: it requires the establishment of some kind of authoritative regime that can organize common solutions to common problems and spread out the costs fairly. This is why many scholars and activists concerned with acute global problems support some form of world government. These advocates are not so naïve as to believe that such a system would put an effortless end to global warming, terrorism, or human rights atrocities, just as even the most effective national governments have not totally eradicated pollution or crime. The central argument in favor of a world government approach to the problems of globalization is not that it would easily solve these problems but that it is the only entity that *can* solve them.

A less newsworthy issue, but one more central to many advocates of world government, is the persistent possibility of a third world war in which the use of megaton thermonuclear weaponry could destroy most of the human race. During the Cold War, nuclear conflict was averted by the specter of mutual assured destruction (MAD)—the recognition by the United States and the Soviet Union that a war between them would destroy them both. To be sure, this grim form of deterrence could well obtain in future international orders, but it is unwise to regard the Cold War as a promising model for future international politics. It is not at all certain that international politics is destined to return to a stable bipolar order, such as prevailed during the second half of the Cold War, but even if this does happen, there is no guarantee that nuclear deterrence would work as well as it did during the second half of the twentieth century. We would do well to remember that the two sides came close to nuclear blows during the Cuban crisis, and this was over a relatively small issue that did not bear upon the basic security of either state. As Martin Amis has written, the problem with nuclear deterrence is that "it can't last out the necessary timespan, which is roughly between now and the death of the sun."[4] As long as interstate politics continue, we cannot rule out that in some future conflict a warning system will fail, a leader will panic, governments will refuse to back down, a third party will provoke a response—indeed, there are any number of scenarios under which deterrence could fail and thermonuclear war could occur.

It is possible that the United States, if not other nations, can fight against the thermonuclear dilemma with technology. By constructing an anti–ballistic missile (ABM) system, America could perhaps defend itself from a nuclear attack. Also, and more ominously, the United States may be on the verge of deploying an offensive nuclear capability so advanced that it could launch a first strike against a nuclear adversary and disarm it completely.[5] But these are weak reeds. As things currently stand, an ABM system remains acutely vulnerable to inexpensive decoy tactics, jamming, and the simple response of building more missiles. The first-strike option is even more questionable: an aggressive or terrified United States could launch a nuclear war against a major adversary, but no American leader could be sure that every enemy weapon would be destroyed, making the acute risks of initiating such a war (unless a full-scale enemy thermonuclear attack was imminent and certain) likely to outweigh the benefits. Technology is unlikely to solve the nuclear dilemma.

Theorists considering world government regard the thermonuclear dilemma as particularly salient because it epitomizes the dangers of the perpetuation of the interstate system. As long as sovereign nations continue to possess nuclear arsenals, nuclear war is possible, and the only apparent way to put a permanent end to this possibility is to develop some kind of world government, an entity with sufficient power to stop states—not to mention subnational groups—from acquiring nuclear arsenals and waging war with them.

---

[4] Martin Amis, *Einstein's Monsters* (London: Jonathan Cape, 1987), pp. 16–17.

[5] Keir Lieber and Daryl Press, "The End of MAD: The Nuclear Dimension of U.S. Primacy?" *International Security* 30, no. 4 (2006): 7–44. Lieber and Press do not advocate an American first strike against a potential aggressor; they simply argue that the United States has developed a capability to do so.

Global Governance Versus a World State

Scholars nevertheless disagree whether an informal, loose form of governance is sufficient, or whether a more formal world state is necessary. Supporters of global governance argue that the unique dangers created by globalization can be solved by a gradual strengthening of existing international institutions and organizations, making the imposition of a full-blown world state unnecessary. Anthony McGrew, a leading scholar of globalization in British academia, where support for global governance is particularly pronounced, suggests that global problems can be effectively dealt with by liberal international agencies, such as the World Trade Organization; nongovernmental organizations, such as Greenpeace and Doctors Without Borders; and security bodies, such as the U.N. Security Council. McGrew argues that the key is to grant increased and more formal powers to such institutions and organizations, ultimately giving them greater effectiveness and influence on the international stage than nation-states. Another British scholar, David Held, stresses the importance of making international institutions accountable to democratic controls. Held maintains that the world's population must have a direct say in the composition and policies of increasingly powerful international bodies.[6] Held worries, along with others who insist on greater democratic oversight of global institutions, that the current "democratic deficit" afflicting existing international bodies, such as the International Monetary Fund and the U.N. Security Council, could become far worse as they acquire and wield greater and greater power.

The European Union is frequently offered as a model of what could happen at the international level. Gradually, once-hostile European states have cooperated to develop forms of transnational governance without subjecting themselves to the convulsive and possibly violent task of creating a European state. Nations that might refuse to accept the formation of a dominant state have nevertheless readily accepted the establishment of institutions and bureaucracies that slowly create transnational political bonds and reduce their own sovereignty. True, the process of establishing the European Union has been unsure and—for those who want to see a stronger political union—remains incomplete, but it has taken place, and in a peaceful manner. A similar process at the international level, contend advocates of global integration, would constitute a practical way to establish global government.

---

[6] For an overview of McGrew's and Held's positions, see Anthony McGrew and David Held, eds., *Governing Globalization* (London: Polity, 2002), chaps. 13 and 15. American scholars in favor of global governance include Richard Falk, *On Humane Governance* (University Park: Pennsylvania State University Press, 1995); and Anne-Marie Slaughter, *A New World Order* (Princeton: Princeton University Press, 2005). For an innovative treatment of the problem of global democracy, see Luis Cabrera, *Political Theory of Global Justice: A Cosmopolitan Case for the World State* (London: Routledge, 2004).

Theorists who believe that a more formal world state is necessary do not necessarily disagree with the logic of global governance: it is difficult to dispute the claim that the gradual creation of supranational institutions is likely to be more feasible and peaceful than the imposition of a true world state. The "key problem" for the governance argument, however, as Alexander Wendt writes, is "unauthorized violence by rogue Great Powers" (2003, 506). As long as sovereign states continue to exist under a system of governance, in other words, there is nothing to prevent them from using violence to disrupt the international peace for their own purposes. The European Union has created forms of transnational governance, but decision making in the areas of security and defense is still the prerogative of its member states. Thus, the European Union remains effectively powerless to stop violence undertaken by one of its own members (such as Britain's involvement in the Iraq war), not to mention war waged by other nations even in its own backyard (as in Bosnia and Herzegovina). Until this problem is solved, world state advocates argue, any global order will be too fragile to endure. Sooner or later a sovereign state will wage war, and the inability of a regime of global governance to stop it will deprive it of authority and legitimacy. International politics would then revert to the old state system.

In "Why a World State Is Inevitable," Wendt argues that a formal world state—by which he means a truly new sovereign political entity, with constitutional authority over all nations—will naturally evolve as peoples and nations come to realize that they cannot obtain true independence, or what he calls "recognition," without one. In other words, the advent of global technologies and weaponry presents weaker societies with an emerging choice between subjugation to powerful states and globalized forces or participation in an authentic world government. A world state would not threaten distinct national cultures, as pluralist scholars have argued; rather, it is the only entity that can preserve them. Wendt sees this as a teleological phenomenon, by which he means that the logic of globalization and the struggle by all cultures and societies for recognition is bound to lead to a world state whether it is sought or not. Such a state, argues Wendt, would not need to be particularly centralized or hierarchical: as long as it could prevent sovereign states from waging war, it could permit local cultures, traditions, and politics to continue (2003, esp. 507–10, 514–16).[7] But a looser system of governance would not be enough, because societies that seek recognition could not trust it to protect them from powerful states seeking domination.

Daniel Deudney's book *Bounding Power* (2006) provides the fullest and most creative vision yet of formal world government in our age.

---

[7] For the argument that world government would threaten cultural pluralism, see Michael Walzer, *Arguing About War* (New Haven: Yale University Press, 2004).

Deudney argues that the driving force behind world government is the fact that international war has become too dangerous. Unified by a common interest in avoiding nuclear extermination, states have the ability to come together in much the same way as tribes and fiefdoms did in the past when advances in military technology made conflict among them suicidal. Unlike Wendt, Deudney does not see this as an inevitability: states may well choose to tolerate interstate anarchy, even though it will sooner or later result in a nuclear war. But Deudney is also optimistic that a world government created for the purpose of avoiding such a war can be small, decentralized, and liberal. In *Bounding Power*, he develops an elaborate case for the establishment of a world republic, based upon the same premise of restraining and diffusing power that motivated the founders of the American republic in the late eighteenth century.

World state theorists such as Wendt and Deudney stress the danger that advocates of more global governance often downplay: the risk that ambitious sovereign states will be unrestrained by international institutions and agencies, even unprecedentedly powerful ones, and will wage war for traditional reasons of power and profit. For Wendt, military conflict of this sort will simply push along the inevitable process of world state formation, as societies and peoples recognize that a return to interstate anarchy will only unleash more such wars, while a world government will put an end to them and so guarantee their cultural independence. Deudney is less hopeful here. Military conflict in our age can well mean thermonuclear war, an event that could put an end to the pursuit of meaningful human independence and the kind of world government that would respect it.

Is a World Government Possible?

The initial argument against a world state, and even a coherent system of global governance, is the one that anyone can see immediately: it is impractical. How could nations of radically different ideologies and cultures agree upon one common political authority? But the "impracticality" argument disregards historical experience. The history of state formation from the days of city-states to the present era is precisely the history of warring groups with different ideologies and cultures coming together under a larger entity. While the European Union is not at all yet a state, who would not have been denounced as insane for predicting a political and economic union of France, Germany, and other European states seventy years ago? For that matter, how "practical" would it have seemed forty years ago to foresee the peaceful end of the Cold War? As Deudney argues, smaller political units have always merged into larger ones when technology has made the violence among them unsustainable.

The surprising thing, he maintains, would be if this did *not* happen at the global level.

The more important objections to world government posit not that it is impractical but that it is unnecessary and even undesirable. According to one such argument, the world should be governed not by a genuinely international authority but rather by the United States: a Pax Americana.[8] This school of thought stresses two main points: that an American seizing of global power would be far less violent than the formation of an authentically international world state; and (as neoconservative writers particularly stress) that a world run by the United States would be preferable to a genuinely transnational world government, given the superiority of American political, economic, and cultural institutions.

The case against a Pax Americana, however, can be boiled down to one word: Iraq. The war in Iraq has shown that military operations undertaken by individual nation-states lead, as they have always done, to nationalist and tribal reactions against the aggressor that pay no heed to larger claims of superior or inferior civilizations. The disaster in Iraq has emboldened other revisionist states and groups to defy American will, caused erstwhile allies and friends of the United States to question its intentions and competence, and at the same time soured the American people on future adventures against states that do not overtly threaten them. In conceiving and executing its war in Iraq, it would have been difficult for the United States to undermine the project of a Pax Americana more effectively had it tried to do so. American leaders could choose in future to rally other states behind them to deal with a genuinely global threat that must be vanquished. But, as Wendt implies, to do that successfully is effectively to begin the process of world state formation.

Another objection to world government was first identified by Immanuel Kant. In articulating a plan for perpetual peace, Kant stopped short of advocating a world state, for fear that the state could become tyrannical. In a world of several nation-states, a tyranny can be removed by other states or be overthrown from within. At least it could be possible for oppressed citizens of that state to flee to less repressive countries. But a sovereign world government could be invulnerable to such measures. It could not be defeated by an external political rival; those who would overthrow it from within would have nowhere to hide, no one to support them from the outside. Kant concluded that these dangers overrode the permanent peace that could be had with world government, and he ended up advocating instead a confederation of sovereign, commercial states.

---

[8] See, for example, Niall Ferguson, *Colossus: The Rise and Fall of the American Empire* (New York: Penguin, 2004).

One can raise two points in response to Kant's deeply important concern. First, Kant wrote in the eighteenth century, when the specter of war was not omnicidal and the planet did not face such global crises as climate change and transnational terrorism. International politics as usual was not as dangerous an alternative to his vision of perpetual peace as it potentially is today. Second, as Deudney argues, there is one central reason to believe that a world government could avoid the temptations of tyranny and actually exist as a small, federal authority rather than a global leviathan (2006, esp. chap. 6 and conclusion). This is the indisputable fact that—barring extraterrestrial invasion—a world government would have no need for a policy of external security. States often become increasingly tyrannical as they use external threats to justify internal repression and authoritarian policies. These threats, whether real or imagined, have throughout history and to the present day been used by leaders to justify massive taxation, conscription, martial law, and the suppression of dissent. But no world government could plausibly make such demands.

Will the world government movement become a potent political force, or will it fade away as it did in the late 1940s? To a degree the answer to this question depends on the near-term future of international politics. If the United States alters its foreign policy and moves to manage the unipolar world more magnanimously or, alternatively, if a new power (such as China) arises quickly to balance American power and instigate a new Cold War, the movement could fade. So, too, if existing international organizations become more effective in ameliorating climate change, fighting terrorism, and preventing humanitarian crises and other global problems. On the other hand, if the United States continues to pursue a Pax Americana or if the transnational problems worsen, the movement could become a serious international cause.

These considerations aside, as Reinhold Niebuhr, Hans Morgenthau, and others discerned during the height of the Cold War, the deepest argument for world government—the specter of global nuclear war—will endure as long as sovereign nation-states continue to deploy nuclear weaponry. Whatever occurs over the near-term future, this is a fact that is not going away. The great distinction between the international system prevailing in Niebuhr and Morgenthau's day and the system in our own time is that the chances of attaining some form of world government have been radically enhanced by the end of the Cold War and the emergence of a unipolar order. This condition, however, will not last forever.

Acknowledgments

This chapter was first published (in slightly different form) in *Ethics and International Affairs* 22, no. 2 (Summer 2008): 133–42.

References

Deudney, Daniel H. 2006. *Bounding Power: Republican Security Theory from the Polis to the Global Village.* Princeton: Princeton University Press.

Wendt, Alexander. 2003. "Why a World State Is Inevitable." *European Journal of International Relations* 9, no. 4:491–542.

4

STRUCTURING GLOBAL DEMOCRACY: POLITICAL COMMUNITIES, UNIVERSAL HUMAN RIGHTS, AND TRANSNATIONAL REPRESENTATION

CAROL C. GOULD

Introduction

Where it is not rejected altogether, global democracy is often thought of in either/or terms: either it entails the implementation of full-scale world government or else it should be limited to innovations within the existing system of nation-states and international organizations—for example, loose federations of nation-states at regional levels or new international institutions such as a Global People's Assembly at the United Nations (Falk and Strauss 2000). This characterization of the options, however, omits a distinctive feature of contemporary globalization, namely, the emergence of cross-border communities and transnational associations, which I suggest require new ways of thinking about the norms involved in democracy in a globalized world. I have developed such a framework in *Globalizing Democracy and Human Rights* (Gould 2004), which also gives a major role to human rights fulfillment, including social and economic rights as much as civil and political ones. This sort of framework can help to harmonize the claims of existing political communities or associations (including new cross-border ones) with the increased democratic scope needed to give input on the part of distant others into decisions that crucially affect them.

In the first part of this chapter, I attempt to develop further the two criteria that I have already advanced for addressing the range and character of desirable democratization in transnational contexts—*common activities* and *impact on basic human rights*—and I analyze their relation to each other, arguing that they are compatible. In the second part, I go on to consider some of the practical implications of these criteria for institutional transformation and design, with special reference to some new directions for *transnational representation*.

1. Political Communities and Human Rights Impacts in Transnational Democracy

Existing Conceptions of Global Democracy

Many critics dismiss the project of transnational or global democracy on the grounds that it is either impossible, given the current state system, or else undesirable, since it would entail a single government for everyone. It is pointed out that we lack a global demos and a strong global public sphere, both of which are thought to be required for democracy (based on our experience in nation-states). In fact, I think that these criticisms are well taken, but I would deny the hasty conclusion that we can make no sense of viable transnational democracy. I would suggest that if we remain with the current interpretation of political communities as sovereign nation-states, then globalizing democracy is probably impossible. And if we take it to mean a world government, then it is undesirable, for the reasons discussed below. Moreover, these critics are also correct that there is no global demos, in which everyone can participate equally as a citizen in a single world polity, and no effective global public sphere. But I think that it is faulty to seek such a global demos and globalized public sphere, and that it is an impoverished view of transnational democracy that would see it as entailing a world government replacing all smaller forms of associations. In fact, I would suggest that the emerging multiplicity of transnational public spheres and their overlapping nature might actually make possible a richer, and potentially more democratic, form of transnational association.

The single world government idea is undesirable mainly because of the possibilities it would introduce of world tyranny. Just as authoritarian regimes can come to power via elections in sovereign nation-states, so a similar possibility cannot be ruled out for a world government, despite the safeguards that would be introduced. But it is more difficult to fault the other prevalent suggestions of loose federations of nation-states at regional and international levels, or else the strengthening of international institutions with, for example, a Global People's Assembly. In regard to the first of these, the most interesting direction is perhaps to be found in the further development of *regionalism*, following on the lead of the European Union, though the primary innovation concerns the introduction of regional agreements on human rights, as I indicate below. But the problem with simple federal or confederal views is that they do not speak to the emergence of transnational associations that extend beyond and across regions. Indeed, to the degree that the regional federations are built up as aggregations of nation-states, where the latter remain the decisive units, the federations do not adequately address the new cross-border communities within them. Further, crucial global justice issues that separate world regions into relatively well-off or impoverished ones are not adequately dealt with by this regional proposal. And global corporations too, which are often problematic actors under current globalization, tend to escape the reach of regional bodies as well as of nation-states. Yet another limitation of such regional federations concerns the difficulty they face of dealing with ecological impacts of a more fully global nature, most especially global warming.

A more limited contemporary approach emphasizes adding to current international institutions new forms of representation of people as global citizens. A key proposal along these lines is for a People's Assembly in the U.N., which would be popularly elected rather than serving to represent governments (Falk and Strauss 2000). This is probably a worthwhile innovation for improving the short-term situation. But it is hard to see how this one body could deal with the myriad new issues that confront a more globalized world, particularly given the powerful nation-states that would continue to dominate international relations on this model.

So, the question that faces us is what sort of perspective can do justice to the emerging cross-border communities and transnational associations that are growing in importance as the sovereignty of traditional nation-states is partially eroded. Particularly with the development of economic globalization, as well as with communities growing up around ecological interests, with migration, and with new transnational social movements, it is necessary to consider what forms would be conducive to more democratic participation by people involved in these new phenomena. Whereas much of economic globalization seems to entail transnational power beyond the control of individuals, and with ecological impacts becoming ever more problematic over time, the issue of democratizing these phenomena is of central contemporary importance.

My standpoint in the remainder of the first part of this chapter is rather forward looking. I am interested in how we can think about democracy given the growth of cross-border interrelations and transnational interdependence, and where eventually we can suppose that nation-states will no longer remain the prime actors in global affairs. In this context, we can also appeal to a normative critique of the functioning of sovereign nation-states, which I have developed elsewhere (Gould 2006). It is clear, then, that these reflections go beyond a current or short-term perspective, in which nation-states are clearly the predominant players, as Allen Buchanan and Robert Keohane have forcefully reminded us (Buchanan and Keohane 2006). Further, my main concern is with clarifying some philosophical principles that are helpful in thinking normatively about these new directions. And, drawing on my previous work, I would even say that an adequate social ontology of communities and of global actors is helpful in figuring out these new directions. In the second part of the chapter, I draw back to a perspective somewhat closer to the present and argue that democratic accountability is relevant to the new international institutions, though in a circumscribed sense, and I discuss some new directions for transnational representation.

Common Activities

In my view, the consideration of the appropriate scope for democratization makes appeal to two concepts, one that I have called common activities and the other, the idea of human rights (Gould 2004). Although these rights have a variety of complex relations to democratic decisions (including legitimately constraining them), my appeal to them here is as a specification of the notion that "those importantly affected" by a given decision or policy should have input into it in global contexts. I explain these notions and defend them further in this section.

In previous work, especially in my books *Rethinking Democracy* and *Globalizing Democracy and Human Rights*, I have argued for a principle of democracy rather different from the more standard "all affected" one (see Gould 1988, esp. chap. 1, and Gould 2004, esp. chaps. 1, 7, and 9), in part because the all affected principle taken in a blanket sense would seem to be hopelessly vague, particularly when applied to global contexts. As I have argued elsewhere, globalization is marked by the interconnection of people and their activities such that innumerable people are affected by decisions and actions at a distance, even leaving aside future generations.[1] Thus, taken in its generality, the all affected principle does not provide much guidance for democratic participation and representation in emerging global institutions. (I do, however, propose what I see as a useful delimitation of it in the second conception of scope, to be discussed shortly.)

Instead of simply considering the effects of decisions and policies, I propose another relevant criterion for determining the scope of democracy, as an interpretation of the very general characterization of it as rule by the people or popular control. In this approach, the democratic principle requires equal rights of participation in decisions concerning the *common activities* in which people engage, where such common or joint activities are understood to be defined by shared goals and practices. To put the argument very briefly, justice is interpreted as a principle of equal positive freedom, or prima facie equal rights to the conditions of freedom as self-transformative activity, whether individual or collective. Since engaging in common activities is one of the main conditions for freedom, it follows that individuals must be self-determining in such activity. But since these activities are collective in character and no participant has more of a right than the others to make the decision for the collectivity (if domination is to be avoided), then decisions about such common activities necessarily take the form of codetermination of the

---

[1] I argued to this effect especially for domestic contexts in Gould 1988; the argument is even more compelling given globalization, as discussed in Gould 2004, esp. chap. 7.

course of this activity, hence of equal rights to participate in decisions about it. On this view, then, democratic participation is seen as widely required in a range of economic and social institutions, as well as in the recognized political ones.

As opposed to conceptions that see democracy as instrumental to the satisfaction of people's interests, this approach privileges human action, where this needs to be understood as taking both collective and individual forms. Institutions on this account are seen as sets of practices that are constructed; as such human creations, they can also be changed (though not by a single individual). Nonetheless, the individuals operating in these institutions and in communities of various sorts have equal rights to participate in shaping them, because this participation is a condition for the self-transformation of each of them.

The social ontology implied here centers on a conception of individuals-in-relations, who are fundamentally equal and agential. People cannot be adequately construed as bundles of interests, and their agency takes both individual and collective forms as noted. The institutions and communities that serve to meet needs and advance common ends have developed over time and provide practical contexts for people's individual and shared goals. In this sense, the institutions and communities where democracy is relevant are given in our social experience and are in this way exogenous to democracy; they are relevant contexts where rights of democratic participation obtain. And because common activities include various institutions and associations with diverse purposes, democracy is not seen as limited to nation-states but pertains in principle to a wide set of economic, social, and cultural associations as well.

This approach rather easily applies to new cross-border associations and communities, since it does not prioritize the nation-state in its fundamental conception. To the degree that forms of common activities with shared ends are becoming increasingly cross-border, it follows that democratic participation and representation are relevant to these new contexts as well. Indeed, there have already been interesting developments along these lines, not only in the large-scale and increasingly established context of the European Union but also in emerging smaller-scale communities, both of a locally cross-border sort—whether ecologically or economically based—or in new forums enabled by Internet communications, for example, among political activists or in some discussion-based groups. It is not currently the case, however, that this model of common activities or preexisting communities of interest or "fate" extends globally in a way that would require a single demos with traditional democratic participation and representation. And I have suggested that this is not a bad thing, because I share the worry about introducing world government or even a unified global democracy (since, as noted, such a unified body might more easily permit global tyranny or domination, despite efforts to safeguard against it).

But there are several potential problems with this common activities view, which need to be considered briefly here. One set of concerns has been aptly posed by Pablo Gilabert: given the variety of common activities, what is to be done when they overlap and conflict with each other? Which communities should be given priority? In addition, it might seem that the concept is so broad that it proliferates communities and could become indeterminate in much the same way that the unrestricted all affected principle is (Gilabert 2006). I think that the second part of this objection—concerning the proliferation of communities—is not decisive, since the proposal is in fact one for radical democracy, endorsing a requirement for it in a range of associations and communities beyond those currently recognized (where this is admittedly a highly normative and distant possibility). That it would be desirable to have such networks of overlapping communities further mitigates the problem here, I think, since they could be mutually enriching and stand in solidarity with each other, as I have discussed elsewhere (Gould 2007).

The first problem is more difficult, however—namely, what to do when communities or spheres of common activity conflict with each other. It is presumably partly because of this situation of conflict that states have evolved over time. Broader frameworks, such as those provided by nation-states, can provide important adjudicative functions. But that fact does not establish that nation-states are different in kind from other institutions and communities as potential arenas for democratic decision making, although the range of their activities and the range of shared goals and projects that states embody are broader. Further, even institutions smaller in scale than the state, such as transnational corporations, have to deal with and adjudicate internal conflicts, where some of these are not only between individuals but also among smaller-scale organizations that make them up.

Another set of objections comes from those who think an emphasis on political agency is too demanding, particularly with globalization. Thus Daniel Weinstock objects to this emphasis as unrealistic and as ineffective in meeting people's interests. On his view, a rather delimited set of institutions of global governance could be justified if they were instrumental to meeting people's fundamental interests (Weinstock 2006). But I would suggest that the criticism Weinstock gives in fact misconstrues the argument for rights of democratic participation. It is not that participation is simply good in itself—indeed, it is only rights of participation, not an obligation to participate, for which I argue. Democratic participation serves freedom on the account I give, and some of what Weinstock counts as fundamental interests come in either as aspects of or as conditions for freedom. Thus democracy is also in this sense instrumental to people's goals and projects on my own view. I think, however, that an emphasis on equal agency and its conditions is to be preferred to the bundle of interests view. Indeed, the importance of agency is brought in by Weinstock as well, though in what might seem a rather backhanded way. Specifically, he identifies nondomination as among people's fundamental interests (Weinstock 2006, 12). I suggest that this implicitly recognizes the importance of the freedom and equality of agency to democracy that is at the core of my account.

Human Rights and Affectedness

The "common activities" criterion does in fact have a significant limitation, and this is its incompleteness as an account of the scope of democracy. Thus the model sees democratic modes of decision as applicable wherever people are organized (either voluntarily or traditionally) into institutions or communities. And such a model does indeed have increasing applicability to cross-border or transnational contexts, as I consider further in part 2. As suggested, it would apply to new communities that are literally cross-border, for example, where ecological interests are shared among neighboring communities across nation-state or more local borders, and to noncontiguous transnational communities of limited purpose, such as those that may develop on the Internet. But interpreting the principle of democracy in this communal way does not suffice to address the need to open the institutions of global governance (or indeed even the decisions of traditional political communities) to input from people increasingly affected by their decisions, who often reside in locations rather remote from these institutions and the major participants within them. So there is a need for an additional principle beyond the common activities one in order to determine the scope of democratic input into decisions.

We have seen, however, that a main candidate for this—the all affected principle—will not suffice, since at least in its most general form it is hopelessly vague. So, to what principle can we appeal in this new context? I have elsewhere proposed that there is in fact a specification of the all affected principle that can help to delineate those at a distance who have prima facie rights of input into the decisions of the multilateral organizations of global governance, if not always full-fledged rights of participation. In particular, I have suggested the following delimitation: When people at a distance are impacted in regard to their possibilities for fulfilling their basic human rights because of the decisions of the institutions of global governance, they have rights of input into those decisions (Gould 2004, chap. 9).

This principle—which takes those affected as determined by impact on basic human rights—speaks to that aspect of democracy in which it is not only required by justice (as equal positive freedom) but also serves to realize it. On my view, human rights have priority in this account, inasmuch as they specify the conditions that people need, including economic and social ones, to realize their projects, whether individual or collective, and to develop capacities. Given the status of these human rights as valid claims that we each make on others for the conditions that we need for our freedom and dignity, it follows that social, economic, and political institutions, including those in the international sphere, need to be designed to make it possible for all to fulfill these basic rights. The significance of these rights also supports an interpretation of people's being importantly affected by decisions of multilateral or transnational institutions precisely when they are affected in their capacity to realize human rights, at least the basic ones. "Basic" denotes those required as conditions for any human action whatever, and "nonbasic" those required for the elaboration of this activity in forms of self-development or self-transformation over time (Gould 1988, esp. chaps. 1 and 8).

Because of the centrality of democratic participation in people's having the ability to realize and protect their human rights, including economic and social ones—an argument initially presented by Henry Shue (1980)—it follows that they should have substantial input into those decisions that affect rights fulfillment. Thus, if these transnational institutions impact the possibility of people meeting basic needs for means of subsistence, for example, those so affected should have input into the functioning of these institutions. The role of democratic input can also be gleaned by considering that people are themselves usually best able to identify and characterize their own needs. This suggests the superiority of a democratic interpretation of providing input over the weaker notions of stakeholder theory, in which it is sufficient for decision makers in corporations or in the institutions of global governance to imagine for themselves what people at a distance think about the proposed issue. On the view here, democratic input is required, even if it can often not take the form of democratic participation in a full sense. In the next part of the chapter, I briefly consider some of the new forms of participation and representation that can facilitate this input.

2. Transnational Representation: Extending Participation in Cross-Border Decision Making

Contemporary analysts of international affairs have most often tended to assume that democratic participation and representation are inapplicable to international and transnational organizations, including intergovernmental organizations and networks, international nongovernmental organizations, various multinational institutions, and transnational corporations. For example, even authors otherwise sympathetic to instituting greater accountability in world politics, such as Ruth Grant and Robert Keohane in a joint article, dismiss any claim to the relevance of democratic representation in that domain as wholly unrealistic and even undesirable (Grant and Keohane 2005). But we have already seen the outlines of an argument for just such relevance of democratic norms of participation and representation in that more global context, provided due attention is paid to the difficult questions of delimiting the scope of the communities of participants in these democratic decisions. In view of the contending approaches to representation within political theory, I want now to consider some of the possible directions for introducing democratic participation and representation both in near-term contexts and by way of longer-term institutional innovation and transformation.

Democratic Participation and Accountability and the Problem of Scope

Grant and Keohane recognize a category of accountability that they call democratic accountability, understood as arising from democratic participation (optimally) and representation (secondarily). But they relegate this to the traditional domain of the nation-state, apparently for both theoretical and practical reasons. Practically, requiring democratic accountability from international organizations like the World Trade Organization, the World Bank, and the U.N. is regarded as too difficult and thus too far-fetched a demand. Theoretically, they emphasize the inherently wide scope of those affected by the decisions of these organizations and conclude that this renders democratic accountability irrelevant. In their view, this is so also because of the undesirability of moving in the direction of a global polity and its presumed correlate of a world government. But granted that international organizations have an impact on large numbers of people situated at a distance, and that we seek democratic forms that can empower people through a degree of input into such organizations, what can we say about the implications of the two criteria for democratic participation discussed in the first part?

Grant and Keohane state that the criterion for the relevance of democratic participation in decisions is what I denoted as "the all affected principle," that is, that all affected by a particular decision have a right to participate in making it. But as we have seen, this is too broad, because the set of all affected is very large, even larger than a polity, a feature exacerbated in the context of globalization. Tacitly, these authors actually appeal, I would suggest, to a more delimited interpretation of the all affected principle that those *subject to* the laws of a polity should have a role in participating and deliberating about them, either directly or through their representatives.[2] Whatever one may think about the possible advantages of "subject to" over "affected by" in the context of nation-states, the issue clearly becomes quite difficult in the case of transnational or international organizations, whether in the making of regulations, policies, or individual decisions. Here, there are no estab-

---

[2] Note, however, that sometimes this criterion of "subject to" or "governed by" is distinguished from that of "being affected," as in Cohen 1996, esp. 95 and 114 n. 1.

lished polities, or clearly demarcated demoi or publics for whom democratic participation and representation are clearly relevant. Yet, as
already suggested, the effects of decisions by the organizations of global
governance, especially the WTO, the World Bank, and the International
Monetary Fund, are felt by those at a distance, and their decisions
profoundly affect the conditions of existence and the life chances of many
millions, if not billions, of people around the globe.

Before turning to the question of representation in these new contexts,
we can observe that Grant and Keohane are in fact hasty in concluding
that democratic accountability in the sense of participation and representation is inapplicable to the institutions of global governance.
As noted, the main problem they describe is the lack of a global public
or people organized into a polity, which they see as the sole context for
democratic accountability in the strong sense in which it would arise from
participation and representation. But their argument simply rules out this
possibility in advance by wrongly taking such democratic rights as
coming into being only when those affected are organized into a polity
or demos, as in sovereign states. In this sense, their argument is question
begging, since it amounts to the claim that because there is no sovereignty
in global governance there can be no democratic accountability in that
sense. But the issue is in fact whether democratic accountability
is possible given the new diminution and restraint on sovereignty posed
by these institutions, so the issue can certainly not be resolved by
definition.

In contrast to the approach of Grant and Keohane, I have suggested
that there are two senses of democratic participation that are indeed
relevant to these new contexts. One concerns the multiplicity of communities, institutions, or publics, including new cross-border or transnational ones, within which processes of codetermination of common
activities remain relevant. The second concerns a more delimited interpretation of being affected by decisions, which gives rise to rights of
democratic input, if not always full-scale participation, namely, where
people are affected in their ability to realize their basic human rights by
the functioning of these global institutions.

Relating Participation to Representation

What are the implications for representation of these two principles—of
common activities and the human rights interpretation of being affected?
The democratic requirement, at least on the common activities model, is
one of equal rights of participation and deliberation in decisions concerning these activities. I see such participation as compatible with
representation in large-scale institutional contexts. But given the applicability of democratic modes to smaller-scale institutions and communities
as well, we can retain the possibility of recognizing rights of direct

participation in those cases, not only representation. Thus I am not inclined to follow those who propose that all valuable participation occurs only in connection with representation or, as David Plotke puts it, that representation just *is* democracy (Plotke 1997). While Plotke is right to point to the features of autonomy or agency and of mutual interest on both sides of the representative-represented relation, it is only by a reduction of the argument for direct participation that the possibility and desirability of such participation can be denied. That is, Plotke errs by supposing that participation necessarily requires that everyone eligible must actually take part in a decision (focusing his remarks on Benjamin Barber's early statement of this view [Barber 1984]). Rather, participation properly requires only that people have rights to take part, not duties to do so.

The practical argument advanced against the possibility of direct forms of participation only makes sense if democracy is taken to be restricted to the large-scale political contexts of nation-states. But this restriction tends to be assumed without much argument, and there clearly are small communities, even cross-border ones, where direct deliberation and participation by people are possible. Such democratic processes are evidently also applicable within small-scale social and economic institutions. This is not to deny, of course, that representative forms may in fact be most appropriate in complex political communities. But as Plotke and others note, such representation should ideally involve strong participative elements, in terms of people's two-way contacts with their representatives, in view of the fact that people can normally best articulate their own interests and needs, as well as their conceptions of common interests. Further, any analysis of representation must come to grips with a difficulty that Plotke completely omits: namely, that in winner-take-all systems, the minority in fact voted against the particular representative. Thus while representatives presumably strive to represent all their constituents and can be held accountable for their activities, they are only in a partial sense to be regarded as chosen by all of them.

In the approach proposed here, then, participation remains essential in the shared determination of the direction of common activities and indeed does not lose its preeminence. Moreover, in the common activities model, we can say that there is no barrier in principle to democracy (whether formal or substantive) coming to embody genuinely *equal* rights of participation. But what about our other principle, which establishes a democratic requirement for those who are affected in their possibilities of realizing human rights? Does this version of the democratic principle also require participation, at least as a regulative ideal, or will representation suffice for its achievement? Indeed, we may ask whether equal participation in fact is possible in the global context, given that people are normally *differentially* affected by the decisions of the international organizations in which we are proposing they should be able to participate or be represented.

My inclination is to call for substantial input, rather than full participation, on the part of people affected in their human rights into the functioning of these transnational institutions. The democratic rights in this case seem most congenial to the selection of representatives, especially because of the large number of people involved and how widespread they are and distant from the centers of power. Nonetheless, some participation is required in the sense that people need to be consulted in regard to their understanding of their basic needs and interests and key projects; they are the ones to give expression and shape to understanding these. This suggests that a system of representation concerning these fundamental interests within transnational institutions has to be developed, but one that would facilitate participation wherever possible. In fact, as I briefly consider in the concluding section, communications technologies open up new possibilities for facilitating direct participation in some of these decisions.

In this new transnational context, however, the problem of equality of participation is a difficult one, even in regard to selecting and authorizing representatives. These representatives could be either standing or ad hoc, and the issue of equality is more urgent in the case of determining standing representatives. I suggest, as something that can be implemented in the near term, that international institutions and transnational corporations be required to prepare *human rights impact assessments* as a regular part of their development of policies and rules. (These would be comparable in some ways to those now mandated in regard to technology assessments or environmental impact statements, but would require the development of a new form suited to its subject matter.) These human rights assessments would specify likely impacts of the proposed policies on specified groups, which would often vary from case to case. If these impacts were differential, it may be possible to construct ad hoc representation to meet the needs of each case. This would go part of the way to giving expression to the principle that people importantly affected by a given policy or plan, namely, people affected in their human rights, have rights of input into these decisions, directly or through representatives. Such a new direction would only work if appeals were possible in both regional and more fully global contexts, especially to established or new courts of human rights. And such regional human rights courts, constructed through region-wide agreements, would also serve to provide structure for the small-scale cross-border associations within their domains.[3]

---

[3] Yet another avenue of appeal could be provided by extending the right to petition to these international institutions (see Nickel 2005, 211–12). This right of petition, included in the American Bill of Rights, could usefully be extended to the transnational realm.

Directions for Transnational Representation Within Human Rights Frameworks

We have moved to the terrain of institutional innovation. It is not possible to deduce institutional models from a concept here, because we are dealing with an emerging and dynamic international and increasingly global system, where change is ultimately rooted in people's transformative processes. Rather, I want to consider the sort of institutional innovations to which the two principles of democratic expansion discussed here might conduce.

Unsurprisingly, the principle that those engaged in common activities—in economic, social, or political institutions—have rights of participation in making decisions about them extends democracy to new cross-border communities, whether territorial or not, and whether they be constituted voluntarily or not. In this model, as we have seen, democratic rights follow upon people's cooperative activities with others and reflect the growing interdependencies among them. Here, democratic processes are ideally deliberative and substantive, in that they are founded on reciprocity among participants. Perhaps most controversially, this model extends democratic decision making to firms and other economic institutions.[4] The elaboration of this model would also involve an expansion of democratic decision making in new ecologically based communities, such as between the northern Midwestern U.S. states and Canada, or, in a different context, in new communications forums on the Internet. It is also plausible to see the model exemplified in the development of regional associations, beyond those in the European Union, involving cooperative democratic arrangements within sets of nation-states in the Americas or in Africa, and in the first instance among contiguously situated nation-states. This process should not primarily be seen as exclusively political or as confined to matters traditionally addressed by nation-states. The democratic principle advanced would also sit well with a variety of functional associations, for example, of an economic (as well as political or social) nature, where the economic associations are themselves divided by sector, with membership drawn from all those active in that particular sector, and where they cooperatively join with others from their region in decision making.

---

[4] The argument for this, developed in Gould 1988 and other writings, turns on the idea that codetermination is required in all institutional contexts of joint activities if people are to be agential and nondominated, and that there is no distinction in principle between governments and smaller-scale institutions in this respect. The requirement gains additional force from the centrality of meaningful work in people's lives, in a sense that involves control over cooperative work activities, as well as from practical considerations that participation in management is motivating and can be highly successful (as in the case of Mondragon, a worker self-managed enterprise that is also one of the largest and most successful corporations in Spain).

Representation would play a key role in new democratic arrangements within contexts of economic, social, and political life, where such representation could either be informal, as it is now with civil society organizations, especially international nongovernmental organizations, or it could become more formalized. It seems clear, however, that the civil society organizations would themselves have to develop more democratic modes of decision making, in order to gain fuller legitimacy in such forms of representation. The critique to which such civil society organizations have been subject, namely, that they are wholly unaccountable, seems incorrect in the main. Some of these organizations already incorporate democratic procedures; especially the grassroots organizations are clearly more accountable than the dominant international organizations. The latter tend to be responsive to large transnational corporations (and thus may display conflicts of interest in their regulations) or to the officials who have appointed them (where these officials themselves are subject to democratic deficits in regard to their own election or appointment). Yet, it must be admitted that NGOs and the institutions of civil society could, generally speaking, introduce more fully democratic procedures for electing representatives and permit greater participation in their decisions on the part of those for whom they claim to speak.

Beyond the multiplicity of regional and cross-border communities or other new bodies that can permit participation and representation regarding cooperative or common activities, there have been proposals for strictly political transnational assemblies. Among these proposals, the principle I presented is friendly to those that call for reciprocal representation within regional associations, as in Philippe Schmitter's idea for such interparliamentary representation (Saward 2000). In addition, it may even be possible eventually to implement joint elections for some representatives within regional political bodies (El Menyawi 2004). Certainly, regional human rights courts would provide an important framework for these developments, as noted earlier. And the model of democracy advocated here can certainly accommodate the proposal for a Global People's Assembly within the U.N., as promoted by Richard Falk and Andrew Strauss (2000). Such a more representative second assembly within the U.N., with representatives chosen at large, would be an advance over the present situation. Yet, if it is thought to involve a single global assembly or parliament with very substantial power, one can worry whether it would provide sufficient space for a diversity of cultural perspectives, and also whether it raises the possibility of a global misuse of power, in view of human error. In this respect, the development of regional associations, particularly for the purposes of human rights protection and fulfillment, along with new representative institutions at regional levels, might enable fuller recognition of the diversity that currently exists globally and could constitute a more multicentric approach to transnational representation.

In terms of the institutions of global governance, the second democratic principle I discussed, which takes into account the impact of decisions on people's fundamental human rights, would seek enhanced representation for distant people within these institutions, including economic ones, such as the World Bank and the WTO, or within their eventual more democratic replacements. Such representation would need to go beyond the present relatively weak proposals for consultation by these international organizations with INGOs. Beyond simply certifying these civil society organizations, it would be necessary to work out established modes of representation for people impacted by the various policies, rules, and regulations enunciated by these organizations. On this democratic principle, this sort of representation is of even greater consequence than the accountability of these organizations to the nation-states that have agreed to set them up. This feature follows from the normative priority of human rights in global affairs, specifically from the idea that political, economic, and social organizations ought to be structured so that people can fulfill their human rights through the functioning of these organizations. The democratic principle would therefore support expansive and regularized representation for people (or perhaps for nation-states), especially from poor countries within these organizations. It might also support ad hoc representation procedures based on specific human rights assessments of prospective policies, rules, and plans. Clearly, this principle also supports proposals for reform of the U.N. and its agencies, to reduce the democratic deficit that is evident in its current functioning and to make it an effective force in realizing human rights, including the economic and social ones in its purview.

Finally, we can observe that the Internet and other information and communications technologies can help to increase both democratic participation and representation in the functioning of transnational institutions. There is of course no guarantee that they will do so, and they are equally capable of facilitating widespread manipulation, along with centralized, or even authoritarian, control. Nonetheless, efforts to develop programs for enhanced deliberation via the Internet are well under way. These include discussion software for deliberative forums, with a less controlling role for moderators or facilitators. Deliberative criteria can also be built into the software in ways that permit discourses among people with divergent and diverse views, in distinction to the preponderance of like-minded online communities currently in evidence. Such deliberation can be used to facilitate the transnational discussions within the *epistemic communities* of experts, such as those that took place regarding the Law of the Sea or the currently ongoing discussions concerning climate change. But it can also be used to facilitate input by NGOs or by members of the public into these discussions and processes.

In addition, there is the important development of open source software, "wikis," and what we might call an "open source model" of deliberation on the Internet, with options for participants freely to set and modify agendas and to alter the terms of arguments, all without a moderator. Collaborative editing software can be used by groups to work out joint policies and projects. Already, activist political groups and movements related to the World Social Forum have made use of the Internet to facilitate more consensual modes of decision making; and sites like Indymedia use open posting to spread information that can in turn set conditions for democratic organizing and deliberation. The further development of these promising models would be of considerable importance, especially (for our purposes) their extension to include new ways of providing input to representatives from their constituents, whether these representatives are of the old-fashioned territorial variety or in new transnational communities or organizations.

Of course, a problem with these various uses of the Internet or other information and communications technologies for participation, deliberation, and representation remains that of the oft-observed "digital divide." Though shrinking somewhat, this divide still exists. It clearly sets limits on the degree to which we can rely on the Internet for increased representation in global institutions. Nonetheless, with the further development of video and its fuller integration into these technologies, we can expect that computer-mediated democratic communication can become less text based and perhaps eventually more global in scope. Nonetheless, the degree to which the democratization of the institutions of global governance takes place will not depend on technologies in any case but will instead depend on social choices and on a renewed commitment to realizing democratic participation and human rights.

Acknowledgments

Earlier versions of this chapter were presented at the Workshop on Democracy in a Globalized World, International Institute for the Sociology of Law, Onati, Spain, April 20, 2007, and at the XXIII World Congress of Philosophy of Law and Social Philosophy (IVR), Special Workshop on Global Democracy and Global Exclusion, Kraków, Poland, August 2, 2007. I would like to thank the participants in those workshops, as well as Francis Raven, for helpful comments and suggestions.

References

Barber, Benjamin. 1984. *Strong Democracy*. Berkeley: University of California Press.
Buchanan, Allen, and Robert O. Keohane. 2006. "The Legitimacy of Global Governance Institutions." *Ethics & International Affairs* 20, no. 4:405–37.

Cohen, Joshua. 1996. "Procedure and Substance in Deliberative Democracy." In *Democracy and Difference*, edited by Seyla Benhabib, 95–119. Princeton: Princeton University Press.

El Menyawi, Hassan. 2004. "Toward Global Democracy: Thoughts in Response to the Rising Tide of Nation-to-Nation Interdependencies." *Indiana Journal of Global Legal Studies* 11, no. 2:83–133.

Falk, Richard, and Andrew Strauss. 2000. "On the Creation of a Global Peoples Assembly: Legitimacy and the Power of Popular Sovereignty." *Stanford Journal of International Law* 36:191–220.

Gilabert, Pablo. 2006. "Global Justice, Democracy and Solidarity." *Res Publica* 12:435–43.

Gould, Carol C. 1988. *Rethinking Democracy: Freedom and Social Cooperation in Politics, Economy, and Society*. Cambridge: Cambridge University Press.

———. 2004. *Globalizing Democracy and Human Rights*. Cambridge: Cambridge University Press.

———. 2006. "Self-Determination Beyond Sovereignty: Relating Transnational Democracy to Local Autonomy." *Journal of Social Philosophy* 37, no. 1:44–60, special issue entitled *Democracy and Globalization*, edited by Carol C. Gould and Alistair Macleod.

———. 2007. "Transnational Solidarities." *Journal of Social Philosophy* 38, no. 1:148–64, special issue entitled *Solidarity*, edited by Carol C. Gould and Sally J. Scholz.

Grant, Ruth W., and Robert O. Keohane. 2005. "Accountability and Abuses of Power in World Politics." *American Political Science Review* 99, no. 1:29–43.

Nickel, James. 2005. "Gould on Democracy and Human Rights." *Journal of Global Ethics* 1, no. 2:207–13.

Plotke, David. 1997. "Representation Is Democracy." *Constellations* 4, no. 1:19–34.

Saward, Michael. 2000. "A Critique of Held." In *Global Democracy: Key Debates*, edited by Barry Holden, 39–43. London: Routledge.

Shue, Henry. 1980. *Basic Rights*. Princeton: Princeton University Press.

Weinstock, Daniel. 2006. "The Real World of (Global) Democracy." *Journal of Social Philosophy* 37, no. 1:6–20, special issue entitled *Democracy and Globalization*, edited by Carol C. Gould and Alistair Macleod.

5

FEDERATIVE GLOBAL DEMOCRACY

ERIC CAVALLERO

Decisions taken by international organizations like the World Bank, the World Trade Organization, and a proliferation of relatively obscure but increasingly essential transgovernmental regulatory networks significantly affect the way life is lived in every corner of the world. Yet these institutions and networks conduct their affairs largely outside of public view and with little accountability to democratic processes. At the same time, cross-border spillover effects—from greenhouse gas emissions to unstable financial markets—impose significant costs on individuals who have no say in determining the policies that generate these costs. In the past few decades normative political theorists have begun to entertain models of global governance that might redress this global "democratic deficit." While the much-dreaded world state has found few champions, many maintain that a global federative system can provide a solution.[1] The sovereign powers of the state, they argue, should be "unbundled," "disaggregated" or "vertically dispersed" so that control over regional and global affairs may be brought under the democratic control of all affected individuals while control over local matters is decentralized (Pogge 1992; O'Neill 1994; Held 1995; Archibugi 1998; Kuper 2004). This chapter offers suggestions for the conceptualization and design of a global federative model.

In part 1, I discuss six key elements of such a model: sovereignty, territoriality, self-determination, democracy, human rights, and equality. I develop an analysis of sovereignty that is consistent with federative institutions; argue that territory should continue to define the scope of sovereign competences; and suggest that in some cases it could be desirable to retain a significant degree of "bundling" of such competences in order to accommodate the self-determination of national groups that seek it. I argue further that the exercise of sovereign competences at every level should be constrained by an effective global human rights regime incorporating a human right to the equal protection of global legal institutions. This right has implications for justice in the design of global

---

[1] I use "federative" to describe any system of nested sovereign jurisdictions.

institutions governing both immigration policy and cross-border socio-economic inequalities.

Part 2 addresses the question of how sovereign competences constrained by a universal human rights regime should be allocated across the jurisdictions of a global federative system. Following many of the authors noted above, I maintain that an allocation responsive to democratic ideals should accommodate substantial local autonomy while at the same time ensuring that everyone has a voice in the political decisions that affect his interests. Although this "principle of affected interests" has often been criticized as vague and indeterminate, I argue that the relevant class of effects can be fully specified under two headings: those that impose norms of governance on individuals, and those that would otherwise—that is, absent the right of political participation for those affected—impose external costs on them. This specification of affected interests yields a determinate allocation of sovereign powers across the territorially nested jurisdictions of a global federative system.

1. Elements of a Global Federative Model

Sovereignty

State sovereignty is commonly characterized as having an internal and an external aspect. External sovereignty is a set of equal rights, powers, and immunities that each state has vis-à-vis every other (and that no other kind of entity has). Territorial integrity, noninterference, and competence to enter into binding treaty agreements comprise its chief components. Internal sovereignty is the exclusive and irrevocable jurisdiction of a state over those found within its territory. Some maintain that recent history has seen a significant diminution in the sovereignty of the state or even the wholesale disaggregation of its sovereign powers (Slaughter 2004; Gould 2006). These authors, however, are referring to what is sometimes called *de facto* sovereignty or *autonomy*—the effective ability of a state to make and pursue policy aims unconstrained by external agents (Held 2006, 295). While international and transnational organizations and networks have indeed undermined the *de facto* sovereignty of the state, the doctrine of state sovereignty remains largely intact *de jure*. In this section I develop a conception of (*de jure*) sovereignty that abstracts away from the idea of the state so that the concept of sovereignty can be applied to global federative structures.

I begin by carving off the component of external sovereignty, though I will return to it later. For the present I focus on internal sovereignty—the exclusive, irrevocable legal competence to make policy and to govern. Internal sovereignty can be analyzed as a three-place predicate relating a polity, a particular legal competence, and a particular territorial jurisdiction. To say that a polity P has sovereign competence C in territorial jurisdiction J is to say that P, acting through its legal-political institutions, has exclusive and irrevocable legal right to exercise C in J; and that P's actions pursuant to that right are not, across a broad range of the normal exercise of C, subject to review by any higher jurisdiction (cf. Pogge 1992). The analysis enables us to characterize sovereign states as territorially constituted polities in which all or virtually all sovereign competences are concentrated. Yet the analysis also enables us to describe jurisdictional structures in which the sovereign powers of the state have been disaggregated or dispersed within a federative framework.

On this analysis a polity's legal competence is sovereign when it is exclusive and irrevocable for some territory and when the competence is not subject to review *across a broad range of its normal exercise*. Thus I omit a condition sometimes thought to be central to the concept of sovereignty—namely, the condition that a sovereign competence cannot ever be subject to judicial (or other) review by a higher authority. The case of the International Criminal Court can illustrate why that condition is too strong. The jurisdiction of the ICC extends to cases of genocide, serious war crimes, and crimes against humanity. In principle any number of state competences could be used to commit one of these international crimes. The sovereign power of a state to control its borders and airspace could be used (as by the government of Burma at the time of this writing) to prevent the delivery of life-saving assistance to large numbers of needy individuals—arguably a humanitarian crime. The competence to establish and enforce a tax regime could be used to tax a population literally to death. The power to try cases of domestic criminal law and to impose penalties could be used to conduct political mass executions. We should not, however, therefore conclude that state signatories to the Rome Statute have abdicated the sovereign competences to control their borders and air space, levy taxes, or try common criminals. There are many limits on what nations today may legally do within their borders; yet so long as those limits do not encroach on the normal range of exercise of a competence it should still be regarded as sovereign.

Territoriality

The stipulation of territoriality in the foregoing analysis of sovereignty may seem to fly in the face of numerous calls for "nonterritorial" or "functionally individuated" dispersals of sovereignty. The apparent disagreement is largely semantic; but to the extent that it is not semantic the balance of reasons favors a territorial dispersal—or so I will argue. To dispense with the semantic points first, we should observe the familiar distinction between a "vertical" dispersal of sovereign powers over territorial jurisdictions and a "horizontal" or "nonterritorial" dispersal of sovereign powers over branches of government, agencies, or spheres of activity. The latter sort of dispersal is commended by several proponents of a global federative system (O'Neill 1994, 72; Slaughter 2004, 34–35, 268; Kuper 2004, 31ff.) They conceptualize sovereignty when dispersed in the horizontal dimension as vesting in *agencies* or *organs of government* rather than in polities as my analysis requires. Thus a nonterritorial global dispersal of sovereignty in the sense they intend is essentially *a separation of powers*. To say that sovereignty should be dispersed in this sense is to say that agencies regulating different spheres of activity worldwide should be independent and autonomous rather than subordinate to a unitary global executive authority. Yet all of the authors who call for this sort of nonterritorial dispersal of sovereignty agree that these autonomous agencies should be accountable to a democratic global polity. In the terms of my analysis, therefore, the sovereign competences these agencies exercise are vested in a global polity—in other words, one that is territorial in the limiting case.

There is a second way in which an apparent difference between my account and others is actually only semantic. Sometimes authors who call for a nonterritorial dispersal of sovereignty are suggesting that a global system could incorporate territorially dispersed *representative constituencies*. Globally dispersed groups whose interests might otherwise be underrepresented in the democratic processes of a global polity—native peoples, sexual minorities, and refugees, to name a few possibilities—could receive special representation in the democratic processes of a global polity. It has also been suggested that special representation or some special role in a democratic process could be given to advocacy groups, nongovernmental organizations, transnational corporations, or other institutions of global civil society (Kuper 2004, 106ff., 165ff.; Gould 2004, 213–14). If any of these constituencies or stakeholder groups were vested with an irrevocable right to be specially represented or to play a special role in a global democratic process, then they might be described as "sovereign" in a sense. They would not, however, be vested with any sovereign competences and would not be sovereign polities in the sense of my analysis.

There remains the somewhat more radical possibility of constituting sovereign polities that actually *are* nonterritorial—meaning that they have global standing and are vested with sovereign competences, yet their members are territorially dispersed among other polities. Global labor unions, national diasporas, and the like might be candidates for nonterritorial polities in this sense. When assessing such arrangements, a distinction should be made between, on the one hand, a territorially dispersed community that has been vested with some irrevocable legal rights, powers, or prerogatives under the constitution of a territorially based polity and, on the other hand, a dispersed community with global standing as a sovereign polity. The Belgian constitution vests its three linguistic communities with certain constitutional rights and prerogatives. These communities, however, have no global standing. Thus, were the constitution of Belgium to be amended so as to revoke the autonomy of the communities, that would be recognized as an exercise of Belgian sovereignty and not as a violation of international law. I do not deny the right of a sovereign territorial polity to vest with a measure of autonomy territorially dispersed groups within its borders. I claim only that territorially dispersed communities should not be recognized as sovereign polities with global standing.

To see why not, we should consider the question whether members of a territorially dispersed polity with global standing should have a right of exit from it. To deny that right would seem to be functionally the equivalent of denying the right to emigrate from a territorial polity, which is a recognized human rights violation. Moreover—assuming that the legitimate use of coercive force is a natural monopoly for a given territory—the enforcement of a territorially dispersed polity's law (or the defense of its rights or prerogatives) would necessarily fall to the local monopoly. Thus, the local territorial polity that holds that monopoly would be legally obligated to impose on its members different bodies of law, on the basis of characteristics those individuals have not chosen. On the face of it this would be a denial of the equal protection of the law of that polity, another recognized human rights violation. Such arrangements would entail that territorial polities whose members include members of a dispersed polity could not be constituted of citizens who are political equals. This could in turn have deleterious consequences for the democratic processes and political culture of territorial polities. These seem to be unacceptable consequences.

On the other hand, if members of a dispersed polity have a right of exit at will—and since exit would entail none of the legal and other burdens (often prohibitive) of physical emigration—such a "polity" would seem more closely to resemble a voluntary organization like the Boy Scouts of America or the Catholic Church. Members of such organizations may be required as conditions of membership to contribute to them financially and to conform to their rules; and such organizations may be vested with certain prerogatives by the territorial states in which they operate (tax exemptions, for example, or "faith-based" government funding of their charitable activities). Yet they remain voluntary associations because members have an "easy" right of exit (this may in fact be the better way of describing arrangements like community autonomy in Belgium, where membership in a community is strictly a matter of self-identification by citizens deemed equal under the law). I conclude that sovereign polities— meaning ones with global standing and vested with irrevocable competences—should be territorially constituted.

Self-Determination

It is sometimes suggested that one of the aims of a global federative model should be to avoid the concentration of sovereign powers in any given territorial jurisdiction. Thomas Pogge argues that sovereignty should be "widely" dispersed over territorially nested jurisdictions, with the consequence that individuals are "citizens of, and govern themselves through, a number of political units of various sizes, without any one political unit being dominant and thus occupying the traditional role of state. And their political allegiance and loyalties should be widely dispersed over these units: neighborhood, town, country, province, state, region and world at large. People should be politically at home in all of them, without converging upon any one of them as the lodestar of their political identity" (1992, 58). While we may expect there to be localities or regions in which circumstances recommend and individuals favor broad dispersals of sovereign powers in the manner Pogge commends, I do not believe that an especially broad dispersal should be a goal or a guiding principle of design for a global federative model. As others have shown elsewhere in this collection of chapters, there is no good reason to assume an antagonism between nationalist ideals and supranational structures of governance (De Schutter and Tinnevelt 2009). National self-determination can be realized within a federative system provided that significant concentrations of sovereign power can be vested in national polities. Some national groups may favor a concentration of power as a means of maintaining their distinctive public institutions, culture, traditions, ways of life, or forms of association. Such things can be of moral importance not only because individuals sometimes value them but also because they can be essential to the achievement of autonomous lives for individuals socialized into those particular traditions, ways of life, and forms of association (Kymlicka 1995, 75ff.). Finally, the political integration of national groups can be valuable because the bases of national identity (commonalities of history, political culture, language, religion, ethnicity, and so forth) can also be bases of solidarity and thus instrumental to the maintenance of stable and just public institutions (Miller 1995; 2000). For these reasons, federative structures should not be designed to undermine the concentration of sovereign power in national polities.

With no mechanism to thwart such local concentrations of sovereignty, their emergence in some localities should be expected as the result of democratic choice within a federative model. This expectation arises from the peculiar significance of the competence to use coercive force. The sovereign power to keep the peace through day-to-day law enforcement is generally recognized to be a natural monopoly for a given territory. Thus it is a reasonable assumption that any stable global federative system will comprise multiple exclusive jurisdictions with sovereign coercive authority on their territories. Each coercive jurisdiction will be a part of a global jurisdiction and possibly also of one or more nested regional ones. And each may also contain smaller ones whose legislative competences are sovereign but whose enforcement capabilities, if any, are merely administrative—that is, delegated by the sovereign coercive power much as the authority of a municipal police force is delegated to it by state or national authorities. Thus there is in principle no reason why sovereign competences could not be widely dispersed up and down such a multitiered system. Yet in many places both democratic ideals and public sentiment are likely to favor more rather than less congruence among those who, through their democratic institutions, make the law; those against whom it is enforced; and those to whom the agency of enforcement is accountable. A concentration of sovereign competences at the level of the coercive jurisdiction is simply the corollary of such congruence. Where national sentiment is strong, democratic choice will tend to focus this concentration of competences at the level of the national polity.

Democracy

I assume that different sorts of democratic institutions will be appropriate for different levels of governance and that no very specific conception of democracy—whether of its normative grounds or of its proper institutional forms—should guide the design of institutions at every level. Daniel Weinstock (2006) distinguishes *agency accounts* of democracy from *interest accounts*. The former regard democratic institutions first and foremost as means of enhancing individual agency and autonomy, while the latter see them primarily as means of ensuring that governments remain responsive to the interests of the governed. Both kinds of account can play a role in the design of a global federative system. Institutions that encourage and facilitate broad deliberative and electoral participation are appropriate in circumstances where individual agency can in fact be enhanced thereby. Under other circumstances, responsiveness to interests may become the dominant concern in the design of democratic institutions.

For example, it seems unlikely that the autonomous agency of the world's most impoverished individuals could be enhanced by enlisting their meaningful participation in civic debate, deliberation, and participation in representative electoral institutions at the global level. The interests of these individuals might be better represented in global or regional forums by the nongovernmental organizations that are today their most effective advocates globally. To be sure, a reliable responsiveness to the interests of these individuals would require mechanisms that give them some sort of *systematic control* of political outcomes that affect them (Kuper 2004). Yet this can be accomplished through means other than familiar electoral and representative institutions. Transparency, checks and balances among independent agencies with "interlocking competencies," and indirect accountability to local electoral institutions may sometimes provide better mechanisms for ensuring responsiveness (Kuper 2004, 100ff.; Persson et al. 1996).

Local democratic institutions may show as much variety as global ones. The question for a global federative model that aspires to democratic ideals, however, is not "Which local forms of government are democratic?" but rather "Which local governments may legitimately exercise the sovereign rights vested in their polities—including the right to participate in regional and global democratic processes?" I suggest that respect for human rights (including political human rights) and the effective capacity to keep the peace are jointly sufficient for the legitimacy of any government that exercises coercive force.[2] No government can satisfy these conditions without a substantial base of popular support, and their satisfaction may even suffice for democracy in the expansive conception of it that some have espoused (e.g., Gould 2004, 181).

Human Rights

Normative democratic theorists generally acknowledge that there are things democratic majorities may not legitimately do. Whether these limits are internal to democratic ideals, share a common root with them, or represent fundamentally different moral concerns, a democratic system should recognize certain rights of individuals, and of minority groups, as constraints on the outcomes of democratic processes. It is to be expected that many jurisdictions in a global federative system will adopt and entrench by means of their own democratic processes adequate protections of human rights. There may, however, be cases where local majorities unconstrained by external norms and institutions would violate human rights or fail to protect them adequately. I argued above that a legal competence can be sovereign while also being subject to judicial review. Here I suggest that the sovereign powers of all polities within a global federative framework should be subject to judicial review by a world court of human rights. Original jurisdiction for human rights cases should rest with more local polities, while the global court would hold final appellate jurisdiction in matters of human rights. For familiar reasons the activities and rulings of such a court should be free from interference by other organs of government and to a certain degree insulated from democratic processes. The court would nonetheless be indirectly subject to democratic control through the procedures of adoption and amendment of human rights covenants and through the processes of appointment and removal of judges.

The functioning of a global human rights court does not entail a coercive global enforcement capability. The European Court of Human Rights functions effectively without relying on a pan-European coercive enforce-

---

[2] Article 25 of the International Covenant on Civil and Political Rights provides that "every citizen shall have the right and the opportunity ... to take part in the conduct of public affairs, directly or through freely chosen representatives; to vote and to be elected at genuine periodic elections which shall be by universal and equal suffrage and shall be held by secret ballot." This stops well short of a human right to democracy, and is consistent with the public affairs of, for example, Cuba or Iran.

ment agency. It is a matter for the democratic processes of a global polity to determine whether or not it will maintain enforcement capability. The power to impose economic and diplomatic sanctions and in cases of grave abuse to authorize intervention on the part of willing militarized polities may suffice to protect human rights adequately worldwide.

Equality

The coercive enforcement of municipal immigration law perpetuates cross-border inequalities of wealth, income, and opportunity. Borders are legal institutions, coercively enforced against individuals who are expected as individuals and collectively through their governments to respect and uphold the international legal framework that recognizes and validates the borders. No one can be expected to respect and uphold institutions of law that coercively impose profound disadvantages on her on the basis of a morally arbitrary characteristic such as place of birth. The basic injustice in the relation between borders and socioeconomic inequality is not the violation of a right to equal distributive shares or equal opportunity. Rather, it is the violation of the more basic right not to be *denied equal opportunity by institutions of law to which one is subject* (Cavallero 2006).

While I believe that this is today the most important individual right not codified in positive human rights law, its importance becomes even more manifest in the context of a global federative system. As Nobel laureate in economics Thomas Schelling remarked in 1992, "If we were to contemplate gradually relinquishing some measure of sovereignty in order to form not a more perfect union, but a more effective legal structure, what familiar political entity might be our basis for comparison? I find my own answer stunning and depressing: South Africa" (Schelling 1992). This observation succinctly expresses the moral imperative for a global federative system to decouple the coercive enforcement of political boundaries from inequalities of life opportunity. The recognized human right to the equal protection of the law of one's country must be extended, within a global federative order, to include the basic right of individuals to the equal protection of global legal institutions. This right is violated whenever someone is systematically disadvantaged on the basis of his place of birth by the enforcement of international borders.

A global right to equal protection could be promoted by opening all borders to migration (Carens 1987) or alternatively by a system of global redistribution that would equalize opportunities worldwide. Yet there are significant moral reasons to reject both remedies. An unregulated influx of immigrants could undermine a self-determining polity's bases of common identity and could destabilize its just political institutions. On the other hand a global redistributive system adequate to equalize opportunities worldwide would confront a dilemma. If local polities were permitted to regulate their own main social and economic institutions, free-rider problems would arise in response to an equalizing redistributive system; on the other hand, highly intrusive regulation of local polities by global authorities would undermine local autonomy. Withholding aid from polities that refuse to use it effectively can avoid both horns of the dilemma but does nothing to remedy the systematic disadvantage of those who continue to be coercively excluded from polities that offer superior opportunities.

Thus there is an apparent conflict between, on the one hand, the legitimate interests of political communities in regulating their membership and in determining the structure of their own social and political distributive institutions and, on the other hand, the basic right of individuals not to be systematically disadvantaged by institutions of law to which they are subject. Elsewhere I have proposed institutional mechanisms that can resolve this conflict while at the same time holding political communities appropriately responsible for the consequences of their policy choices (Cavallero 2006). I have defended this model as appropriate in the context of the existing international states system; its application, however, is general and extends to a global federative model. Transposed into the latter context and briefly summarized, the proposal is as follows:

(1)   Any polity may legitimately claim the sovereign competence to grant or deny entry to immigration seekers at its discretion.

(2)   Any polity may legitimately claim the sovereign competence to regulate its local distributive institutions within the constraints stated in (3) to (6).

(3)   Better-off polities that find themselves under positive immigration pressure are under legal obligation to fund development assistance for polities that generate immigration pressure.

(4)   The amount of mandated assistance is, with an exception to be noted, the amount needed to meet a near-term target of immigration pressure equilibrium. (Equilibrium obtains between two polities when the same proportion of individuals in each manifests a preference to migrate to the other, as determined by demographically representative sampling of populations).[3]

(5)   The exception to (4) is as follows: If meeting the equilibrium target in the near term would be to the long-term disadvantage of the worst off globally, then a Pareto-superior alternative target supersedes the immigration pressure equilibrium target. The alternative mandates development assistance at

---

[3] For the sake of simplicity, the formula is here expressed in terms of a hypothetical two-polity world. For a more general formulation that can be applied to systems containing more than two polities, see my 2006.

the level that yields the most favorable human development projections for the worst-off countries.

(6) Assistance should be subject to conditions of fair and effective use in recipient polities.

Incorporated into the human rights regime of a global federative system, these principles secure local autonomy (at an appropriate cost to localities) while avoiding a global apartheid regime.

2. Allocation of Sovereign Competences over Territorial Jurisdictions

This chapter began with the familiar observation that a growing "democratic deficit" has attended the processes of economic globalization. A global federative system suggests itself as a means of redressing this deficit. Democratic decision-making would occur at the level of larger, more centralized units in order to enable participation by all who will be affected by a given decision (Pogge 1992). At the same time, decisions that exclusively or disproportionately affect relatively local regions can be taken by smaller polities, thus rightly excluding those who are not affected in order to "maximiz[e] each person's opportunity to influence the social conditions that shape his or her life" (Pogge 1992, 65; cf. Held 2004, 375). In this part of the chapter I defend a principle governing the (vertical) dispersal of sovereign competences across territorially nested jurisdictions. In its basic outline, the proposal builds on that of Pogge: "The authority to make decisions of some particular kind should rest with the democratic political process of a unit that (i) is as small as possible but still (ii) includes as equals all persons significantly and legitimately affected by decisions of this kind" (Pogge 1992, 67). Part (i) of this allocation principle states a version of what I will call "the locality condition," while part (ii) is a version of what is often called the "all-affected principle" or "principle of affected interests." Similar allocation principles incorporating both elements have been proposed and designated variously as "principles of distributive subsidiarity and democracy" (Kuper 2004), "the Principle of Inclusiveness and Subsidiarity" (Held 1996), "the principle of equivalence of publicness" (Kaul and Mendoza 2003), and "the principle of democratic inclusion" (Marks 2000, 109ff.). In each case the principles have been characterized abstractly and are not sufficiently specified to yield a determinate allocation of sovereign powers. In this part I aim to formulate plausible interpretations of the locality condition and of the principle of affected interests, and to specify them sufficiently to yield a determinate allocation of sovereignty.

Locality

Pogge's allocation principle requires that decision-making of a given type should be allocated to "a unit that is as small as possible" while at the same time satisfying the principle of affected interests. This requirement could be interpreted two ways. The smallest possible unit could be the smallest *already constituted* political unit that contains all the individuals affected. On the other hand the requirement could mean that if a unit smaller than any existing one and containing all affected individuals *could be* constituted, then that new unit *should be* constituted and vested with the sovereign competences that affect its members alone. The most plausible interpretation of the locality condition is that it operates over existing, independently constituted polities, which I will designate "fundamental." The allocation principle then mandates new "composite" polities by combining fundamental ones as needed to satisfy the principle of affected interests. Fundamental polities are simply taken as given from the standpoint of the allocation principle. This presumes some other principle that governs the constitution and territorial demarcation of fundamental polities—a matter that lies beyond the scope of this chapter (but see Pogge 1992).

The allocation principle should operate over existing fundamental polities because to use it as a standard by which fundamental polities are constituted and their boundaries drawn would result in a welter of crisscrossing and noncontiguous single-issue jurisdictions and intermingled one-issue polities. Critics have repeatedly pointed to the proliferation of one-issue (or even one-decision) polities as a fatal defect of any principle that relies solely on scope of effects for the drawing of political boundaries (see Whelan 1983; Saward 2000). If we regard the allocation principle as operating over existing, territorially constituted fundamental polities, then these difficulties are avoided.

Necessarily this approach permits individuals to have a say sometimes in matters that do not affect them. Yet that can be fully justified in terms of the very intuitions that motivate the locality condition. To see this, we can conceptualize the unworkable, crisscrossing, one-issue polities of actually affected persons as *virtual polities*. An "original" right of democratic participation for a given competence can be supposed to inhere in the virtual polity comprising all and only those who are affected by the exercise of that competence. Assuming that the costs to members of administering and participating in each of these virtual polities would be inordinate, their members can be presumed to tacitly delegate the exercise of their original right to the smallest *existing* polity of which they all are members. The underlying commonsense point is that members of democratic polities freely and knowingly cast their lot together with the understanding that all will have an equal say in matters that may sometimes affect only some—and there is nothing necessarily to be regretted about this.

While very much in the spirit of Pogge's proposal, Kuper and Held formulate their locality conditions in terms of the principle of *subsidiarity*. That principle provides that smaller units should govern themselves in matters that affect them alone, "unless allocating them to a higher level central unit would ensure higher comparative efficiency or effectiveness" (Føllesdal 1998, 190). While the motivation for this condition is clear, its purposes can be accomplished without actually building an efficiency condition into the allocation principle. Here we must emphasize the distinction between a *sovereign competence* and what I referred to above as an *administrative competence*. Most countries are governed at multiple levels—city or town, district or county, department or province, and national government. This sort of division of administrative authority does not entail any division of sovereignty, because the competences of the subordinate jurisdictions can be and often are nonexclusive or are revocable by the center. Just as a sovereign jurisdiction may delegate specified administrative authority to its divers localities without alienating its sovereignty, so it may also delegate such authority "upward" to a regional or global authority. An upward delegation, with or without voluntary alienation, might be desirable on grounds of efficiency or for some other reason. Thus relatively efficient distributions of administrative authority can generally be expected to arise through democratic choice without building a comparative efficiency condition into the principle by which sovereign powers are allocated. If efficient distributions do not arise, then the mere fact that centralizing authority would be more efficient should not override the contrary democratic preference of a polity to govern itself in matters that affect its members alone.

Affected Interests

The first and main challenge that confronts any defender of the principle of affected interests is to specify which kinds of effects are relevant and which are not. As Robert Keohane notes, "Merely being affected cannot be sufficient to create a valid claim. If it were, virtually nothing could ever be done, since there would be so many requirements for consultation and even veto points" (2003, 141). To date no adequate account of relevant effects has been proposed.

Pogge disqualifies one sort of effect that seems plainly irrelevant: we cannot credit such a claim as "I should be allowed a vote on the permissibility of homosexuality, in all parts of the world, because the knowledge that homosexual acts are performed anywhere causes me great distress" (1992, 64 n. 28). It seems safe to generalize that effects resulting from other-regarding preferences—bigoted, altruistic, or otherwise—are not the sort of effects that ground a right of democratic participation. While this narrows the class of relevant effects in an important dimension, it does not yet suffice to give us a plausible principle of democratic inclusiveness. Suppose, for example, that the United States was considering a renewable energy policy that would reduce greenhouse gas emissions by 50 percent within a decade. Those who work or invest in fossil fuel industries or who live in major oil or natural gas exporting countries could be substantially (and adversely) affected by this decision. Yet it seems wrong to conclude that Saudis, Nigerians, Venezuelans, and the (non-American) shareholders of Shell and Exxon Mobil should for that reason have a say in decisions about U.S. energy policy (though they and everyone else deserve a say for *other* reasons—for example, because everyone is affected by climate change caused by greenhouse gas emissions).[4] Similarly, it seems wrong to suggest that the people of China should have an equal say in a decision by the United States to promulgate consumer safety standards that will adversely affect sales of Chinese imports. These kinds of effects, while not based on other-regarding preferences, nonetheless seem irrelevant.

Carol Gould, a critic of the principle of affected interests, maintains that a qualified version of it has an important role to play in extending democracy to a global context. She maintains that individuals should have some democratic say in decisions that *importantly* affect them— where "a person is to be regarded as importantly affected if the decision in question impacts the basic freedom, needs, or central interests that are protected by human rights" (Gould 2006, 212). While capturing an important range of legitimate democratic rights, Gould's version of the principle is underinclusive. If two countries share a river, for example, it seems reasonable that citizens in the country downstream should have some say in determining what kinds and levels of pollutants are permitted to be discharged into the river upstream—even if unregulated discharges will not actually impact anyone's basic needs or human rights. Gould's version of the principle also seems overinclusive. It seems inappropriate that the millions of Chinese whose basic needs are met at the margins of the export sector should thereby acquire the right to participate in the democratic processes that determine American product safety regulations.

Gould defends a second principle of political inclusion, also said to be sufficient to ground rights of participation. When basic needs are not at stake, "rights of democratic participation derive from rights to self-determination in the context of common or joint activities" (2006, 175). A common activity is simply one in which "individuals join together to effect a given end" (2006, 78). Thus, the common activities of upholding a legal system, facilitating mutually beneficial international trade arrangements, and producing automobiles ground rights of democratic participation for those who engage in these activities. Yet while expanding the democratic franchise appropriately in many dimensions, the joint-activities account still fails to ground a right of participation for members of the downstream community in the example above, on whom significant external costs may be imposed by activities in which they do not participate.

[4] Moore 2006, 36, offers a similar example.

In the remainder of the chapter I develop an analysis of relevant effects such that those relevantly affected by an activity should have a say in the democratic processes that ultimately regulate (or fail to regulate) it. I defend a two-part interpretation of the principle of affected interests. According to this interpretation, an individual is relevantly affected by the exercise of a sovereign competence if (1) its exercise imposes governance norms on her or (2) its exercise could otherwise reasonably be expected to impose external costs on her. To distinguish it from other interpretations, I will refer to this as *the principle of self-governance and internalization.* I discuss each part in turn.

(1) Governance Norms

As nations faced with a rapidly integrating global economy seek to harmonize and coordinate their laws and policies, binding legal norms and other norms of governance increasingly issue from international forums. Individuals worldwide are subject to the policies and directives of institutions like the WTO, the World Bank, and the G8 finance ministers' summits. In addition, a relatively obscure but proliferating sphere of agency-to-agency networks—the Basel Committee on Banking Supervision and the International Organization of Securities Commissioners are examples—exercises a growing influence on policy worldwide (Slaughter 2004). These organizations and networks develop policy initiatives, coordinate regulatory regimes, promulgate binding rules and memoranda of understanding, and act as sources of legal and quasi-legal governance, guiding and constraining the actions of governments, corporations, investors, and other actors large and small. The activities of these organizations thus structure and organize the lives of individuals worldwide, with consequences for the nature of work, the transmission of culture, and the distribution of wealth and political power both within and across political borders. Norms and agents of governance that affect individuals in such profound and pervasive ways should be accountable to all who are subject to them.

This forms the basis of the *self-governance condition.* An individual, Q, has a right of democratic participation in the process by which norms of (legal or quasi-legal) governance are made if:

(a) Q is a member of polity P, and members of P are unavoidably subject to those norms; and

(b) there exists no smaller polity P* that contains all of the members of P who are subject to those norms but that does not contain Q.

The self-governance condition captures an important part of Gould's conception of self-determination in the context of joint activities. The self-governance condition, however, is not as expansive a democratic requirement as Gould defends. It is restricted to norms issuing from public authorities. Thus it does not ground a right of democratic participation for those who, while engaged in joint activities, are subject to such norms as industry standards and "best practices," the organizational hierarchies of business firms, religious rules and instructions, private university codes of conduct, and so on. Perhaps Gould is correct that such organizations should be governed more democratically. Yet ideally, at least, the norms and hierarchical structures of the private sector arise from voluntary association and contracts among individuals with real alternatives. It is arguable that, properly regulated by just public institutions, private hierarchies and the norms that issue from them can express the autonomy of their participants. The fact that they so often fail to do so in the actual world may be a reason to seek to organize them democratically as Gould suggests. On the other hand it may simply be a reason to situate them in a context of just public institutions. Such institutions would ensure that those who participate in private hierarchical organizations and who are subject to their norms have freely chosen to do so. The key point is that, ideally, norms of the private sector can be avoided by free agents, while governance norms—just or unjust—are unavoidable for those subject to them. From a democratic perspective the latter are justified only if each person subject to them has an equal say in the processes by which they are made or revised.

(2) Externalities

Being subject to norms of governance is sufficient but not necessary to ground rights of democratic participation. A second sufficient condition consists in being made to bear external costs. An individual, Q, is relevantly affected by the exercise of a sovereign competence C and has a right of democratic participation in the processes by which C is exercised if

  (a) Q is a member of a polity P and there is a significant chance that policy decisions that will be made repeatedly or sustained on an ongoing basis under C will otherwise impose significant external costs on members of P; and

  (b) there is no smaller existing polity P* that contains all of the members of P who would bear these costs but that does not contain Q.

I will call this the *internalization condition*, since it requires that certain otherwise external costs be internalized through the constitution of composite polities comprising all who bear those costs. Before specifying more fully the relevant idea of an external cost, I note two important features of the internalization condition (features that extend to the principle of self-governance and internalization as a whole). First, this condition operates over sovereign competences insofar as there is a *significant chance* that their exercise will impose external costs *repeatedly or on an ongoing basis*. These qualifiers are necessary because for any given kind of policy decision, democratic institutions must be put in place to implement or administer those decisions, and the necessary administrative structures cannot be conjured up ad hoc in response to rare and unusual spillover effects. Robert Goodin observes that costs can be internalized in either of two ways: by extending control over an activity to all who are affected, or by compensating those who are affected by activities they cannot control (Goodin 2007). The interests of those who may be affected by negative externalities that arise from a type of decision that only rarely generates them are better handled through an arbitrated system of fair compensation than through democratic inclusion.

Second, for reasons noted above in the discussion of locality, the internalization condition operates over individuals *qua members of already-constituted polities*. In other words, if any members of a polity are significantly at risk of bearing costs generated by the exercise of a given competence—and provided there is no smaller polity containing all of the directly affected parties—then every member of the polity is deemed to have been affected in the relevant sense and to have a right of democratic participation. This is consistent with an individualistic moral methodology for reasons also noted above: individuals can be presumed for prudential reasons to have delegated their exclusive democratic control over matters affecting them alone to the smallest actually existing polity of which they are members.

The remaining challenge in specifying the internalization principle will be to characterize the relevant sense of an external cost more fully. Every precise definition of external costs that has been proposed by economists has been controversial (Cornes and Sandler 1986, 29). Here I propose a definition that is tailored to the purpose at hand; it may be of little use for other purposes, and is in no way intended as a contribution to the science of economics. The definition comprises five conditions such that a negative effect is an external cost if it satisfies all of them. They are (1) the baseline condition; (2) the publicness condition; (3) the tangibility condition; (4) the market-efficiency exemption; and (5) the public-goods exemption.[5]

1. The baseline condition. This condition has two parts. First, an external cost must leave those who bear it worse off in some regard than they were before the activity that generated the cost. The mere

---

[5] The external costs with which we are here concerned are costs imposed on one polity by another. Thus, while the proximate cause of an external cost might be, for example, an industry or an industrial facility, the internalization principle regards the cost as imposed by the sovereign jurisdiction empowered to regulate that industry or facility.

failure to make individuals better off when it is within one's power to do so does not count as an imposition of external costs. Thus a decision by a developed nation to devote resources to space exploration when they could have gone to development assistance does not impose external costs of space exploration on those who would or could have benefited from development assistance. The second part of the baseline condition states that an agent cannot impose external costs on others simply by ceasing to provide them with a benefit (where a *benefit* cannot be construed as the mere absence of a cost but must be an outcome of activities that leave beneficiaries better off than they were). It is significant that the baseline condition requires that individuals be made worse off *in some regard* than they were before. The condition does not require individuals be made worse off overall. Thus the greenhouse gases emitted in the manufacture of mosquito nets and fertilizer in Europe can count as external costs born by individuals in other parts of the world, including individuals who may subsequently use those products and thereby be made better off overall by their manufacture.

2. *The publicness condition.* To count as a negative externality in the relevant sense the cost must be one that is borne by the public. It must be what economists call a "public bad"—a cost that is to some significant extent both "nonexcludable" and "nonrival." A cost is nonexcludable insofar as it is difficult to avoid for those who bear it, and is nonrival to the extent that one person's bearing more of it does not cause another to bear less (Kaul and Mendoza 2003, 154 nn. *a* and *b*). Thus costs incurred by firms, institutions, or individuals through normal market and other voluntary transactions cannot *as such* be negative externalities in the favored sense—though they can be so in aggregate, when viewed from a macroeconomic, public health, or other public perspective. I discuss macroeconomic externalities further below, in the context of conditions 4 and 5.

3. *The tangibility condition.* This requires that a negative externality must with two exceptions to be noted be a *tangible* negative effect borne by the public. The sphere of the tangible can be defined by enumeration: it includes (a) effects on the natural and physical environment, including effects on climate, air, and water quality; on physical common-pool resources and on physical public goods like shipping lanes and canals; (b) effects on the human utilization of plants, animals, and other living things; (c) health effects for human populations; (d) security effects; and (e) a circumscribed range of macroeconomic effects, to be discussed below.[6] Substantial risks of tangible effects should themselves be deemed tangible effects; for example, a nuclear power facility may pose a risk of

---

[6] Thus, the present notion of an externality is broader than that of Arrow (1984), who regards externalities as necessarily products of a competitive economy.

radiological catastrophe to neighboring polities, and that risk should be regarded as a tangible effect.

The tangibility condition captures our earlier conclusion that effects on individuals caused by their own other-regarding preferences are irrelevant. The tangibility condition, however, also carves off a range of other effects, including aesthetic abhorrence; the influence of a "bad example"; the (perceived) indignity of (perceived) insults to one's race, nation, or religion; ghastly cultural spillovers (fundamentalist ideology, microwavable popcorn with artificial butter aroma, Karaoke); and any other effects that might be characterized as ideological, sociological, cultural, or the like. The exceptions to the tangibility condition are of two types: effects on biodiversity and effects on natural or cultural heritage (see Pogge 1992, 65–66). The extinction or endangerment of a species, or the destruction of rare natural beauty or cultural heritage, imposes external costs on humanity as a whole even when such an event imposes no tangible costs. Although losses of natural and cultural heritage are (unlike extinctions) not objectively definable events, they nonetheless have a conventional basis of definition in international law. The U.N. World Heritage Convention characterizes "world heritage sites" as cultural and natural sites "of outstanding interest" that "need to be preserved as part of the world heritage of mankind as a whole" (United Nations 1972). The convention establishes mechanisms for designating relevant sites. Activities that degrade them—including sites already designated and those for which a successful case can be made in the appropriate forum—can be regarded as generating negative externalities for all of humanity.

4. The market-efficiency exemption. An undistorted outcome of the price mechanism cannot, as such, be a negative externality in the favored sense even when viewed from a macroeconomic perspective; nor in general can efficient market outcomes as such.[7] Thus, if demand for rice in China drives up prices for Egyptians, that is not an external cost of Chinese rice consumption. Similarly, if a more favorable business environment in the Philippines induces corporations to move facilities there from Mexico, the loss of Mexican jobs is not an external cost of Philippine regulatory, tax, and labor law. On the other hand, prices or other market outcomes may sometimes *transmit* external costs. For example, if climate-altering greenhouse gas emissions cause drought in Australia, reducing the supply of Australian rice on world markets, then the consequent increases in price are among the external costs imposed by countries that are major emitters of greenhouse gases.

5. The public-goods exemption. In general terms, the legitimate business of government consists mostly of imposing burdens—primarily by levying taxes—in order to provide public goods. Street lights, law and order, health care, public assistance, the conditions of autonomous lives,

---

[7] Thus the present notion of an externality is narrower than that of Meade 1973.

and even socioeconomic equality can be public goods. Adverse macro-economic effects (though not other kinds of tangible effects) that are borne by one polity as a result of another's provision of public goods are not external costs in the favored sense. For example, if the United States were to place substantially higher taxes on gasoline consumption in order to provide the public goods of clean air, climate stability, and less-crowded roads, negative macroeconomic effects on oil exporting countries would not be external costs of U.S. tax policy. Similarly, U.S. consumer protection regulations that adversely affect the Chinese export economy do not impose external costs on China, because the regulations provide Americans with the public good of safer products.

On the other hand, incompetent regulation of the U.S. financial industry has imposed external costs on individuals worldwide by creating a liquidity crisis and general financial instability whose full consequences are yet to be seen. Insofar as such instability is caused by bad public policy, it cannot be said to have provided any public good for Americans, and therefore macroeconomic effects on other polities of bad U.S. industry regulation should be regarded as external costs in the favored sense. Similarly, the artificial oversupply of agricultural commodities on world markets caused by subsidies to U.S. producers imposes external costs on countries that would otherwise have a more competitive agricultural sector. These count as external costs not because the subsidies distort markets but because the subsidies provide no public goods for Americans.

In sum, the baseline condition, the tangibility condition, the publicness condition, the market-efficiency exemption, and the public-goods exemption serve to define negative externalities in a way that is suitable for use in specifying a principle of democratic inclusiveness. If individuals could be affected by the exercise of a sovereign competence in the sense of having external costs imposed on them in the favored sense, then those individuals are entitled to participate in the democratic processes through which that competence is exercised.

Conclusions

Increasingly, international norms of governance affect the lives of individuals worldwide, and local activities generate external costs that are borne regionally and globally. A global federative system can redress the growing democratic deficit that attends these phenomena. The sovereign powers of the nation-state should be dispersed across territorially nested jurisdictions so that all who are subject to norms of governance, or who would otherwise bear external costs, have an effective right of political participation in the processes that thus affect them. The exercise of sovereign competences at every level should be constrained by a global human rights regime incorporating a human right to the equal protection of international law. This right will be secured only when individuals are no longer systematically disadvantaged by the coercive enforcement of international borders. A federative global model is compatible with local concentrations of sovereign powers sufficient for the self-determination of national groups that seek it. Where national sentiment does not dominate, a wider dispersal may be the result of democratic choice.

Acknowledgments

I am grateful to Ronald Tinnevelt and Helder De Schutter for comments on a previous version of this chapter.

References

Archibugi, Daniele. 1998. "Principles of Cosmopolitan Democracy." In *Reimagining Political Community*, edited by Daniele Archibugi et al., 198–230. Stanford: Stanford University Press.

Arrow, Kenneth J. 1984. "The Organization of Economic Activity: Issues Pertinent to the Choice of Market Versus Non-market Allocation." In *The Collected Papers of Kenneth Arrow, Volume 2: General Equilibrium*. Cambridge, Mass.: Harvard University Press.

Carens, Joseph. 1987. "Aliens and Citizens: The Case for Open Borders." *Review of Politics* 49, no. 2 (Spring): 251–73.

Cavallero, Eric. 2006. "An Immigration Pressure Model of Global Distributive Justice." *Politics, Philosophy & Economics* 5, no. 1 (2006): 97–127.

Cornes, Richard, and Todd Sandler. 1986. *The Theory of Externalities, Public Goods and Club Goods*. Cambridge: Cambridge University Press.

De Schutter, Helder, and Ronald Tinnevelt. 2009. "Is Liberal Nationalism Incompatible with Global Democracy?" *Metaphilosophy* 40, no. 1 (January): 1–7. Included in this collection.

Føllesdal, Andreas. 1998. "Subsidiarity." *Journal of Political Philosophy* 6, no. 2:190–218.

Goodin, Robert E. 2007. "Enfranchising All Affected Interests, and Its Alternatives." *Philosophy & Public Affairs* 35, no. 1: 40–68.

Gould, Carol C. 2004. *Globalizing Democracy and Human Rights*. Cambridge: Cambridge University Press.

———. 2006. "Self-Determination Beyond Sovereignty: Relating Transnational Democracy to Local Autonomy." *Journal of Social Philosophy* 37, no.1 (Spring): 44–60.

Held, David. 1995. *Democracy and the Global Order*. Stanford, Calif.: Stanford University Press.

———. 1996. *Models of Democracy*. 2nd ed. Cambridge: Polity Press.

———. 2004. "Democratic Accountability and Political Effectiveness from a Cosmopolitan Perspective." *Government and Opposition* 39, no. 2 (Spring): 364–91.

———. 2006. *Models of Democracy*. 3rd ed. Stanford, Calif.: Stanford University Press.

Kaul, Inge, and Ronald U. Mendoza. 2003. "Advancing the Concept of Public Goods." In *Providing Global Public Goods*. edited by, Inge Kaul et al., 78–112. Oxford: Oxford University Press.

Keohane, Robert O. 2003. "Global Governance and Democratic Accountability." In *Taming Globalization*, edited by David Held and Mathias Koenig-Archibugi, 130–59. Cambridge: Polity Press.

Kuper, Andrew. 2004. *Democracy Beyond Borders*. Oxford: Oxford University Press.

Kymlicka, Will. 1995. *Multicultural Citizenship*. Oxford: Clarendon Press.

Marks, Susan. 2000. *The Riddle of All Constitutions: International Law, Democracy and the Critique of Ideology*. Oxford: Oxford University Press.

Meade, J. E. 1973. *The Theory of Economic Externalities: The Control of Environmental Pollution and Similar Social Costs*. Leiden, Netherlands: Sijhof.

Miller, David. *On Nationality*. 1995. Oxford: Oxford University Press.

———. 2000. *Citizenship and National Identity*. Cambridge: Polity Press.

Moore, Margaret. 2006. "Globalization and Democratization: Institutional Design for Global Institutions." *Journal of Social Philosophy* 37, no. 1 (March): 21–43.

O'Neill, Onora. 1994. "Justice and Boundaries." In *Political Restructuring in Europe*, edited by Chris Brown, 69–88. New York: Routledge.

Persson, Torsten, Gérard Roland, and Guido Tabellini. 1996. "Separation of Powers and Accountability: Towards a Formal Approach to Comparative Politics." London: Center for Economic Policy Research. Discussion paper no. 1475. Available at http://ideas.repec.org/p/cpr/ceprdp/1475.html (accessed Nov. 16, 2008).

Pogge, Thomas. 1992. "Cosmopolitanism and Sovereignty." *Ethics* 103, no. 1 (October): 48–75.

Saward, Michael. 2000. "A Critique of Held." In *Global Democracy: Key Debates*, edited by Barry Holden, 32–46. London: Routledge.

Schelling, T. C. "The Global Dimension." In *Rethinking America's Security: Beyond Cold War to New World Order*, edited by Graham Allison and Gregory F. Treverton, 196–210. New York: Norton.

Slaughter, Anne-Marie. 2004. *A New World Order*. Princeton: Princeton University Press.

United Nations. 1972. *Convention Concerning the Protection of the World Cultural and Natural Heritage*. Available at http://whc.unesco.org/archive/convention-en.pdf (accessed June 18, 2008).

Whelan, F. G. 1983. "Democratic Theory and the Boundary Problem."
  In *Liberal Democracy*, edited by J. R. Pennock and J. W. Chapman,
  13–47. New York: New York University Press.
Weinstock, Daniel. 2006. "The Real World of (Global) Democracy."
  Journal of Social Philosophy 37, no. 1 (Spring): 6–20.

6

INTERACTION-DEPENDENT JUSTICE AND THE PROBLEM OF INTERNATIONAL EXCLUSION

RAFFAELE MARCHETTI

The Problem of International Exclusion

Political history can be interpreted as a long journey marked by battles for the equal right to participate in the decision-making process of political life; that is, for political enfranchisement. Indeed, the description of the development of political life over the centuries coincides in significant part with the description of the fights for the inclusion of those political subjects who were kept apart in a subaltern status. Differences of social class, ethnicity, gender, and skin color have long represented insurmountable barriers deployed to exclude people from political and social power. Social categorizations of ethnic and religious minorities, indigenous peoples, women, the elderly, homosexuals, the young, the poor, and, by proxy, future generations were used as exclusionary mechanisms to maintain a condition of political deprivation. These ostracized individuals consequently suffered a disadvantaged and profoundly unjust life in comparison with those endowed with full political membership, and with their lives thus almost invariably characterized by a high degree of social vulnerability, those so dispossessed were motivated to advance claims to redress their political entitlement. And so they struggled for political inclusion.[1]

"Foreignness" constitutes another typical category of exclusion, and (unlike the categories previously mentioned) despite the intense criticism which the priority traditionally granted to fellow citizens over aliens has received over the past two decades, it is a category that is still powerfully effective in discriminating between included and excluded individuals. In fact, the very idea of a self-defining group implies exclusivity, that is,

---

[1] Norberto Bobbio, *L'età dei diritti* (Turin: Einaudi, 1990); Michael Walzer, "Exclusion, Injustice and the Democratic State," *Dissent* 40, no. 2 (1993): 55–64; John S. Dryzek, "Political Inclusion and the Dynamics of Democratization," *American Political Science Review* 90, no. 3 (1996): 475–87; Robert Goodin, "Inclusion and Exclusion," *Archives Européennes de Sociologie* XXXVII, no. 2 (1996): 343–71; Jürgen Habermas, *The Inclusion of the Other: Studies in Political Theory* (Cambridge, Mass.: MIT Press, 1998); Iris Marion Young, *Inclusion and Democracy* (Oxford: Oxford University Press, 2000).

the existence of public characteristics effectively delimiting the boundaries of a community. Every such society needs to assume a selective criterion in order to self-define its jurisdictional constituency, thus simultaneously keeping out nonmembers. The demarcation of group identity entails drawing a line between those who are in and those who are out, between those individuals who are recognized as equal and those who are treated unequally. Such a mechanism of limited inclusion creates a system of social exclusion shaped according to differing spheres of justice, the thresholds of which depend on the scope of application of the principle of impartiality.[2] The degree of impartiality that each group applies in its relationship with aliens thus represents a good indicator of the degree of inclusion of nonmembers.[3]

At the moment, such discrimination on the grounds of national membership is nowhere more visible than on the border between national and international jurisdictions concerning political participation. Increasingly, decisions taken in one country affect people in other countries who do not have the possibility to express their consent because of their subaltern status as non-fellow, ergo disenfranchised, citizens. The fracture between socioeconomic reality, which is transnational in its effects, and the political system, which is still fundamentally anchored to a community-based model, is widening. Environment, migration, finance, commerce, health, and security are just a few examples of how the link between actions and consequences extends across borders. And yet those who bear the effects of decisions taken abroad are not typically entitled to have a political voice in the process.[4] Both in cases where decisions taken in a given country have border-crossing consequences and in those where decisions taken at the international level have correspondingly international effects, most often the individual consequence bearer does not have significant power to register her consent (or, indeed, dissent). Assuming she has the power to register her consent at the domestic level (which is rarely the case), she nevertheless does not have a voice at all in the domestic decisions of other countries and has little voice in international forums, even when they are public. In public international organizations, the only political voice available to her is through the double representation offered by national parliaments, which (if entitled) subsequently elect international representatives with differing actual powers. Should she come from a poor country, in fact, she can expect to have an especially weak voice in intergovernmental organizations.

---

[2] Walzer 1985; Robert B. J. Walker, *Inside/Outside: International Relations as Political Theory* (Cambridge: Cambridge University Press, 1993).

[3] Accordingly, exclusion is maximal when impartiality is minimal. An extreme case of partiality is given by the Nazis' attitude toward some of their victims, who, deemed *Untermenschen*, were denied moral standing. O'Neill 2000, 193.

[4] See the works of Richard Falk, David Held, and Tony McGrew, Walden Bello, Joseph Stiglitz, Anne Claire Cutler, and George Monbiot.

Using these observations as a starting point, one can argue that current international affairs are characterized by a high degree of exclusion and disenfranchisement. Were this international scenario of multiple disenfranchisement translated into a domestic setting, it would not be tolerated by any version of democratic theory. Any democrat would be ready to accept the principle that any citizen should be entitled to have a voice on the decisions concerning public issues, above all those that affect him. Accordingly, the democrat would not accept that decisions taken by, for instance, a private club with restricted membership could significantly affect the life prospects of the remaining citizens without these citizens having the legal possibility to contest the outcomes. However, this is the common understanding, not to mention the usual practice, of international affairs—even though a vast part of the discussion on international political theory rests on the assumption of democratic principles. This incongruity is possible because political scientists conventionally work on a double supposition, one that yields huge social consequences in international affairs. On the one hand, national decisions are to be respected to the extent that they are the product of democratic self-determination within sovereign jurisdictions; and on the other, international decisions taken by intergovernmental organizations are to be observed, since they are ultimately taken to be the indirect expression of the same democratic self-determination. Leaving aside their practical implausibility, such suppositions remain highly illegitimate according to the perspective presented here because they warrant and preserve a political system that structurally excludes relevant political subjects from political agency.

The dichotomy of political exclusion versus political participation illustrates a core component of international political theory in that it highlights a crucial element of political incompleteness in the current political arrangements at the international level. From a normative perspective, the inclusion of vulnerable agents into public and impartial decision-making processes at the international level represents a unique chance to improve the democratic legitimacy of the entire political system, both domestically and globally. The widely accepted creed of democracy remains in fact fundamentally flawed unless it is complemented with an international dimension of democratic engagement. Until a criterion is found that allows for the justifiable delimitation of membership according to constituencies that effectively reflect public interests, rather than national or private boundaries, no democratic regime can be truly democratic. I maintain in this chapter that a major international democratic deficit remains a key characteristic of the current political system, and that this system needs to be revised in order to end the resulting unjust exclusion of a vast portion of the world population from transnational decision-making processes and thereby improve the overall implementation of the democratic ideal (Marchetti 2008a and 2008b).

Following this introduction to the general contours of the present investigation, the next three sections examine the arguments in the debate on global justice that most crucially demand to be contested with regard to the issue of exclusion and the international democratic deficit, the arguments determined by the paradigm of interaction dependency.

Interaction-Dependent Justice: Failing Responses or Contributing Factors?

The ground for the high level of reciprocal exclusion that currently characterizes the international domain is built, to a large degree, on the prevailing model of interaction among sovereign states. Despite some recent movements toward tighter intergovernmental coordination through forms of multilateralism and global governance, the fundamental structure of international relations remains anchored in the Westphalian model of independent, self-contained states with sovereign jurisdictions. This paradigm, which became dominant in part as a reaction against the increasing instability brought on by the decline of the universal powers of the Middle Ages, envisages, briefly stated, no duties beyond borders except those generated from modes of interaction. Thus, any international duties are at bottom functional imperatives for self-regarding coordination. This remains true despite the intensifying recognition of the legitimizing status of the human rights regime, which is based on a different universalistic axiom and, were it effectively accepted and enforced, could potentially destabilize the fundaments of the system.

Interaction-dependent justice is the normative paradigm underpinning such a model of international reciprocal exclusion. A model of justice is interaction-dependent if its prescriptions arise from and apply only to the interaction of the agents under consideration. A duty of justice, in this vein, has its normative source in the intercourse among agents, and it is only relevant for them, for where no intercourse occurs, no duty of justice applies. Consequently, no externally originated duties or external agents are taken into primary account in the normative assessment of the situation. In particular, from an international perspective, intercourse is typically determined within the context of a bounded state, and those members who (or parts of humanity which) exist outside this context are accorded only the thin principles of beneficence. A highly counterintuitive stance derives from this according to which the moral agent is under no duty of justice to create *ex novo* an interaction in at least two crucial cases. That is, justice does not bind the moral agent to build up a relationship either (a) to help other needy agents or (b) to promote a better overall outcome regardless of her personal benefit. In both cases, rather than a strict duty of justice only a thin and imperfect obligation of beneficence applies, with its correlate of conditional blame and guilt. Since ethics always applies to actions or omission among agents, the establishment of new relationships constitutes a critical issue. Do the duties of justice extend to the duty to enter into an interaction, or do they only kick in once it is established? This determination is what really marks the practical distinction between interaction-dependent and interaction-in-dependent normative theories of justice.

The set of principles embedded in interaction-dependent normativity is of paramount importance for it represents a (if not *the*) principal component of Western liberal theories of justice, both ethical and legal. Doubtless, such a paradigm has contributed greatly toward the reduction of domestic social and political exclusion, for it grounded the stance enabling many political movements to advance their emancipatory claims within the borders of the national state. Liberal societies have reached a high level of inclusion thanks to the adoption of such a nondiscriminating principle of closed impartiality. At the international level, however, the situation is turned upside down, in that the very same principle reveals its closure clause, which in turn weakens any progressive force to include excluded individuals. It is used to excuse international exclusion, for it normatively legitimizes the preservation of a state of subalternity and vulnerability. An examination of the interaction-based theories of justice is thus of the utmost importance when the issue of international exclusion is at stake, both for its failure to respond to and its indirect contribution to warranting such a discriminatory situation.

The following examination develops two of the most compelling and influential interaction-based theories of justice—the contextualist and universalist theories of justice—in order to highlight their inadequacy. Contextualist theories are unresponsive to others' demand for justice insofar as not sharing the governing cultural and political background precludes inclusion in the realm of ethical and political consideration. Conversely, while universalist interaction theories have a more inclusive approach toward nonmembers, they still exclude all those agents with whom no intercourse occurs. Through the distinction between justice and beneficence, in fact, they draw the threshold of impartial treatment toward foreign people to a point that, despite universally prohibiting exploitation, still allows for significant exclusions. Both variants thus remain insufficiently attentive to the universal claims of aliens. The examination begins with the contextualist theories because, of the two kinds of interaction-dependent theories, they diverge farthest from a truly democratic global order. The examination then proceeds to scrutinize universalist theories of interaction-based justice, the most challenging paradigm in the field of international ethics.

Interaction-Dependent Contextualist Theories: Statism and Nationalism

Despite being profoundly different in other respects, realist and nationalist theories are here considered jointly on account of their reliance on the interaction paradigm, and the subsequent international consequences of their exclusive inclusiveness. Sharing a group-limited focus—the state in the case of realism and the cultural community in the case of nationalism—these theories draw the boundaries of justice according to a conventionalist paradigm. From their contextualist perspective, justice in any given society is determined by the socially defined, and thus shared, belief about the meanings of the goods to be distributed among the members of the community (Walzer 1985). In this way, both statist realism and nationalist communitarianism hold that the limit of thick duties of justice is the horizon of domestic interaction, with their prescriptions toward nonmembers varying from a thin obligation of beneficence, to a set of traditional modus vivendi principles of nonharm and nonintervention, to even a license for aggressive and expansionist policies. The issue of inclusion/exclusion is at its clearest here, for the normative paradigm of realism and nationalism is based on the notion of limited inclusion as meaningfully contrasted to the political outranking of nonmembers. As aptly noted by a commentator, the idea of spherical justice yields the intrinsic risk of generating global injustice and exclusion.[5]

In international political terms, the state and nation paradigms are the normative basis for the two principal interpretations of the principle of sovereignty, which is in turn considered to be a constitutive and ordering rule of international organization. Following a traditional definition according to which sovereignty is "the institutionalization of public authority within mutually exclusive jurisdictional domains,"[6] the state paradigm recognizes this domain with reference to territory, the nation with reference to the population.[7] Using such conventional categorization, this section develops its analysis by adopting the alternative of state versus nation, as illustrated by the two paradigms of realism and nationalism.

Since at least Thucydides' times, the paradigmatic interpretation of international relations has been realist: based on the idea of exclusion and competition among the various political agents.[8] Based on a negative

---

[5] Brian Barry, "Spherical Justice and Global Injustice," in *Pluralism, Justice and Equality*, edited by David Miller and Michael Walzer, 67–80 (Oxford: Oxford University Press, 1995).

[6] John G. Ruggie, "Continuity and Transformation in the World Polity: Toward a Neorealist Synthesis," in Keohane 1986, 131–57; qtd.143; Stephen D. Krasner, *Sovereignty: Organized Hypocrisy* (Princeton: Princeton University Press, 1999).

[7] Sam Barkin and Bruce Cronin, "The State and the Nation," *International Organization* 49 (1995): 107–30.

[8] Examples of this genre include works by Hans Morgenthau, Kenneth Waltz, and Felix Oppenheim. For commentaries see Keohane 1986; Kenneth Kipnis and Diana T. Meyers, eds., *Political Realism and International Morality: Ethics in the Nuclear Age* (Boulder: Westview Press, 1987); David A. Baldwin, ed., *Neorealism and Neoliberalism: The Contemporary Debate* (New York: Columbia University Press, 1993); Pier Paolo Portinaro, *Il realismo politico* (Rome-Bari: Laterza, 1999).

anthropology of power and hostility à la Hobbes, the realists' ultimate political objective remains the preservation and increase of state power in an environment characterized by the absence of any significant cooperative or inclusive international structures. Whether they take the perpetual conflict behind all of this to be generated by the self-seeking nature of human beings (natural realism) or by the anarchical structure of international relations (structural realism), realist explanations overlap in concluding that the constitutive function of power relationships inevitably implies the exclusion of the others from power.

Following from these assumptions, almost no space is left for justice intended as an impartial and inclusive mechanism of conflict settlement. Typically, given the choice between impartial justice and state interest, the realist scholar is always for the second—though this may sometimes be dissimulated—since the realists take the demands of justice to be merely a weak ideology serving a weak actor. It is a common realist creed that justice exists only, if it exists at all, by the grace of the powerful, and the weak rely upon it at their peril. If moral demands, such as respecting human rights, are advanced, they remain completely subordinate to the imperatives of foreign policy. Moral assessments are relevant only in instances in which state representatives decide on something other than national interest, and any such moral decision must conform to the national interest. The principal normative stance of realism regards the duties of the governor as the preservation and increase of national power to the detriment of non–fellow citizens.

Beyond the representation of the international realm as an external competitive environment, also of particular significance within the discussion of exclusion is the mechanism of the externalization of domestic conflict adopted by the realist school. While personal ambition can sometimes be redirected and tamed through domestic socializing mechanisms such as law, ethics, customs, and sport, a principal tactic of "realist" governments consists in the externalization of personal ambition where these overlap with the national interest and expansionist tendencies. In this sense, for realists there is an inevitable correlation between internal pacification and the externalization of conflict. On this point, an obvious reference is Carl Schmitt, who maintains that political unity presupposes the real possibility of an enemy, and therefore an antagonistic political unity. Hence, for one state to exist, more than one needs to exist; consequently a world state is not conceivable, for the political scene is intrinsically pluriverse.[9] Conversely, the neutralization of internal conflicts can also derive from external threats.

These considerations suffice here to characterize the realist position as one of the major supporting ideologies of the current level of interna-

---

[9] Carl Schmitt, *The Concept of the Political* (Chicago: University of Chicago Press, 1996). (Originally published in 1932.)

tional exclusion. However, realism does not exhaust the range of normative options within the contextualist category of interaction-dependent theories of justice. Its counterpart, nationalism—and more generally communitarianism—represents another source that has made an almost equal contribution to the establishment of the present exclusionary system of international relations. The rationale for exclusion within the community-based theories of political justice is in fact almost as old and almost as influential as the realist argument.[10] After the long-term realist hegemony attending the cold war, nationalism resumed a politically relevant place in the late 1980s, and exploded in the 1990s. Its theoretical foe is undoubtedly represented by universal liberalism, with its correlate of disembedded or unencumbered individual rights.

While the term "state" represents a legal concept describing a social group that occupies a defined territory and is organized under common political institutions and effective government, "nation" depicts a social group that shares a common ideology, common institutions and customs, and a sense of homogeneity. In this sense, a nation can be seen, then, as a community of sentiment or an "imagined community." While the exact content of this sentiment—that is, what constitutes a nation—remains highly controversial, a significant component of all its multidimensional definitions consists in an exclusionary clause to effect the delimiting of the boundaries of the national community. According to Anthony Smith for instance, national identity involves some sense of political community, which in turn implies at least a definite social space and a fairly well-demarcated and bounded territory, with which the members identify and to which they feel they belong, as opposed to other nations.[11]

Another influential interpretation of nationality that is centered on political inclusion is that elaborated by David Miller. In Miller's view, a national identity entails the feeling of belonging to a community that is constituted by mutual beliefs, extended in history, active in character,

---

[10] For references to the political phenomenon, see the studies of Hans Kohn, Benedict Anderson, Ernest Gellner, Eric Hobsbawn, and Anthony Smith. For a philosophical analysis, see Alasdair MacIntyre, "Is Patriotism a Virtue?" (paper presented as the Lindley Lecture, Philosophy Department, University of Kansas, 1984); Yael Tamir, *Liberal Nationalism* (Princeton: Princeton University Press, 1993); Charles Taylor and Amy Gutmann, *Multiculturalism: Examining the Politics of Recognition* (Princeton: Princeton University Press, 1994); Michael Walzer, *Thick and Thin: Moral Argument at Home and Abroad* (Notre Dame: University of Notre Dame Press, 1994); David Miller, *On Nationality* (Oxford: Oxford University Press, 1995); Margaret Canovan, *Nationhood and Political Theory* (Cheltenham: Edward Elgar, 1996); Robert McKim and Jeff McMahan, eds., *The Morality of Nationalism* (New York: Oxford University Press, 1997); Will Kymlicka and Christine Straehle, "Cosmopolitanism, Nation-States, and Minority Nationalism: A Critical Review of Recent Literature," *European Journal of Philosophy* 7 (1999): 65–88; Catherine M. Frost, "Survey Article: The Worth of Nations," *Journal of Political Philosophy* 9, no. 4 (2001): 482–503.

[11] Anthony Smith, *National Identity* (London: Penguin, 1991).

connected to a particular territory, and distinguished from other nations by its members' distinct traits. In addition, Miller's theory of nationality generates three cardinal claims: national identities are properly part of personal identities; they ground circumscribed obligations to fellow nationals; and finally, they justify aspirations to political self-determination. Nationality is, consequently, valued for two principal reasons. National identity is constitutively good insofar as it is endowed with an ethical value that crucially contributes to the full development of personal identity. Furthermore, national identity is instrumentally good as a provider of social conditions needed for the implementation of domestic social justice. Losing such identity would loosen a number of solidaristic ties, which are necessary for an effective social project.[12]

At the basis of this lies Miller's concept of particularistic ethical obligations, which originate from the recognition of the intrinsic values of the modes of relations within the community and are centered on the concept of loose reciprocity, built on the possibility of identification and on the feeling of membership. According to such a contextualist theory of ethical identity, the contents of justice are culturally shaped, so that those who are not part of the social game are not considered valid recipients of the same kind of moral attention reserved for members.[13]

Both Smith's and Miller's theories confirm the intrinsically exclusionary character of nationalist theories, rendering them fundamentally consistent with the realist position on the issue of inclusion/exclusion. While a similar argument also applies to other kinds of relativist or communitarian theories, such as those of Michael Walzer and Alasdair MacIntyre, these theories are not analyzed here, for lack of space as well as lack of anything significant they could add to the issue of exclusion. Now that we have ascertained the position of the contextualist interaction-dependent theories of justice, we need to examine the other strand of interaction-dependent theories, the universalist one, in order to complete the depiction of the set of normative arguments that support exclusion at the international level.

Interaction-Dependent Universalist Theories: Contractarianism, Nonharm Theories, and the "Cosmopolitan Democracy" Project

Endorsed by the Rawlsian school of thought, the notion of interaction-based justice can be considered the mainstream in current political philosophy. In fact, the principle of reciprocity—as opposed to good samaritanism—is now widely accepted by many contemporary scholars

[12] David Miller, "The Ethical Significance of Nationality," *Ethics* 98, no. 4 (1988): 647–62, "In Defence of Nationality," *Journal of Applied Philosophy* 10, no. 1 (1993): 3–16, and Miller 1995.

[13] David Miller, "National Self-Determination and Global Justice," in *Citizenship and National Identity*, edited by David Miller, 161–79; esp. 168–71 (Cambridge: Polity, 2000).

of global ethics as the fundamental principle of justice.[14] Furthermore, as already noted, in being consistent with the principle of noninterference the interaction-based principle of justice can be considered a central component of liberalism, and thus of modern Western—especially Anglo-Saxon—political thought.[15] While this principle of justice offers a number of important normative resources for tackling relevant social problems, such as exploitation, it fails when it comes to others that are especially pertinent to the problem of international exclusion. Thus, in providing crucial "support" for liberal-democratic versions of international democracy, such as the project of "cosmopolitan democracy," the paradigm of interaction dependence ultimately generates a club-based version of democracy, which renders these versions deficient in terms of capacity for inclusion and participation.

The principle of reciprocity forms the basis of interaction-dependent versions of justice. Being a rights-based theory of justice, interaction-based justice does not aim to promote the good; rather, it aims to ensure that a number of principles often expressed as individual rights are honored. Moral agents are not, according to this view, in charge of positive obligations of beneficence (which remain in the domain of supererogation); rather, they are simply under a negative duty of non-harm and noninterference. Beyond this strict duty of nonharm and the relative duty of compensation, individuals are not recognized as having any further "natural" obligation except for that of reciprocity, which applies in the case of cooperative practices. Were they to pursue an advantage in entering into a social relationship, this voluntary step in their personal interest would then compel them to comply with a fairness principle of justice. If an agreement is stipulated, one has a duty to keep to it, but there is no duty to stipulate it ab initio. Much like the principle of *pacta sunt servanda*, the principle of reciprocity maintains that "if one benefits from some co-operative practice, one should not be a 'free rider' by taking the benefits while failing to do one's part in sustaining the

---

[14] Charles R. Beitz, *Political Theory and International Relations* (Princeton: Princeton University Press, 1979); Gauthier 1986; Charles R. Beitz, "Social and Cosmopolitan Liberalism," *International Affairs* 75, no. 3 (1999): 515–29; Rawls 1999; Thomas Pogge, *World Poverty and Human Rights: Cosmopolitan Responsibilities and Reforms* (Cambridge: Polity, 2002); David Held, "Democratic Accountability and Political Effectiveness from a Cosmopolitan Perspective," *Government and Opposition* 39, no. 2 (2004): 364–91. For a critical consideration of the notion of justice as reciprocity, see Thomas Scanlon, "Contractualism and Utilitarianism," in *Utilitarianism and Beyond*, edited by Amartya Sen and Bernard Williams, 103–28 (Cambridge: Cambridge University Press, 1982); Brian Barry, *Theories of Justice: A Treatise on Social Justice*, vol. 1 (Hemel Hempstead: Harvester-Wheatsheaf, 1989), Barry 2005, and Barry, *Justice as Impartiality* (Oxford: Oxford University Press, 1995).
[15] Alan Ryan, "Liberalism," in *A Companion to Contemporary Political Philosophy*, edited by Robert Goodin and Philip Pettit, 291–311 (Oxford: Blackwell, 1993).

practice when it is one's turn to do so" (Barry 2005, 530). Still, there is no duty of justice to enter a cooperative practice.

The principle of reciprocity is usually characterized as that which sets justice apart from beneficence, which is in itself a deontologically biased presentation clearly favoring reciprocity over beneficence.[16] According to this view, the promotion of others' well-being is meritorious but not strictly speaking required, and thus is nonenforceable. Acts of beneficence are then regarded as acts of charity rather than ethical imperatives, as imperfect obligations concerning which the vulnerable can advance claims, but to nobody in particular. Conversely, the principle of nonharm and reciprocity generates perfect duties of justice, which are enforceable, in that it produces obligations whose compliance can be demanded of somebody specifically, that is, the harm-doer or the practice cooperator. A much-studied case in relation to the distinction between beneficence and justice is the penetrating example originally formulated by Peter Singer of someone witnessing a child drowning in a pond (Singer 1972). According to the "justice" view presented so far, the duty to rescue the child depends on the relationship between the child and the witness. For the duty to exist, either both parties have to be members of the same community or social enterprise, or the witness has to be causally connected with the child (which implies a duty to repair and compensate for the rescuer's wrongdoing). Outside these two cases, only thin obligations of beneficence—good samaritan actions among fellow members of humanity—remain.[17] Moreover, usually relying on the "restricted causation claim," a claim according to which only direct and intentional causal consequences count for attributing responsibility, such a view on justice maintains the distinction between action and omission, according minor relevance to justice for the latter by comparison with the former.

The collective correlate of the principle of reciprocity and nonharm is the interaction-dependent institutionalism that forms the common ground of many, mainly liberal-contractarian, contemporary political theories.[18]

---

[16] Peter Singer, "Famine, Affluence, and Morality," *Philosophy and Public Affairs* 1, no. 3 (1972): 229–43; Allen Buchanan, "Justice and Charity," *Ethics* 97 (1987): 558–75.

[17] For a discussion on samaritanism, see John Kleinig, "Good Samaritanism," *Philosophy and Public Affairs* 5, no. 4 (1976): 382–407; Jonathan Glover, *Causing Death and Saving Lives* (Harmondsworth: Penguin, 1977); Erik Mack, "Bad Samaritanism and the Causation of Harm," *Philosophy and Public Affairs* 9, no. 3 (1980): 230–59; Jeff McMahan, "Killing, Letting Die and Withdrawing Aid," *Ethics* 103, no. 2 (1993): 250–79; H. M. Malm, "Liberalism, Bad Samaritan and Legal Paternalism," *Ethics* 106 (1995): 4–31; O'Neill 2000, chap. 10.

[18] The republican theory also suffers a similar limitation, as in the studies of Pettit, Pocock, Skinner, and Viroli. At the normative level, it is possible to detect in this school of thought the same kind of weakness based on the interaction paradigm. For a republican state to be just, it suffices for it to be both nondominated and not interfered with, or alternatively nondominating and noninterfering. This criterion of legitimacy, however, does not prevent a certain degree of indifference toward peoples and countries with which no

Before exposing to critique their failure to capture the ethical and political relevance of the exclusion factor, however, it is necessary to point out the specific feature of these theories that generates this failure. This can best be observed through their discussion of political justice, which almost invariably begins from the historically false consideration of a "closed system isolated from other societies."[19] The most emblematic case of such a community-based approach is certainly Rawls's notion of a mutually beneficial co-operative enterprise. Central to this is the disanalogy of the principles of justice according to which those principles that apply within a society do not apply between societies, and consequently no substantial duty of redistributive justice exists at the international level (Rawls 1999). In this sense, the Rawlsian position offers eminent evidence of the inadequacy of the contractarian theory of justice in dealing with problems that pertain to multiple levels of political action. In being anchored to a state model of societal organization, these theories fail to detect the relevancy of other transborder spheres of social conduct.[20] Since the principle of fair play and reciprocal justice is conditional, "the most Rawls can say about a society that does not have such a scheme is that it suffers from collective irrationality in that it is passing up a chance to do itself some good" (Barry 2005, 531).

Other scholars theorize along similar lines. For instance, despite representing two different traditions of thought, David Gauthier and Thomas Pogge both fundamentally rely on the assumption of a self-contained community, however expanded.[21] Pogge, in particular, holds that the duty of justice toward every other person, which can be discharged merely by not cooperating in the imposition of an unjust institutional scheme upon him, is conditioned on the contingent presence of social interaction and consequently does not exist with respect to the plurality of self-contained communities. Pogge admits that prior to any trading there would still be fairly weak duties of morality in terms of beneficence, but he is firm in maintaining that there would be no duties of justice.[22] One of the challenges raised by Pogge's argument lies in the

---

relations of domination or interference exist. For republicanism, as for all other interaction-based theories, there is not sufficient sensitivity to prevent the vulnerable from suffering independently from the relationship with them. This remains the case despite recent attempts to link republicanism and cosmopolitanism. James Bohman, "Cosmopolitan Republicanism: Citizenship, Freedom and Global Political Authority," *Monist* 84, no. 1 (2001): 3–21; Ryoa Chung, "The Cosmopolitan Scope of Republican Citizenship," *Critical Review of International Social and Political Philosophy* 6, no. 1 (2003): 135–54.

[19] John Rawls, *A Theory of Justice* (Cambridge, Mass.: Harvard University Press, 1971), 8.

[20] Samuel Scheffler, *Boundaries and Allegiances: Problems of Justice and Responsibility in Liberal Thought* (Oxford: Oxford University Press, 2001), 33–4.

[21] Gauthier 1986, chap. 9; Thomas Pogge, "Cosmopolitanism and Sovereignty," *Ethics* 103 (1992), 51, and "The Bounds of Nationalism," *Canadian Journal of Philosophy* supplementary volume 22 (1998): 463–504.

[22] Thomas Pogge, "On the Site of Distributive Justice: Reflections on Cohen and Murphy," *Philosophy and Public Affairs* 29, no. 2 (2000): 137–69; esp. 166–67.

capacity to distinguish between a positive and a negative responsibility. For him, any ethical theory unable to accommodate the fundamental commonsense difference between acting and omitting would prove implausible. While an interaction-dependent theory of justice such as consequentialism can accommodate this requirement by way of differentiating between action and omission[23] in terms of instrumental value, it is important to stress that attaching intrinsic value to this distinction inevitably leads toward interaction-dependent justice, with its correlate of exclusion so far exposed.

Before proceeding to a consideration of the particular significance of the interaction-based paradigm for the international realm of politics, a note of clarification on the issue of global interdependence is due. While the ever-increasing worldwide interdependence occasioned by recent global transformations has certainly been a key factor in awakening global moral consciousness, it cannot play an independent normative role in any argument about international political theory and global justice. In particular, important as interdependence may be in the moral assessment of current international duties,[24] it is not the decisive factor for what concerns positive duties.[25] From the currently held consequentialist perspective, that we now influence each other to such a high degree only serves to clarify that we are in a relevant position to influence outcomes that affect others; it does not constitute a deontic principle in itself. If it did, the result would be a contingent ethics recognizing only a duty to those upon whom we depend, and "indeed, a wealthy nation that wished to exempt its populace from having any obligation to redistribute part of its wealth to impoverished nations might simply withdraw from economic exchanges with those nations."[26]

Internationally speaking, the political correlate of the interaction-based paradigm of justice entails a club-based interpretation of democracy, as embodied in the proposal associated with the project of cosmopolitan democracy and more recently with the model of stakeholder democracy. In holding to a notion of democratic congruence based not on an ideal of universal constituency but instead on the strict relation between those who make the rules and those who directly suffer the

[23] Related to this is the concept of omission, which here designates the renunciation of performing an act that the agent is able to perform.

[24] Christien van den Anker, "The Role of Globalisation in Arguments for Cosmopolitanism," *Acta Politica* 35, no. 1 (2000): 5–36.

[25] Andrew Hurrell, "Global Inequality and International Institutions," in *Global Justice*, edited by Thomas Pogge, 32–54; qtd. 34 (Oxford: Blackwell, 2001).

[26] Russell Hardin, "From Bodo Ethics to Distributive Justice," *Ethical Theory and Moral Practice* 2 (1999): 399–413; qtd. 410. For a similar point, see Liam Murphy, "Institutions and the Demands of Justice," *Philosophy and Public Affairs* 27 (1998): 271–75, esp. 272; Andrew Linklater, "The Evolving Spheres of International Justice," *International Affairs* 75, no. 3 (1999): 473–82; esp. 476–77; Peter Singer, *One World: The Ethics of Globalization* (New Haven: Yale University Press, 2002), 197.

consequences of them, cosmopolitan democracy tends toward a club-based system of democracy.[27] The strict notion of congruence, in fact, can be more easily associated with the decision-making method of a democratic club than with a democratic political system, in that it prevents the exploitation of those it chooses to include but does not allow for those not designated as "members" to be included in a public decision-making process. Thus, those "nonmembers" who are only indirectly or "publicly" involved in sociopolitical interaction are shut out. This system also shares a number of elements with the corporativist model of political participation, as characterized in particular by the two following features: interest groups can only take part in those political discussions specifically dealing with the interests they represent; and their representatives have an issue-constrained political mandate.[28]

In suggesting a net of narrowly circumscribed institutions, cosmopolitan democracy refuses citizens outside such structures a guarantee of representation. In particular, this corporativist model excludes three crucial categories of stakeholders: those who represent (a) nonformally organized interests, (b) future interests, and (c) general or public interests.[29] In the attempt to identify a threshold according to which only those who are relevantly affected are taken into consideration, the paradigm sometimes deploys the harm principle, restrictively intended, and at other times deploys the principle of nonimposition of unjust institutional settings. In both cases, however, those who are indirectly (but for them, perhaps, critically) affected are twice excluded: in being left out from the public decision-making process in charge of assessing the degree of the causal relation and later from the mechanism of compensation for the harm suffered.

In sum, what the analysis of the paradigm of interaction-dependent justice developed in the previous two sections has shown is that the possibility of legitimately not entering into, or legitimately withdrawing from, a relationship can be identified as a major generator of political ostracism. When, as has just been done here, universalist and contextualist interaction-dependent theories of justice are considered together in light of their specific prescriptions toward international exclusion, an image of the mighty normative armature providing everyday politics with the ideological support for such political outranking is clearly revealed. Ultimately, this attitude equals indifference to injustices not immediately occasioned by the moral agent in question. To use the famous case of a bystander passive at the sight of a child drowning in a pond: it is this

---

[27] David Held, *Democracy and the Global Order: From the Modern State to Cosmopolitan Governance* (Cambridge: Polity, 1995).

[28] Norberto Bobbio, *Teoria generale della politica* (Turin: Einaudi, 1999), 410–28.

[29] Luigi Einaudi, *Il buongoverno* (Rome: Laterza, 1973), 1:30–33. (Originally published in 1919.)

passive stance, the *justly* walking-away attitude, that this chapter has aimed to discredit.

Conclusions

In this chapter the principal boundaries of the research on international justice with reference to the issue of exclusion have been drawn both in their empirical aspects and in their normative fundaments. In opposition to the current international political fragmentation that generates political exclusion and vulnerability, a different paradigm of justice needs to be developed in order to avoid the evil of international exclusion.[30] An interaction-independent theory needs to be framed that is able to envisage a cosmopolitan system in which all world citizens are included within a scheme of a direct representative participation under an overarching authority governing the process of democratizing world affairs. It is, in fact, only through an all-inclusive world system that the drawing of jurisdictional boundaries can be implemented democratically and the problem of political exclusion be avoided. Exclusion would then be considered legitimate only when boundaries were collectively decided though an all-inclusive procedure. As is already recognized in the domestic case, only when an individual is entitled to participate in the delineation of jurisdictional boundaries can he or she not feel excluded, for he or she has a valid and publicly recognized voice to claim inclusion in a relevant jurisdictional domain.

The pursuit of the democratic ideal would then be implemented through a reworked notion of citizenship as global, multilayered, and all-inclusive. In essence, this entails an expansion of the domestic model of democracy to the international level, structured on several layers that take into account different jurisdictional boundaries as coordinated through a world democratic system. Only through the radical project of stretching the paradigm of democratic inclusion to the extreme limits encompassing the whole of humankind, together with recognizing the legitimacy of multiple political allegiances, not simply those of state governments, can the inhuman mechanism of inclusion as a generator of exclusion be avoided. If the phenomenon of illegitimate political exclusion is to be escaped, the authority to define jurisdictional boundaries needs to be reallocated from groups with a circumscribed scope to a global public democratic mechanism. Hence, universal inclusion and

---

[30] For a discussion of the paradigm of interaction-independent justice as applied to global democracy see Raffaele Marchetti, "Consequentialist Cosmopolitanism and Global Political Agency," in *Global Ethics and Civil Society*, edited by John Eade and Darren O'Byrne, 57–73 (Aldershot: Ashgate, 2005), "Human Rights as Global Participatory Entitlements," in *Between Cosmopolitan Ideals and State Sovereignty: Studies on Global Justice*, edited by Ronald Tinnevelt and Gert Verschraegen, 159–69 (London: Palgrave Macmillan, 2006), and Marchetti 2008a and 2008b.

multiple allegiances represent key components of a genuine project of global justice through global democracy.

Acknowledgments

Useful comments on an earlier version of this chapter were provided by David Held, Kimberly Hutchings, Dorothea Kast, Paul Kelly, Tony McGrew, Thomas Pogge, and Olga Tribulato. I wish to thank all of them. The chapter was previously published (in slightly different form) in *Constellations: An International Journal of Critical and Democratic Theory* 12, no. 4 (2005): 487–501.

References

Barry, Brian. 2005. "Humanity and Justice in Global Perspective." In *Contemporary Political Philosophy*, edited by Robert Goodin and Philip Pettit, 525–40. Oxford: Blackwell. (Originally published in 1991.)

Gauthier, David. 1986. *Morals by Agreement*. Oxford: Oxford University Press.

Keohane, Robert, ed. 1986. *Neorealism and Its Critics*. New York: Columbia University Press.

Marchetti, Raffaele. 2008a. *Global Democracy: For and Against: Ethical Theory, Institutional Design, and Social Struggles*. London: Routledge.

———. 2008b. "A Matter of Drawing Boundaries: Global Democracy and International Exclusion." *Review of International Studies* 34, no. 2:207–24.

Miller, David. 1995. *On Nationality*. Oxford: Oxford University Press.

O'Neill, Onora. 2000. *Bounds of Justice*. Cambridge: Cambridge University Press.

Rawls, John. 1999. *The Law of Peoples: With The Idea of Public Reason Revisited*. Cambridge, Mass.: Harvard University Press.

Singer, Peter. 1972. "Famine, Affluence, and Morality." *Philosophy and Public Affairs* 1, no. 3:229–43.

Walzer, Michael. 1985. *Spheres of Justice: A Defence of Pluralism and Equality*. Oxford: Blackwell.

7

COSMOPOLITAN DEMOCRACY AND THE RULE OF LAW

WILLIAM E. SCHEUERMAN

What are the likely consequences of globalization for democratic theory and practice? In a series of path-breaking publications that have garnered a remarkable amount of scholarly attention in a brief span of time, the political theorist David Held and a group of interlocutors (most important, Daniele Archibugi and Anthony McGrew) have tackled this question by means of an audacious model of "cosmopolitan democracy," according to which the democratization of transnational politics now belongs at the top of the agenda.[1] Working in cooperation with an interdisciplinary group of scholars, Held and his intellectual compatriots argue that the ongoing transnationalization of key forms of human activity calls out for the development of no less transnational modes of liberal democratic decision making.[2] A host of recent social trends (the globalization of the economy, for example, as well as the growing significance of cross-border environmental problems) not only demonstrates that the existing nation-state is ill prepared to deal with the regulatory imperatives of our times, but also raises fundamental questions about the traditional attempt to weld liberal democracy onto the framework of the modern nation-state. Modern liberal-democratic theory typically presupposed the existence of substantial symmetry and congruence between citizen-voters and decision makers at the national level, and the key categories of consent, constituency, participation, and representation were accordingly conceived within the parameters of the nation-state (Held 1999, 81). As national borders become ever more

[1] Archibugi 1992; 1995; 1998; 2000; Archibugi and Held 1995; Archibugi, Held, and Koehler, 1998; Held 1991; 1992; 1995a; 1995b; 1998; 2000; McGrew 1997; 1998; Held and McGrew 1993.
[2] Their research was conducted, at least for a period of time, under the auspices of the European Commission-funded Network of European Scholars on the Political Theory of Transnational Democracy: Citizens, Minorities, and People in Europe. The project was interdisciplinary in scope, and a number of other scholars (including David Beetham, Mary Kaldor, Martin Koehler, Andrew Linklater, and Richard Falk) have played important roles in contributing to the theory of cosmopolitan democracy, whose fundamental core has been sketched out most clearly by Archibugi and Held in a number of essays, books, and jointly edited volumes. I should also note that the theory of cosmopolitan democracy has influenced some of Habermas's recent reflections on globalization (Habermas 1998, 159–63).

porous, however, a series of difficult and thus far unanswered questions force themselves onto the agenda of democratic theory: "What is the proper constituency, and proper jurisdiction, for developing and implementing policy issues with respect to ... the use of nuclear energy, the harvesting of rain forests, the use of non-renewable resources, the instability of global financial markets, and the reduction of the risks of nuclear warfare" (Held 1998, 22) in light of their profound cross-border consequences? Held's and his interlocutors' answer to this question is that we need to update the liberal-democratic vision by undertaking a series of dramatic institutional reforms. Stated in the simplest terms: those policy arenas whose transnational scope overwhelms existing nationally based liberal democratic institutions require a dramatic strengthening of nascent forms of transnational liberal-democratic authority (under the auspices of the United Nations, but also regional organizations such as the European Union or North American Free Trade Agreement) along with the establishment of new forms of transnational decision making (for example, cross-border popular referenda).

The resulting model of "cosmopolitan democracy" has generated significant interest among political theorists, and a number of useful recent publications have already been devoted to critically analyzing Held's proposals from a host of different theoretical perspectives.[3] Here I cannot hope to offer an adequate critical summary of that increasingly multisided debate, in which communitarian-inspired attempts to deflate cosmopolitan democracy's universalistic Kantian features play an especially prominent role (Bellamy and Castiglione 1998; Kymlicka 2000; Thompson 1998; Wendt 2000). For now, let me just state that I find the communitarian response unconvincing (Scheuerman 2001a). Nonetheless, it is striking that little critical attention has been paid to cosmopolitan democracy's purported fidelity to classical conceptions of the "rule of law." Held repeatedly suggests that "cosmopolitan democratic law" builds on the best of the Western legal tradition, even going so far as to dub his updated version of liberal democracy a cosmopolitan "democratic *Rechtsstaat*" (Held 1995a, 221–38; 2000, 106–7).

As I hope to show here, this claim not only obscures the extent to which Held and his colleagues in fact break with traditional conceptions of the "rule of law," but the weaknesses of their legal argumentation also point to the existence of immanent flaws within their overall vision of transnational democracy. Both Archibugi and Held insist that one of cosmopolitan democracy's main appeals is that it circumvents the ills of unacceptable models of a hypercentralized "planetary Leviathan" or world-state likely to prove incapable of doing

---

[3]   Archibugi, Held, and Koehler 1998; Coates 2000; Dahl 2000; Dryzek 1999; Görg and Hirsch 1998; Hirst and Thompson 1996; Holden 2000; Schmitter 1999; Shapiro and Hacker-Cordon 2000; Thompson 1999; Zolo 1997, 2000; Zuern 1998, 248–49.

justice to cultural, religious, and ethical diversity (Archibugi 1995, 132–35; 1998, 215).[4] They proudly assert that their model of "cosmopolitan democratic law" not only can succeed in effectively restraining the exercise of political power on the global level but would continue to provide significant room for decision making at the local and national levels. Presumably there is no legitimate reason to fear cosmopolitan democracy law as a potential cover for a new and potentially onerous form of imperialism, and opponents of centralized world government would do well to join forces with those committed to realizing transnational democracy in accordance with their ideas.[5]

Unfortunately, the legal ills of cosmopolitan democracy undermine precisely those features that initially make it so attractive. These flaws suggest that we would do well to pursue more modest—but nonetheless important—experiments in buttressing democracy at the global level. I first provide an exegesis of the conceptual foundations of the idea of a cosmopolitan democratic Rechtsstaat (section 1), before turning to examine its conceptual weaknesses (section 2).

1

Cosmopolitan democracy is predicated on the plausible notion that a growing range of policy concerns explodes the confines of both the traditional nation-state and the Westphalian system of international relations in which the nation-state long has been embedded. In light of a host of phenomena providing evidence of a "rapid growth of complex interconnections and interrelations between states and societies" along with the growing "intersection of national and international forces and processes," existing nation-states increasingly seem poorly equipped to tackle the most pressing political concerns of our times *either* unilaterally *or* by means of traditional forms of interstate cooperation (Held 1998, 12).[6] National legislation too often is of limited effectiveness in the face of

---

[4] Most participants in the ongoing debate on transnational democracy share similar reservations about world government. A perceptive critical discussion of this idea is offered in Narr and Schubert 1994, 233–47. See also Kelsen's criticisms of it in Kelsen 1944, 12.

[5] In a similar vein, Ingeborg Maus (1998) endorses neo-Kantian models of international relations, but she worries that contemporary Kantian models of global governance suffer from substantial conceptual and political confusion. Like Maus, I am worried that core features of the idea of the "rule of law" are obscured by Held. In some contrast to Maus (1992), I am less interested in making sure that we identify the "right" interpretation of Kant's legacy for contemporary political and legal theory. But I am very much indebted to a characteristically enlightening conversation with her in Frankfurt, when she planted some doubts in my mind about cosmopolitan democracy's rule-of-law credentials. This chapter represents an attempt to follow up on those doubts.

[6] In this account, globalization is a multidimensional (economic, environmental, cultural, legal, and political) phenomenon (Held et al. 1999). Its most obvious manifestations are probably economic (the growth of multinational firms, global currency markets, free trade) and environmental (ozone depletion, global warming).

transnational problems; regulations passed by impressive second-tier powers (France, Germany, Italy), or even a world power like the United States, are unlikely to immunize them against ozone depletion, for example, or the problematic side effects of global trade. The heightened significance as well as the lasting character of many transnational policy tasks render traditional forms of treaty making inadequate; the temporary and ad hoc character of most treaties meshes poorly with the regulatory undertakings at hand. From a normative perspective, the profound impact on domestic politics of global financial markets or the environmental crisis makes it difficult to accept the traditional view that *inter*national matters can be left in the hands of small groups of (typically nonelected) foreign policy elites: if we are to take liberal-democratic notions of legitimacy seriously, we need to conceive of new ways to democratize decision making concerning issues no longer narrowly "international" in the traditional sense of the term.

In a similar vein, it is unclear how conventional Realist "reason of state"–oriented views of interstate politics offer satisfactory conceptual resources for tackling the imperatives of transnational policy making, especially in light of the fact that contemporary Realism's dogmatic insistence on the primacy of the "national interest" decreasingly makes sense conceptually in a world in which the border between "national" and "transnational" interests becomes blurred (Held 1998, 22; Archibugi 1998, 205–6). Realist theories of international politics miss the boat in part because they reify precisely that institutional constellation, the modern nation-state, currently exhibiting signs of decay.

Cosmopolitan democracy's exponents propose that "[d]eliberative and decision-making centers beyond national territories are [to be] appropriately situated when those significantly affected by a public matter constitute a cross-border or transnational grouping, when 'lower' [local or national] levels of decision-making cannot manage and discharge satisfactorily transnational ... policy questions, or when the principle of democratic legitimacy can only be properly redeemed in a transnational context" (Held 1998, 22–23). Since many issues continue to affect constituencies primarily local or national in character, this recommendation should by no means entail the hypercentralization of decision making. Thus, Archibugi and Held repeatedly describe themselves as advocates of a multitiered political system in which new forms of transnational liberal-democratic authority, concerned exclusively with those issues possessing genuinely transnational effects, would *complement* existing forms of liberal democratic decision making. They also seem assured that this proposal amounts to more than yet another doomed "liberal idealist" pipedream inconsistent with the fundamental laws of international politics.

Though critical of its widely acknowledged democratic deficits, they not only see the E.U. as an important stepping stone to more ambitious models of global governance but also interpret it as a present-day approximation of their own quest to develop transnational political authority "midway between the confederal and federalist models" of transnational governance (Archibugi 1998, 215). Like the E.U., experiments in cosmopolitan democracy require closer ties among its units than those typically characteristic of loosely connected confederations of sovereign states (for example, NATO), since globalization increases the need for permanent forms of democratically legitimized transnational cooperation. Yet cosmopolitan democracy would avoid the relatively high degree of centralized power exhibited by existing federal systems (the United States, for example, or the Federal Republic of Germany), since "it is undesirable to go beyond a given threshold of centralization on a scale as vast as a global one" (Archibugi 1998, 216). The E.U. example is also illuminating, since it suggests the possibility of complex political institutions able to realize novel forms of sovereignty inconsistent with the traditional "hierarchical relationship between central institutions and individual states" (Archibugi 1998, 216). In this account, there is no principled reason to underscore potential tensions between regional and global forms of political authority: not only do regional liberal-democratic political blocs represent useful experiments in transnational democracy, regional decision making would also continue to play a decisive role in a more universal global network of liberal-democratic decision making when interests affected are genuinely regional in scope and thus require a regionalized solution.[7]

What, then, is the role of *law* in this model? Archibugi and Held advocate a system of *cosmopolitan* "democratic public law" in some contrast to existing *inter*national law in part because they envision a more ambitious form of jurisprudence than implied by the traditional notion of a "law between states." Since the Nuremberg Trials, international rights protections have tended to demote the role of the nation-state while anticipating, albeit incompletely, the possibility of transnational citizenship built on an unmediated relationship between individuals and global institutions. A key task of cosmopolitan democratic law is to further this cause. New forms of regional and global liberal-democratic decision making would rest directly on an emerging transnational "community of fate," and an unmediated legal relationship between individuals and transnational decision-making bodies would come to operate in a manner thus far only hinted at within existing forms of international law. Transnational courts would ultimately gain jurisdiction over many key conflicts pitting individuals against existing nation-states. In order to help ground this transformation of *inter*national law into *trans*national law, Archibugi and Held appeal to Kant's famous notion that "universal hospitality" represents a universal right transcending the claims of

---

[7] Other observers are less sanguine about the relationship between regional and global law (Cassese 1986).

particular nations and states and legitimately extending to all members of the human community.[8] But they radicalize Kant's claim by provocatively suggesting that "in a highly interconnected world" universal hospitality entails a more far-reaching set of rights than Kant originally had in mind. Given the process of globalization, universal hospitality today allegedly implies nothing less than the "mutual acknowledgement of, and respect for, the equal and legitimate rights of others to pursue their own projects and life-plans" (Held 1995a, 228; also Archibugi 1992, 310–17). Reinterpreted in accordance with present-day social and economic imperatives, Kant's cosmopolitan right to hospitality points the way to an audacious model of transnational law committed to realizing an extensive set of basic rights.[9]

More fundamentally, cosmopolitan democracy builds directly on the liberal-democratic tradition insofar as it aspires to realize both the principles of self-determination and limited government. It promises protection from arbitrary power as well as meaningful possibilities for self-determination, individual self-development, and economic opportunity, and its commitment to upholding "cosmopolitan democratic public law" is essential to its liberal-democratic credentials (Held 1995a, 150). Only by exercising political power in accordance with a legal "structure that is both constraining and enabling" can transnational liberal democracy, like its nationally based cousin, realize both self-determination and a commitment to the ideal of the rule of law (Held 1995a, 147).

Held has gone furthest in offering a detailed account of the model of law at the base of this vision. In his view, cosmopolitan democratic law ultimately rests on liberal democracy's underlying "principle of autonomy," whose chief characteristics are already embedded in the liberal-democratic practices and traditions of the West (1995a, 148). The principle of autonomy represents the "constitutive basis of democratic public law" and thus serves as an indispensable basis for political legitimacy in any liberal-democratic political community (153, 163). Influenced by Rawls's conception of political liberalism, Held considers it possible to pursue his Kantian intuitions without committing himself to controversial philosophical justifications, and he expressly distances himself from Habermas's attempt to ground a similar model of democratic politics in a demanding "theory of communicative action" (166). In

---

[8] Kant was already able to observe that "[t]he peoples of the earth have thus entered in varying degrees into a universal community, and it has developed to the point where a violation of rights in *one* part of the world is felt *everywhere*. The idea of a cosmopolitan right is therefore not fantastic and overstrained; it is a necessary complement to the unwritten code of political and international right, transforming it into a universal code of humanity" (1970, 105–6).

[9] On Kant's relevance for contemporary models of global governance, see the important essays collected in Lutz-Bachmann and Bohman 1997 as well as Maus's comparatively heretical—and provocative—statements (Maus 1998).

this view, the liberal-democratic vision of autonomy requires a commit-ment to diverse clusters of rights that alone make it possible for "people to participate on free and equal terms in the regulation of their own associations" (191). Making T. H. Marshall's famous account of the evolutionary dynamic of (legal, political, and social) rights look relatively cautious (Marshall 1950), Held argues that a legitimate interpretation of cosmopolitan democratic public law centers around a bold set of seven types of rights (health, social, cultural, civic, economic, pacific, and political). These include traditional liberal-democratic rights such as due process, equal treatment before the law, freedom of thought and expression, freedom of religion, adequate and equal possibilities for political deliberation, and universal political participation, as well as social-democratic, environmental, and even feminist rights to physical and emotional well-being, universal childcare, a guaranteed minimum income, sustainable environment, control over one's own fertility, uni-versal education, lawful foreign policy, and political accountability, as well as a mixed economy consisting of diverse forms of consumption and production (190–201).

Held is well aware of how unrealistic some of these rights are likely to appear in the existing political climate, and he concedes that it may be impractical to expect them all to be fully realized at the present time (Held 1995a, 210). But this generates no real intellectual anxiety on his part: a substantial concretization of them is currently attainable, and thus they can legitimately function as a yardstick according to which political action should be evaluated (206–16). Although basic rights "must be defined broadly" in order to assure their abstract and general character "to guide and resolve disputes among . . . interests in particular conflict situations," they lay "down an *agenda* for democratic politics, but necessarily leave . . . open the exact interpretation of each of the items on the agenda" (200–201). The justiciable charter of rights proposed here constitutes the basis for a "rule of law" to the extent that it remains legitimate to expect "[r]ules, laws, policies and decisions" to be made within their confines (205). Held clearly believes that they can successfully set "the form and limits of public power" in such a way as to make his vision deserving of the noble title of "democratic *Rechtsstaat*" (216). His proposed charter of rights thus offers "an agenda for change and direction for policy to which 'offending' institutions, laws and policies could, in principle, adapt if they are claim justifiably the mantle of democracy" (205). To the extent that rights *enable* the exercise of political power by determining how it is to be properly channeled, while simulta-neously *limiting* the exercise of power by focusing on its proper form and scope, this model allegedly offers an effective structure for a "democratic legal order—[a] democratic *Rechtsstaat*" in which political power is "circumscribed by, and accounted for in relation to, democratic public law" (Held 2000, 106).

In the final analysis, this model of a transnational rule of law consists of the following core components. When faced with issues impacting on genuinely transnational groupings, supranational legislative devices should strive to act in accordance with a detailed—but by no means fully realizable—charter of rights, and these rights thus should "be enshrined within the constitutions of parliaments and assemblies" (Held 1995a, 272). In order to achieve this goal, transnational decision-making authorities would be empowered to pass "framework" legislation whose basic outlines would correspond to the aims of cosmopolitan democratic law, but whose application and implementation should be left in the hands of lower (national or local) levels of governance; on this point as well Held has been inspired by the E.U. and its relatively limited reliance on traditional forms of uniform general legislation, and he seems to accept the view that transnational legislation will need to take a relatively flexible form so as to deal effectively with the challenge of pluralism at the global level (255, 274–75).[10] Transnational courts play a pivotal role in this conception as well. Although cosmopolitan democratic law "empowers" legislators to pursue an ambitious policy agenda, the authority of courts will be extended "so that groups and individuals have an effective means of suing political authorities for the enactment and enforcement of key rights" (200, 272). A system of judicial review would need to be established in order to make sure that legislators exhibit proper fidelity to the rights constitutive of cosmopolitan democratic law. In order to bring about this goal, Archibugi and Held propose that we build on Hans Kelsen's famous proposal to extend the compulsory jurisdiction of international courts. Kelsen's courageous defense of a robust system of international justice has long been neglected, but Archibugi and Held believe that globalization provides Kelsen's hopes with a fresh impetus (Held 1995a, 272; Archibugi 1995, 146–48; Kelsen 1944, 3–67).

2

Archibugi and Held conveniently fail to mention a striking difference between their championship of compulsory jurisdiction and Kelsen's. To be sure, Kelsen hoped that international courts would undergo invigoration, and he proposed that individuals (for example, war criminals) could be held more or less directly punishable on the basis of international legal norms. Kelsen was no enemy of either an ambitious welfare state or social democracy (Kelsen 1955). Whereas cosmopolitan democracy institutionalizes mandatory jurisdiction for a vast range of political, social, economic, and environmental rights, however, Kelsen's defense of compulsory jurisdiction for international courts focused on the *fundamental issue of war and peace*, and a careful reading of his discussion of this issue

---

[10] In a similar vein, see Zuern 1998, 345.

suggests that he endorsed a more modest—yet indisputably innovative—model of compulsory jurisdiction for global courts.[11] Indeed, Archibugi's and Held's enormously ambitious proposals arguably leave them vulnerable to Kelsen's wise admonishment that the reformer of international law would do well not to compromise "great ideals" while simultaneously accommodating "his postulates to what is politically possible" (Kelsen 1944, viii). Progress in international law is only achievable if we avoid directing our suggestions "toward a goal which, if at all, can be reached only in a distant future; this is unreal and therefore politically less than nothing" (Kelsen 1944, viii). Archibugi and Held certainly offer "great ideals," but their recommendations for the international state system should at least raise the question of whether Kelsen's insistence on the virtues of a "slow and steady perfection of the international legal order" undertaken in a sober and "realistic" tone has been sufficiently heeded (Kelsen 1944, ix). To the extent that cosmopolitan democracy means dismantling core components of the international state system, it points the way to revolutionary changes in contemporary political life.

My main aim here is to criticize neither cosmopolitan democracy's utopian overtones nor its misleading reliance on Kelsen. I mention these differences vis-à-vis Kelsen only in order to raise initial doubts about cosmopolitan democracy's legal credentials. As I hope to demonstrate, cosmopolitan democracy's legal weaknesses go well beyond a minor misappropriation of the leading light of twentieth-century liberal international law.

The notion of the "rule of law" has been widely contested in the history of legal thought (Bobbio 1987, 138–56; Neumann 1986). Within the modern liberal tradition, however, it generally has taken the form of requiring that state action rest on legal norms that are (1) general in character, (2) relatively clear, (3) public, (4) prospective, and (5) stable. In this standard liberal view, only norms of this type assure a minimum of certainty and determinacy within legal decision making, help guarantee the accountability of power-holders, promote the principle of fair notice, and contribute to achieving equality before the law. As Franz L. Neumann pointed out many years ago, this model often coexists with a particular interpretation of the liberal commitment to basic rights. Liberalism rests on the notion of a "presumption in favor of the rights of the individual against the coercive power of the state" (Neumann 1996, 198). The rule of law in part provides a minimal but indispensable standard for helping to determine the legitimate scope of state intervention in the sphere of individual rights. Although liberalism conceives of rights as essential for assuring liberty, rights nonetheless always require legal regulation or restraint, though they never can be obliterated by legal means; even ardent defenders of free speech, for example, must accept the

---

[11] See Kelsen's famous discussion in Kelsen 1944, 71–123.

necessity of regulating free speech, even if it only entails establishing minimal basic rules for registering demonstrations or publishing newspapers. By necessity, rights are interpreted, institutionalized, and contested by a panoply of state bodies and agents, and the task of making sure that the interpretation and regulation of individual rights can be rendered normatively acceptable traditionally has been linked to the notion of the rule of law. In this view, "individual rights may be interfered with by the state only if the state can prove its claim by reference to an indeterminate number of future cases; this excludes retroactive legislation and demands a separation of legislative from judicial functions" (Neumann 1996, 200).

Fidelity to the rule of law virtues noted above is essential if we are to make sure that the interpretation and regulation of basic rights (for example, free speech) takes a relatively predictable and consistent form. In contrast, if state bodies are permitted to regulate basic rights in accordance with inconsistent, ambiguous, open-ended, or retroactive norms, excessive discretionary authority is likely to accrue to state authorities, and the sphere of individual liberty will suffer significant damage. From this traditional perspective, the rule of law performs many admirable functions, but one of its more worthwhile purposes is to work alongside the liberal defense of basic rights in order to preserve meaningful possibilities for individual liberty.

Of course, even those of us sympathetic to this conventional interpretation of the rule of law typically are forced to acknowledge its limitations; Neumann himself conceded that it was unrealistic to expect every aspect of the legal order to take the form of general, clear, public, prospective, and stable norms (1996, 203–4). In addition, traditional liberal jurisprudence raises a host of difficult institutional questions, and the multiplicity of ways in which liberal democracy has sought to institutionalize the idea of the rule of law suggests that these questions are likely to remain controversial. Nonetheless, we would do well not to throw out the baby with the bathwater, as too many critics of liberal jurisprudence tend to do. Despite the familiar dangers of overstating the merits of this traditional view, it provides a fruitful starting point for critically interrogating Archibugi's and Held's vision of cosmopolitan democratic law.

Notwithstanding constant appeals to the notion of the Rechtsstaat, Archibugi and Held seem unfamiliar with the traditional notion of the rule of law. At the very least, the only features of cosmopolitan democratic law clearly overlapping with it are their demand for rights to due process and equal treatment before the law (Held 1995a, 193). The account of the rule of law briefly summarized above is richer than theirs, however, to the extent that it better highlights key functions (for example, assuring fair notice and the accountability of power holders) and more cogently underscores the importance of effectively harnessing the exercise of state authority by demanding that legal norms and standards take a clear, general, prospective, and stable form. From the perspective of traditional liberal jurisprudence, the potential danger with Archibugi's and Held's conceptual lacuna when it comes to this matter is that it may leave cosmopolitan democracy ill equipped to ward off problematic forms of discretionary state authority.

If Archibugi and Held are as worried by the specter of a "planetary Leviathan" as they repeatedly claim, one might expect them to pay closer attention to the liberal legal model's emphasis on the dangers of discretionary and even arbitrary state authority. Unfortunately, they occasionally associate traditional concerns of this type with economic "libertarianism" and the ideas of Friedrich Hayek (Held 1995a, 241–44). A principled commitment to traditional rule of law virtues by no means necessitates loyalty to free-market capitalism, however (Raz 1979, 210–29; Scheuerman 1994). In a similar vein, it is also troubling that cosmopolitan democracy's exponents have little to say about how transnational "framework" legislation would be fleshed out at local and national levels. At one juncture, Held declares that local and national bodies would be outfitted with the authority to "implement" global laws, and that the E.U. "embodies a range of relevant distinctions among legal instruments and types of implementation which are helpful to reflect on in this context" (1995a, 275). Although there is no question either that the legal problem of "translating" transnational directives to the national or local arena is exceedingly complex, or that a great deal can be learned from the E.U. about this matter, Held's appeal to the E.U. experience only begs the question at hand. Even those enthusiastic about the emerging E.U. legal system would likely consider it presumptuous to suggest that E.U. law in its present incarnation represents a fully satisfactory embodiment of traditional rule of law virtues.

Archibugi and Held undertake a conceptual move relatively familiar from recent jurisprudence: the notion of the rule of law is basically reinterpreted as a rights-centered model of jurisprudence in which courts are likely to gain substantial authority to determine a host of controversial matters.[12] At times echoing Ronald Dworkin's famous critique of a positivist "rule-book" conception of law and concomitant espousal of a rights-based jurisprudence in which courts are outfitted with generous interpretative authority, Archibugi and Held similarly redefine the Rechtsstaat in terms of a set of basic rights purportedly able both to "empower" legal actors and to effectively "circumscribe" them (Dworkin 1977, 1985).[13] But here as well courts ultimately are destined to take on weighty discretionary authority.

---

[12] For a provocative critical discussion of this trend, see Maus 1992, 308–36.

[13] Interestingly, Dworkin is only mentioned in passing here (e.g., in Held 1995a, 202, 217).

As we saw above, the "rule of law" here basically means that legislators and courts are supposed to act in accordance with an ambitious set of basic rights. Given the fact that these rights "must be defined broadly," one wonders how they, in fact, might succeed in effectively binding or circumscribing state authority. On the surface, they would seem to provide tremendous leeway for both legislators and judicial actors, especially in light of the fact that Archibugi and Held seem uninterested in how a traditional model of the rule of law might contribute to the task of guaranteeing a modicum of consistency and calculability in the interpretation of basic rights. So how, then, would cosmopolitan democracy make sure that transnational authorities exercise authority in accordance with this charter of rights in a satisfactorily "circumscribed" way? In the final analysis, their answer seems to be that this determination should be placed in the hands of transnational courts: "[T]he influence of judicial 'review boards,' the courts, and designated complaints and appeal procedures has to be extended so that groups and individuals have an effective means of suing political authorities for the enactment or enforcement of key rights" (Held 1995a, 205; see also 270–72; and see Archibugi 1995, 143–48). Although cosmopolitan democratic public law would probably grant impressive legislative power to a variety of transnational political actors, transnational judges would ultimately possess the impressive authority to determine how the rights constitutive of "democratic public law" are ultimately to be concretized and interpreted.

By commenting that we would do well to consider proposals to democratize the judiciary,[14] Held indirectly concedes that this vision risks placing substantial open-ended authority to interpret cosmopolitan democratic law in the hands of judicial personnel: notwithstanding cosmopolitan democracy's alleged break with traditional concepts of sovereignty, it is such judicial experts who seem most likely to exercise far-reaching "sovereign" prerogative power. Discretionary rule by judicial personnel, however, is not the same thing as the rule of law.[15] Neither

---

[14] Held speculates that judicial bodies might consist of people "statistically representative of key social categories" rather than existing judicial personnel (1995a, 206). This proposal also raises fundamental questions for the ideal of the rule of law, to the extent that distinct modes of legal reasoning typically generated by a specialized legal training and culture have long been associated with it. One might argue that this proposal minimizes some of the dangers of "judicial imperialism" that I hope to highlight here. However, discretionary rule exercised by members of statistically representative social groups may deserve to be described as democratic, but it cannot be considered consistent with the notion of the rule of law.

[15] This, of course, is not the same thing as claiming that some measure of judicial discretion and the principle of the rule of law are mutually exclusive. Nor, for that matter, is a simultaneous commitment to constitutionally enshrined rights and the rule of law. But the relationship between these two features of liberal jurisprudence is more complex than Archibugi and Held seem to grasp.

Held nor Archibugi seems to grasp the ways in which their view potentially conflicts with conventional ideas about the Rechtsstaat, or the fact that their account of cosmopolitan democratic law threatens to generate precisely the sort of unharnessed state authority that so worried classical theorists of the liberal rule of law. In their model, that authority will now be exercised on a global scale, and thus ultimately backed up by the prospect of transnationally organized military force (Held 1995a, 279). In a Dworkinian mode, one might praise this demotion of classical rule of law virtues by conceding that the architects of cosmopolitan democracy may be right to downplay the significance of clear, general rules for liberal-democratic jurisprudence. At the level of global decision making, classical conceptions of legislation and judicial interpretation undoubtedly face even greater challenges, in light of the complexity of the regulatory tasks at hand, than they do at the level of the nation-state (Teubner 1997; Scheuerman 2001b).

Nonetheless, Dworkin at least has devoted substantial energy to describing the proper scope of decision making for his famous Herculean judge, whereas Archibugi and Held say little about how their hypothetical transnational judges would be effectively "circumscribed" by cosmopolitan democratic law. The fact that they also claim that cosmopolitan democratic law presupposes no particular conception of the good and thus "does not require political and cultural consensus about a wide range of beliefs, values, and norms" seems reasonable given the challenges of pluralism on the global scale (Held 1995b, 115–16).[16] Yet it arguably compounds the weaknesses of their legal analysis by potentially opening the door to a vast diversity of alternative judicial interpretations of the basic framework of cosmopolitan law. If cosmopolitan democratic law is fundamentally neutral in the face of competing interpretations of the good, what is to prevent judges from fleshing out its complex and multifaceted charter of rights in a rich variety of potentially inconsistent ways? On this point as well, Dworkin's position is arguably superior: whatever our final assessment of his restatement of natural law theory, Dworkin strives to provide a detailed gloss on how his conception of rights-based jurisprudence is to be properly embedded in a particular interpretation of liberal political morality (Dworkin 1986).

It is also easy to see why this reinterpretation of the rule of law may initially seem so attractive. Many nation-states have already committed themselves to a set of ambitious international human rights agreements (for example, in the Universal Declaration of Human Rights). From a liberal-democratic perspective, this historical trend is a positive one; my criticisms here are not directed against the notion of universal human

---

[16] This claim also seems questionable in light of the ambitious social-democratic, feminist, and environmental character of the rights they defend.

rights.[17] Nonetheless, a commitment to universal human rights is probably consistent with a rich variety of distinct institutional versions of
liberal democracy, both on the global level and elsewhere. It remains open
to debate whether the best way either to advance rule of law virtues or
pursue transnational democracy is to demand the justiciability of a bold
and indisputably controversial charter of rights by transnational courts.
We should neither conflate the protection of rights with the rule of law
nor ignore the ambivalent legal and political consequences of a model of
transnational government probably destined to place massive discretionary decision making in judicial hands. Danilo Zolo has accused Held and
his interlocutors of advancing a brand of judicial imperialism blind to the
matter in which cosmopolitan democracy's model of basic rights masks
Western biases and exhibits indifference toward non-Western legal
culture (Zolo 2000, 79–80). Although I see no reason for endorsing either
Zolo's Realist international relations theory or his dismissive attacks on
universalistic concepts of human rights, my argument suggests that he
nonetheless may have stumbled onto a real failing here: in cosmopolitan
democracy, judges would indeed be outfitted with impressive and arguably unprecedented authority concerning a rich variety of highly contest-
able political matters. The charter of rights making up the core of
cosmopolitan democratic law includes issues (for example, ecological
and feminist rights) still considered highly controversial even within the
wealthy welfare state liberal democracies of Western Europe and North
America. Since many of these rights are even more controversial on the
global level, one might ask whether it makes much sense to try to advance
transnational democracy by outfitting transnational judicial personnel
with the authority to rely on an open-ended commitment to them as a
starting point for an "agenda for change" (Held 1995a, 205).

Pace Zolo and his Machiavellian-Hobbesian brand of Realism, the
weaknesses of this model hardly represent necessary byproducts of a
universalistic brand of Kantianism. Instead, they derive from a questionable interpretation of the notion of the rule of law in which some of the
core concerns of traditional liberal jurisprudence have simply been left by
the wayside. Recall that Kant not only envisioned a cosmopolitan right of
hospitality but also took seriously the rule of law virtues of generality,
publicity, and clarity.[18]

---

[17] For a useful defense, see Donnelly, who provides some helpful remarks on the
complex legal status of universal human rights (1989, 13–16).

[18] More than twenty years ago, the human rights advocate Philip Alston perceptively
warned of the dangers of proclaiming ambitious and poorly defined new rights beyond the
basic civil, political, and social and economic rights based in the two International Human
Rights Covenants, pointing out that many of the proposed new rights were typically
characterized by enormous vagueness (for example, rights "to coexistence with nature," "not
to be killed in war," or "to be free to experiment with alternative ways of life"). As Alston
correctly observed, "a proliferation of new rights would be more likely to contribute to a

This criticism also points to real problems for Archibugi's and Held's attempt to distinguish cosmopolitan democracy sufficiently from unacceptable models of a "planetary Leviathan" outfitted with enormous discretionary authority. Their vague statements concerning the precise scope of cosmopolitan law are only like to fan such anxieties. As we noted earlier, Archibugi and Held tend to argue that issues "affecting" transnational groups would alone make up proper objects of transnational legislative and judicial activity. But this deceptively simple claim cloaks a host of complex normative and institutional questions. As Frederick Whelan has pointed out in an astute critical contribution to democratic theory, "[a]n obvious practical difficulty with the all-affected principle is that it would require a different constituency of voters or participants for every decision" in light of the fact that citizens are unlikely to be affected by every decision to the same degree or in the same way (Whelan 1983, 18–19). One of the more controversial aspects of many laws and policies is their likely impact on different categories of people; political controversy often is concerned with *determining* which category of people should be affected by a policy. "Thus to say that those who will be affected by a given decision are the ones who should participate in making it is to ... propose what is a logical as well as procedural impossibility" (19).[19] A prior decision would be required in each case to determine who is to be affected and thus entitled to participate on whatever substantive issue is at hand. But how might this decision be made? It would have to be made democratically by those affected, "but now we encounter a regression from which no procedural escape is possible" (19).

Moreover, it is unclear that we can delineate transnational issues from those properly resolved on the local or national level as easily as cosmopolitan democracy's defenders claim, especially if it is correct to argue that "[g]lobal governance knows no boundaries, geographic, social, cultural, economic, or political. If ... new trading partners are established, if labor and environmental groups in different countries form cross-border coalitions, if cities begin to conduct their own foreign commercial policies ... then the consequences of such developments will ripple across and fan out at provincial, regional, national and international levels as well as across and within local communities" (Rosenau 1998, 31). If we conceive of globalization as resting on a process of "time and space compression" in which instantaneousness and

---

serious devaluation of the human rights currency than to enrich significantly the overall coverage provided by existing rights" (1984, 614). If I am not mistaken, Alston's anxieties take on special significance for the defenders of cosmopolitan democracy, since many of the proposed rights at the core of "cosmopolitan democratic law" seem remarkably reminiscent of those criticized by Alston.

[19] Saward 2000 offers an enlightening discussion of this weakness of cosmopolitan democracy.

simultaneity increasingly make up constitutive features of human activity, it inevitably becomes difficult to specify a relatively limited arena for transnational policy (Harvey 1990). As the time span necessary to connect disparate geographical points declines, space is "compressed": in an age of e-mail, instantaneous computerized financial transactions, and high-speed forms of production and consumption, "there" seems less distant from "here" than it used to be. Given dramatic changes in the phenomenological horizons of present-day human activity, the scope of cosmopolitan democratic law thus is not only likely to be characterized by ambiguity and flux, it seems destined ultimately to cover a potentially enormous range of human activities.

In fairness, Held occasionally makes some brief suggestions about how he hopes to limit the scope of transnational legislation. A test of "extensiveness" would determine the range of people potentially affected by a collective problem; a test of "intensity" would assess the degree to which different groupings are affected by a collective problem; an "assessment of comparative efficiency" would focus on the practical pros and cons of grappling with a particular policy task at different levels of governance (Held 1995a, 236; 1995b, 113–14). But here again cosmopolitan democracy's proponents simply take their suggestions from the E.U. and its tension-ridden experience with the difficult task of determining the proper relationship between transnational and national legislation. But they badly obscure the fact that the E.U. experience with "subsidiarity" raises at least as many difficult questions as it answers.[20] Unless much more is said about how we can properly delineate cosmopolitan democratic law from local and national law, there are legitimate reasons for worrying that cosmopolitan democracy is likely to fail in its noble quest to uphold the traditional liberal notion of a limited law-based government.

3

Notwithstanding its numerous virtues, cosmopolitan democracy suffers from jurisprudential flaws that ultimately undermine its appeal. Does this mean that we should abandon Archibugi's and Held's admirable quest to subject an array of transnational policy arenas to liberal-democratic ideals? Of course not. But my argument does suggest that we will need to develop a concept of transnational democracy better equipped to take the legacy of traditional rule of law-virtues seriously. In light of the prospect

---

[20] Held tends to refer in this context to an article on subsidiarity within the E.U. by Karlheinz Neunreither in order to underscore the soundness of the tests of extensiveness, intensity, and comparative efficiency. But Neunreither's article in fact underlines the *inadequacies* of those tests within the E.U. as devices for generating an adequate conception of subsidiarity, pointing out that they raise difficult questions for those committed to the "uniform enforcement of EC law" (Neunreither 1993, 217).

of awesome forms of global political authority that make the modern nation-state's power capacities pale in comparison, we abandon the traditional notion of the rule of law at our own risk. Mainstream liberal concerns about the specter of untrammeled state authority arguably take on heightened significance as the prospect of global government becomes real. A transnational democracy worth defending will have to find some way of preserving a substantial quotient of traditional rule of law virtues.

How might we accomplish that task? A proper answer to that question points the way beyond the confines of this chapter. But for now, let me just say that a host of more modest—yet nonetheless potentially path-breaking—proposals for deepening liberal democracy on the global level are now being discussed and deserve closer examination.[21] Many of those proposals cohere more clearly with traditional conceptions of the rule of law than the model criticized here. Those of us enamored of Kelsen's thoughtful warnings about the limits of "unreal and politically less than nothing" reform proposals for the international arena can easily identify many *ongoing* political struggles as good starting points for preparing the way for major changes in the international system. The demand for an international criminal court should come immediately to mind, as should the possibility of altering the structure of the U.N. Security Council. Reforms of this type may seem dull when compared to the dream of a global liberal democracy committed to realizing an ambitious set of justiciable liberal, democratic, social-democratic, feminist, and ecological rights, but they better build on Kelsen's sound advice to pursue "a slow and steady perfection of the international legal order" (Kelsen 1944, ix).

Acknowledgments

This chapter was first published (in slightly different form) in *Ratio Juris* 15, no. 4 (2002): 439–57.

References

Alston, Philip. 1984. "Conjuring Up New Human Rights: A Proposal for Quality Control." *American Journal of International Law* 78:607–21.
Archibugi, Daniele. 1992. "Models of International Organization in Perpetual Peace Projects." *Review of International Studies* 18:295–318.
———. 1995. "From the United Nations to Cosmopolitan Democracy." In *Cosmopolitan Democracy: An Agenda for a New World Order*, edited by Daniele Archibugi and David Held, 121–62. Cambridge: Polity Press.

---

[21] Schmitter 1997, for example, proposes that nation-states accord each other seats in their legislatures to representatives of other nation-states with which they are intensely involved (for example, within free trade zones); see also Schmitter 1999; Saward 2000.

——. 1998. "Principles of Cosmopolitan Democracy." In *Re-imagining Political Community: Studies in Cosmopolitan Democracy*, edited by Daniele Archibugi, David Held, and Martin Koehler, 199–228. Stanford: Stanford University Press.

——. 2000. "Cosmopolitical Democracy." *New Left Review* 4:137–51.

Archibugi, Daniele, and David Held. 1995. *Cosmopolitan Democracy: An Agenda for a New World Order*. Cambridge: Polity Press.

Archibugi, Daniele, David Held, and Martin Koehler, eds. 1998. *Re-imagining Political Community: Studies in Cosmopolitan Democracy*. Stanford: Stanford University Press.

Archibugi, Daniele, Sieva Balduini, and Marco Donati. 2000. "The United Nations as an Agency of Global Democracy." In *Global Democracy: Key Debates*, edited by Barry Holden, 125–42. London: Routledge.

Bellamy, Richard, and Dario Castiglione. 1998. "Between Cosmopolis and Community: Three Models of Rights and Democracy Within the European Union." In *Re-imagining Political Community: Studies in Cosmopolitan Democracy*, edited by Daniele Archibugi, David Held, and Martin Koehler, 152–78. Stanford: Stanford University Press.

Bobbio, Norberto. 1987. *The Future of Democracy*. Minneapolis: University of Minnesota Press.

Cassese, Antonio. 1986. *International Law in a Divided World*. Oxford: Clarendon Press.

Coates, Tony. 2000. "Neither Cosmopolitanism nor Realism: A Response to Danilo Zolo." In *Global Democracy: Key Debates*, edited by Barry Holden, 87–102. London: Routledge.

Dahl, Robert. 2000. "Can International Organizations Be Democratic? A Skeptic's View." In *Democracy's Edges*, edited by Ian Shapiro and Casiano Hacker-Cordon, 19–36. Cambridge: Cambridge University Press.

Donnelly, Jack. 1989. *Universal Human Rights in Theory and Practice*. Ithaca, N.Y.: Cornell University Press.

Dryzek, John. 1999. "Transnational Democracy." *Journal of Political Philosophy* 7:30–51.

Dworkin, Ronald. 1977. *Taking Rights Seriously*. Cambridge, Mass.: Harvard University Press.

——. 1985. *A Matter of Principle*. Cambridge, Mass.: Harvard University Press.

——. 1986. *Law's Empire*. Cambridge, Mass.: Harvard University Press.

Falk, Richard. 1995. *On Humane Governance*. State College: Pennsylvania State University Press.

Görg, Christoph, and Joachim Hirsch. 1998. "Is International Democracy Possible?" *Review of International Political Economy* 5:585–616.

Habermas, Jürgen 1998. *Die postnationale Konstellation*. Frankfurt am Main: Suhrkamp.

Harvey, David. 1990. *The Condition of Postmodernity*. Oxford: Blackwell.

Held, David 1991. "Democracy, the Nation-State, and the Global System." In *Political Theory Today*, edited by David Held, 197–235. Stanford: Stanford University Press.

———. 1992. "Democracy: From City-States to a Cosmopolitan Democratic Order?" *Political Studies* 40:10–39.

———. 1995a. *Democracy and the Global Order: From the Modern State to Cosmopolitan Governance*. Stanford: Stanford University Press.

———. 1995b. "Democracy and the New International Order." In *Cosmopolitan Democracy: An Agenda for a New World Order*, edited by Daniele Archibugi and David Held, 96–120. Cambridge: Polity Press.

———. 1998. "Democracy and Globalization." In *Re-imagining Political Community: Studies in Cosmopolitan Democracy*, edited by Daniele Archibugi, David Held, and Martin Koehler, 11–27. Stanford: Stanford University Press.

———. 2000. "The Changing Contours of Political Community: Rethinking Democracy in the Context of Globalization." In *Democracy's Edges*, edited by Ian Shapiro and Casiano Hacker-Cordon, 84–111. Cambridge: Cambridge University Press.

Held, David, and Anthony McGrew. 1993. "Globalization and the Liberal Democratic State." *Government and Opposition* 28:261–85.

Held, David, Anthony McGrew, David Goldblatt, and Jonathan Perraton. 1999. *Global Transformations*. Stanford: Stanford University Press.

Hirst, Paul, and Grahame Thompson. 1996. *Globalization in Question*. Cambridge: Polity Press.

Holden, Barry, ed. 2000. *Global Democracy: Key Debates*. London: Routledge.

Kant, Immanuel. 1994. "Perpetual Peace." In *Kant's Political Writings*, edited by Hans Reiss, second edition, 93–130. Cambridge: Cambridge University Press. (Originally published in 1796.)

Kelsen, Hans. 1944. *Peace Through Law*. Chapel Hill: University of North Carolina Press.

———. 1955. "Foundations of Democracy." *Ethics* LXVI:1–103.

Kymlicka, Will. 2000. "Citizenship in an Era of Globalization: A Commentary on Held." In *Democracy's Edges*, edited by Ian Shapiro and Casiano Hacker-Cordon, 112–26. Cambridge: Cambridge University Press.

Lutz-Bachmann, Matthias, and Jim Bohman. 1997. *Perpetual Peace: Essays on Kant's Cosmopolitan Ideal*. Cambridge, Mass.: MIT Press.

Marshall, T. H. 1950. *Citizenship and Social Class, and Other Essays*. Cambridge: Cambridge University Press.

Maus, Ingeborg. 1992. *Zur Aufklärung der Demokratietheorie*. Frankfurt am Main: Suhrkamp.

———. 1998. "Volkssouveränität und das Prinzip der Nichtintervention in der Friedensphilosophie Immanuel Kants." In *Einmischung*

Erwuenscht? Menschenrechte und Bewaffnete Intervention, edited by Hauke Brunkhorst, 89–110. Frankfurt am Main: Fischer.

McGrew, Anthony. 1997. *The Transformation of Democracy? Globalization and Territorial Democracy?* Cambridge: Polity Press.

———. 1998. "Realism vs. Cosmopolitanism." *Review of International Studies* 24:387–98.

Narr, Wolf-Dieter, and Alexander Schubert. 1994. *Weltökonomie: Die Misere der Politik*. Frankfurt am Main: Suhrkamp.

Neumann, Franz. 1986. *The Rule of Law: Political Theory and the Legal System in Modern Society*. Leamington Spa: Berg. (Originally published in 1953.)

———. 1996. "The Concept of Political Freedom." In *The Rule of Law Under Siege*, edited by William E. Scheuerman, 195–230. Berkeley: University of California Press.

Neunreither, Karlheinz. 1993. "Subsidiarity as a Guiding Principle for European Community Activities." *Government and Opposition* 28:206–17.

Raz, Joseph 1979. *The Authority of Law*. Oxford: Clarendon Press.

Rosenau, James N. 1998. "Governance and Democracy in a Globalizing World." In *Re-imagining Political Community: Studies in Cosmopolitan Democracy*, edited by Daniele Archibugi, David Held, and Martin Koehler, 28–57. Stanford: Stanford University Press.

Saward, Michael. 2000. "A Critique of Held." In *Global Democracy: Key Debates*, edited by Barry Holden, 32–46. London: Routledge.

Scheuerman, William E. 1994. "The Rule of Law and the Welfare State: Towards a New Synthesis." *Politics and Society* 22:195–213.

———. 2001a. "Globalization and Democratic Theory." *Polity* 33:331–42.

———. 2001b. "Reflexive Law and the Challenges of Globalization." *Journal of Political Philosophy* 9:81–102.

Schmitter, Philippe C. 1997. "Exploring the Problematic Triumph of Liberal Democracy and Concluding with a Modest Prospect for Improving Its International Impact." In *Democracy's Victory and Crisis*, edited by Axel Hadenius, 297–310. Cambridge: Cambridge University Press.

———. 1999. "The Future of Democracy: A Matter of Scale?" *Social Research* 66:933–58.

Shapiro, Ian, and Casiano Hacker-Cordon, eds. 2000. *Democracy's Edges*. Cambridge: Cambridge University Press.

Teubner, Gunther, ed. 1997. *Global Law Without a State*. Aldershot: Dartmouth Gower.

Thompson, Dennis. 1999. "Democratic Theory and Global Society." *Journal of Political Philosophy* 7:111–25.

Thompson, Janna. 1998. "Community Identity and World Citizenship." In *Re-imagining Political Community: Studies in Cosmopolitan Democracy*, edited by Daniele Archibugi, David Held, and Martin Koehler, 179–97. Stanford: Stanford University Press.

Wendt, Alexander. 2000. "A Comment on Held's Cosmopolitanism." In *Democracy's Edges*, edited by Ian Shapiro and Casiano Hacker-Cordon, 127–33. Cambridge: Cambridge University Press.

Whelan, Frederick. 1983. "Prologue: Democratic Theory and the Boundary Problem." In *Liberal Democracy*, edited by J.Roland Pennock and John W. Chapman, 13–47. New York: New York University Press.

Zolo, Danilo. 1997. *Cosmopolis: Prospects for World Community*. Cambridge: Polity Press.

———. 2000. "The Lords of Peace: From the Holy Alliance to the New International Criminal Tribunals." In *Global Democracy: Key Debates*, edited by Barry Holden, 73–86. London: Routledge.

Zuern, Michael 1998. *Regieren jenseits des Nationalstaates*. Frankfurt am Main: Suhrkamp.

8

A-LEGALITY:
POSTNATIONALISM AND THE QUESTION OF
LEGAL BOUNDARIES

HANS LINDAHL

Introduction

If the fixed and exclusive territoriality of states has stamped its distinctive mark on the era of nationalism, postnationalism ushers in the de-territorialisation of law. In particular, the emergence of regional and global legal orders loosens the link between territoriality and legal order in at least two ways. First, the relation between, say, the European Union and its member states cannot be grasped in terms of mutually exclusive territories. The E.U.'s member states continue to claim a significant measure of exclusive control over their territory, while also relinquishing part of their sovereignty by participating in a European legal order. In such cases, de-territorialisation amounts to what has come to be called the emergence of "overlapping" legal orders. Global legal orders point to a second, arguably more radical, form of de-territorialisation: de-localisation. However disparate, global legal orders such as the World Trade Organisation, the law merchant, the International Standards Organisation, and multinationals give the nay to the assumption that an order of positive law must be spatially bounded—or so it seems.

Taken together, these two developments demand that legal and political theory reconsider the relation between legal orders and their boundaries—subjective, material, temporal, and spatial. At one level, of course, and assuming that nation-states will not disappear from the postnational scene, the problem is to fashion a concept of legal order that is sufficiently capacious to accommodate the nation-state, while also explaining why law has become more local, more global, and more transversal than the nation-state. While the literature that describes the de-territorialisation of postnational legal orders is massive, there is a dearth of studies dedicated to elaborating a concept of legal order that can integrate the variegated forms of law spawned by postnationalism, while also concretely explaining why and how these different kinds of orders are species of a single genus: legal order. This chapter offers a contribution to such a conceptual enquiry. This is its first task.

But, as will become clear, addressing this task requires dealing with a more fundamental conceptual problem raised by postnationalism—namely, whether "de-territorialisation" amounts to "de-localisation." One of the most influential and refined vindications of this position is, as we shall see, Gunther Teubner's theory of global law. Although, for Teubner, global forms of private self-regulation must certainly close their "meaning boundaries" if they are at all to be law, their validity claims are delocalised by dint of being *global* law. True, global forms of private self-regulation are irreducible to the territorial organisation of a nation-state; but can they avoid organising themselves in one way or another in space? If not, might there be a more fundamental sense in which even global law must be spatially bounded, that is, localised law?

Addressing this question requires looking more closely at the "closure" of legal orders. The question concerning how and why all legal orders, including global legal orders, might be spatially bounded is part and parcel of a more general enquiry, the main object of which is to explore what it means that legal orders are "closed," and how these orders relate to what is beyond their boundaries. It does not suffice, or so I shall argue, to understand the closure of legal orders in terms of the binary code legality/illegality. To the extent that human behaviour does not simply fall tidily on either side of the divide between legality and illegality, legal closure manifests itself primordially in challenges to the ways in which legal orders draw the boundary between legality and illegality: *a-legality*. Spatially speaking, a-legality manifests itself in forms of behaviour that intimate a place that has no place within the distribution of legal places a collective calls its own, yet ought to in some way. So described, a-legality points to a primordial form of spatial closure that is constitutive of all legal orders: the distinction between a familiar distribution of places—an inside—and a strange place—an outside. In this fundamental sense, all legal orders are localised, emplaced. By claiming that de-territorialisation amounts to de-localisation, theories of global law tend to conceal—hence to depoliticise—the spatial closure of such legal orders. The second task this chapter sets itself is, therefore, to contribute to repoliticising the spatiality of global legal orders by calling attention to their spatial boundaries as the object of contestation.

The reference to politics evinces the third and most fundamental set of issues that this chapter would like to discuss. If the unity of legal orders depends on their fourfold closure, to what extent can a legal order accommodate political plurality by redefining its boundaries? Are legal boundaries temporary and defeasible in such a way that a legal order can progressively include what it had excluded, thereby bringing about an ever more inclusive legal unity? This, as we shall see, is the view espoused by Jürgen Habermas in his cosmopolitan reading of the "postnational constellation." By contrast, I shall hold that legal orders deploy a strongly finite responsiveness to a-legal behaviour. While Habermas readily accepts that politico-legal orders cannot include without excluding, I shall go a step further. Although boundaries are more or less transformable because boundaries include what they exclude, the responsiveness of legal orders to political plurality is finite because legal orders cannot include without also excluding, to a lesser or greater extent, *what they include*. This insight parts ways with the normative lodestar of cosmopolitanism, namely, the idea of the realisability, even if indefinitely postponed, of an all-inclusive legal order. And it also parts ways with a communitarian conception of legal boundaries. Variable intertwinements, not expanding concentric circles, or so I argue, is the appropriate metaphor that captures the spirit of postnationalism as the "age of pluralism."

Political Reflexivity and the Boundaries of Legal Order

The national era, as Teubner notes, has been marked by "the historical unity of law and state" (1997a, xiii). With the emergence of global law, contemporary social and legal relations can no longer be adequately described and explained as taking place within—and to some extent between—sovereign states with mutually exclusive territories, populations, and governments. In effect, technical standardisation, multinational enterprises, professional rule production, the law merchant, human rights, and even sports law are forms of global law that "claim worldwide validity independently of the law of the nation-states and in relative distance to the rules of international law" (Teubner 1997a, xiii). In response to these developments, Teubner forcefully resists the reductive move to view global law as an underdeveloped form of state law. Global law, he asserts, is a distinct form of law, namely, a "self-reproducing, worldwide legal discourse which closes its meaning boundaries by the use of the legal/illegal binary code and reproduces itself by processing a symbol of global (not national) validity" (1997b, 14).

I find Teubner's critique of the move to reduce global law to an underdeveloped form of state law compelling. His claim that the emergence of global law poses a considerable challenge to state-centred theories of law is no less compelling, or so I think. But what revision of the concept of legal order could accommodate both national and global law, while also concretely explaining the differences between these orders? The answer to this question turns on the problem of legal closure. While Teubner grants that global legal orders, like all law, require a closure of "meaning boundaries," they distinguish themselves from state law because, by definition, they no longer rely on spatial closure. In contrast to national or even regional legal orders, which remain localised in space, global law heralds the most radical form of de-territorialisation: de-localisation. This does not mean, of course, that global legal orders waive space altogether; how could they? The law governs human behaviour, and human behaviour takes place in space.

Here, precisely, is where my own questioning sets in. I take my cue from a wonderful aside by Ernst Cassirer, who described the fundamental and most general function of order thus: "to limit the unlimited, to determine the relatively indeterminate."[1] If the law orders human behaviour by limiting it, must it not a fortiori limit legally relevant behaviour spatially? If so, might this suggest that even global legal orders are perforce spatially closed—and in this sense localised? Were this the case, what concept of legal order would be sufficiently general to accommodate the spatial closure of states, regional polities, and global law, while also explaining in a concrete manner how these different legal orders are modalities of legal order?

In dealing with this question I assume that reflexivity is typical for (but not necessarily exclusive to) national and postnational understandings of legal order: legislation is enacted in a process of collective *self*-legislation. For the purpose of this chapter, I define legislation very expansively as the enactment of legal norms of whatever sort, whether general or individualised. It encompasses all reflexive forms of lawmaking germane to municipal and international law, such as international treaties, statutory acts, judicial decision-making, and the like. It also includes all forms of minority self-rule within or across nation-states, and all and sundry forms of "private" self-regulation, global or otherwise. Accordingly, I propose to analyse collective self-legislation, thus defined, into its two constituent elements: (i) collective *self*-legislation and (ii) collective self-*legislation*. I do this with a view to explaining why and in what way reflexively structured legal orders might be bounded.

(i) Philip Pettit notes that "the word 'self' derives from the pronominal *se-* whereby we indicate that an attitude or action bears on the agent himself or herself." Drawing on this etymology, he reserves the notion of selfhood "for those agents who can in principle speak for themselves and think of themselves under the aspect of the first-person indexicals 'I' and 'me,' 'my' and 'mine'" (2001, 80). As he later indicates, selfhood is not limited to the first-person singular perspective; the reflexive structure of selfhood includes the first-person *plural* perspective of a "we" as a collective agent: "As there is a personal perspective available only with talk of 'I,' so there is a personal perspective that becomes available only with talk of 'we'" (2001, 80). Importantly, although the first-person plural perspective cannot be reduced to a summation of individual acts, collectives do not exist independently of individuals and their acts. In Michael Bratman's words, "Shared intentions are intentions of the group. But ... they consist in a public, interlocking web of the intentions of the individuals."[2] "Shared intentional activity," as Bratman dubs the basic

---

[1] Enst Cassirer, *Symbol, Technik, Sprache* (Hamburg: Felix Meiner, 1985), 100 (my translation).

[2] Michael Bratman, *Faces of Intention* (Cambridge: Cambridge University Press, 1999), 143.

format of collective action, turns on reciprocity: reciprocity of intentions, to the extent that my intention to act is co-determined by your intention to act, and vice versa, and that we know this of each other; and reciprocity in the enmeshing of our individual acts, in view of bringing about the shared activity. The purpose or interest defining what the group is doing, and what it is about, is determined through reciprocal action between the participants.

Now, in the case of legislation, reflexivity concerns first and foremost those individuals whose reciprocating action is necessary to enact the law—*legal officials*. Legislation is reflexive just to the extent that these officials see themselves as jointly engaging in the ongoing process of articulating, by way of lawmaking, the purpose or interest of the broader collective of which they are part. Notice that this interpretation of reflexivity cuts across the distinction between so-called public and private self-legislation, whether national, regional, or global. No less than in public lawmaking, all modalities of "private" self-regulation require a reference to a common or collective interest that requires articulation through legislation. Precisely for this reason, both "public" and "private" self-legislation are manifestations of *political* reflexivity. For it would be reductive to identify politics with any of its specific institutionalisations, say, a parliamentary system. From the point of view of legal orders, politics denotes the ongoing legislative process of articulating an interest *deemed* to be common, along with the contestation of these claims to legal commonality.[3]

I emphasise the word "deemed" because it condenses the multifaceted problem of representation in reflexively structured legal orders. Most fundamentally, representation concerns an irreducible feature of politics, at least in reflexively structured legal orders: there is no direct access to the collective's common or shared interest, nor, consequently, to the collective as a unity. The unity of a legal collective is always a represented unity, even in what political exponents of a metaphysics of presence call "direct democracy."[4] So, although legal officials claim that by enacting legislation they are articulating the common interest of a collective, such orders vary considerably in the extent to which and the ways whereby they institutionalise the *authoritative attribution* of lawmaking to the

---

[3] Although I focus hereinafter on collective self-legislation, hence on the interface between law and politics, I do not assume that lawmaking exhausts political power and action.

[4] I develop this thesis at length in my "Constituent Power and Reflexive Identity: Towards an Ontology of Collective Selfhood," in Neil Walker and Martin Loughlin (eds.), *The Paradox of Constitutionalism* (Oxford: Oxford University Press, 2007), 9–24. For the metaphysical roots of the simple opposition between presence and representation, as reappropriated in the simple opposition between constituent power and constituted power, see my "Collective Self-Legislation as an *actus impurus*: A Response to Heidegger's Critique of European Nihilism," *Continental Philosophy Review* 41 (2008): 323–43.

members of a collective. For example, whereas constitutional democracies have well-developed institutional frameworks that stipulate the conditions necessary for attributing legislation to collectives, the same is much less true in the case of, say, the broader constituency of international commercial arbitrators, when ruling in the framework of *lex mercatoria*. Moreover, a more fully developed institutional framework for representation in global self-regulatory schemes would arguably have to be quite different to that of constitutional democracies (Teubner 1997b, 4 and 21–22). What interests me here is that mooting the problem of representation makes it possible to define political reflexivity in a way that can accommodate all these different forms of lawmaking. And it allows for considerable disparity in the extent to which, and the ways in which, the key political question, "Who is an interested party to collective self-legislation?" is institutionalised.[5]

(ii) Having outlined in what sense legislation is an act of collective *self*-ordering, we can now examine how legislation is an act of collective self-*ordering*, that is, the different ways in which legal norms regulate human behaviour. Most generally, the law orders human behaviour by setting its boundaries, that is, by determining, explicitly or implicitly, individually or in general, *who* ought to do *what*, *when*, and *where*. These four boundaries are, of course, what the legal doctrine dubs the subjective, material, temporal, and spatial "spheres of validity" of legal norms.[6]

The material and subjective spheres of validity of legal norms are posited in the process whereby, articulating what they deem to be the collective interest, legal officials establish what rights and obligations accrue to whom. This account, however schematic, entails that the subjective and material spheres of validity of legal orders are bounded. The key here is the reference to a common interest. Indeed, a common interest is always *determinate*: legal officials select some interests as worthy of legal protection, and discard others, usually implicitly, as legally irrelevant. The fact that the material sphere of validity of legal norms and orders is bounded means that only a finite schedule of rights and obligations is made available by any given legal order.

The same goes for the subjective sphere of validity of a legal order. A bounded common interest requires determining which categories of individuals are privy to certain rights and subject to certain obligations, thereby discarding other possible combinations of subjects and rights/obligations. This also holds true for membership. To the extent that a

---

[5] See further Van Roermund 2006. My account of political reflexivity owes much to this perceptive article, and to multiple conversations on the topic with Van Roermund.

[6] See Hans Kelsen, *Introduction to the Problems of Legal Theory*, translated by Bonnie Litschewski Paulson and Stanley L. Paulson (Oxford: Clarendon Press, 2002), 12–13. Although I cannot discuss this issue here for reasons of space, a more complete development of legal spheres of validity would require a discussion of the empowerment of legal officials as a subset of boundary-setting.

common interest is necessarily bounded, the emergence of a reflexively structured legal order implies the possibility of identifying who counts as an interested member of the collective, although there may be great disparities in the extent to which such identification is institutionalised, and the extent to which those members are authorised to participate in the process of lawmaking. Additionally, and crucially, the possibility of identifying members entails, as its correlate, the possibility of stripping individuals of membership if they radically contest what is deemed to be the common interest of the collective. A world polity, if it was ever founded, would be no exception to the rule. In this minimal sense, membership in all forms of collective self-legislation is bounded.

If the subjective and material spheres of validity of legislation are reflexively structured and thereby bounded, so also is legal temporality. At one level, the law relies on calendar time, as when it determines the date at which a legal norm enters into force or when it is repealed. But legal time is never only calendar time; the time of the law is first and foremost a subject-relative form of temporality. As legal norms are posited from the first-person plural perspective, they situate human behaviour in the temporal arc spanning the past, present, and future of a collective. These modes of time are irreducible to calendar time. The unity of calendar time manifests itself as the continuum of a before and an after; by contrast, past, present, and future only appear as a unity to the extent that the members of a collective mutually engage in action with a view to realising their common interest: we now "y" to be able to "z" later on, given that "x" took place. Past, present, and future are sutured into the history of a "we" through mutual interaction in the framework of a common project. Because a determinate common interest manifests itself temporally in the form of a determinate common project, historical time is common in the twofold sense of a time that is shared by, and distinguishes, the members of a collective. Precisely for this reason, legal orders unfold a *bounded* temporality. In this fundamental sense of the term, the bounded time of a polity conditions its use of calendar time when setting dates, and in that sense temporal limits, to human action.

Finally, legal space is also reflexively structured and, consequently, bounded. The fact that legal space is reflexively structured means that it arises through a collective self-closure: by positing spatial boundaries, legal officials view themselves as giving spatial form to the common interest of the collective of which they are part. Importantly, the reflexivity of legal space is intimately linked to the claim that it is the common space of a collective. It is a distribution of "ought-places"—that is, places where behaviour ought or ought not to take place—that lends spatial form to the common interest of a community. On the one hand, to the extent that the members of a collective view themselves as the group in whose interest the boundaries of a legal space have been drawn, they claim a bounded space as their *own*. Notice that "own" functions here as a quasi-indexical relative to the first-person plural perspective, not as a legal title in the form of *dominium* or *imperium*. On the other hand, political reflexivity takes the form of an act whereby a collective is deemed to close itself into an *inside*. A claim to an own space and the closure of space into an inside are two sides of the same reflexive act.

A number of counterexamples come to mind that seem to cast doubt on the generality of this account of legal space. A first counterexample would be the "overlapping" legal orders so characteristic of postnationalism. Do they not expose bounded legal spatiality, in the way I have described it, as relying on the mutually exclusive territoriality of states? No. A legal space is never only a geographical surface, never only the material support of one or more legal systems, but rather a concrete articulation of normative and physical dimensions. As a result, the metaphor tends to conceal that even if two distinct legal orders cover precisely the same geographical extension, human behaviour that is relevant to one of these orders, in terms of the interests it defines as common, might be entirely immaterial to the other. Accordingly, someone or something could enter or exit the first of these legal orders *without entering or leaving the other order*. Political reflexivity entails that the spatial unity of a legal order is subject-relative, such that different collectives with different understandings of their common interests draw the normative distinction between inside and outside differently, while sharing all or part of a geographical extension. For example, it is a pseudo-conundrum to ask whether the E.U. is "outside" the member states, or whether the member states are "outside" the E.U. As the politico-legal distinction between inside and outside is always relative to a collective and a common interest, the real question is whether a specific form of human behaviour is to be regulated in the European legal order or in the legal orders of the member states. Accordingly, the mutually exclusive territoriality of states is but a *limiting case* of a broader spectrum of possibilities covered by reflexively structured legal orders.

A second obvious counterexample would be nomadic peoples; does not a bounded legal space presuppose the fixed territory of sedentary collectives? No. Polities are never simply located somewhere "in" space, like, say, a boulder lying in a field. A community must—literally—*find* a place for itself in a continuous process of relating *to* space, even in those comparatively recent cases, historically speaking, when its external borders are cartographically demarcated and stabilised. A relation to an own space, to a distribution of places in which behaviour ought or ought not to take place, is no less constitutive of nomadic communities than it is of "sedentary" communities. And collectives relate to space by emplacing themselves through self-closures that delimit a common space as an inside that stands in contrast to an outside, however indeterminate. As Edward Casey adroitly puts it, nomadic communities "move in place." And he adds: 'When I take a journey, I move *from place to place*.

... In nomadic life ... my movement between places, although frequent and diverse, remains *within* a given region, usually a region claimed or reclaimed at the outer fringes of civilization."[7]

Yet would not the distinction between inside and outside disappear in *global* law, as Teubner suggests? No. Consider the hypothetical case of a world polity, even though Teubner is no champion of this scenario. Whatever else might be required, its officials would need to posit a distribution of places determining where behaviour ought or ought not to take place. Although a world polity would have no outside in the sense of *foreign* places, or at least not initially, the inclusion and exclusion of interests articulated by its spatial boundaries entail that the polity's foundation gives rise, at least latently, to *strange* places—places that do not fit in the distribution of ought-places deemed to be a collective's *own* legal space. Strange places are, in the twofold sense of the term, out-landish. What a world polity could not avoid is to posit boundaries that close it off as an inside—as a *familiar* distribution of places—in contrast to an indeterminate outside. This outside manifests itself through forms of behaviour that, contesting the claim to commonality raised on behalf of a global distribution of places, intimate an ought-place that has no place within that global space, yet ought to in some way. Accordingly, the emergence of global legal orders reveals that the inside/outside distinc-tion, when construed as the distinction between domestic and foreign territories, is historically contingent; legal orders are certainly conceivable that do not require fixed territorial borders like those of a nation-state. But to the extent that a world polity, if it is to be a legal order, must in some way organise the face of the earth as a common distribution of ought-places, any of the boundaries that mark off a *single* ought-place from other ought-places in the world polity also appears, when contested, as marking off the *whole* distribution of ought-places as an inside vis-à-vis a strange outside.

This form of spatial boundedness also holds for global forms of "private" self-regulation, even when the distribution of ought-places to which they give rise remains rudimentary, and continues to depend, in some aspects, on the distributions of ought-places made available by states. For example, it has been argued—plausibly, I think—that multi-nationals constitute a novel form of global law. While multinationals rely in a variety of ways on the positive law of territorially bounded states, their spatial unity is patently irreducible to a simple aggregation of patches of state territories: "The existence of these organizations, each with its unity of command, logic and rules (making use of this multiplicity of supports in positive law while existing as one in their functioning), challenges our understanding of law as a phenomenon intrinsically based

---

[7] Edward S. Casey, *Getting Back into Place: Toward a Renewed Understanding of the Place-World* (Bloomington: Indiana University Press, 1993), 306, 275.

on [territorial] states."[8] If it is nonsensical to explain the spatial unity of a multinational in terms of state borders, so also it is nonsensical to argue that the multinational's spatial unity gives rise to the distinction between inside and outside in the form of the distinction between "foreign" and "domestic" territories.

But there is certainly a minimal sense in which multinationals are a single distribution of places, hence a bounded spatial unity. Take Shell: it comprises a building or set of buildings that is its world headquarters; a number of other buildings that are the national headquarters scattered throughout the countries in which it is active; yet other buildings which house its research and development programs; oil extraction rigs; refineries; service stations; and so forth. Notice that these boundaries are not "fixed": Shell is free to move its headquarters, sell off refineries, acquire concessions to explore and tap expanses of the sea bed, and so on, thereby reconfiguring its spatial confines as it sees fit. Yet even despite this important difference with states, Shell is a *single* distribution of places, organised as such in terms of the overall interest guiding the multinational's various activities. Moreover, and in light of that purpose, different sorts of persons are entitled to enter certain of these places, and different kinds of activity are authorised or forbidden in different sorts of places. In short, qua (more or less movable) spatial unity, Shell consists in a single distribution of *ought*-places.

It is this feature that explains why Shell is not only a bounded space but bounded in terms of the inside/outside distinction. In effect, the occupation of the Brent Spar oil-storage and tanker-loading buoy by Greenpeace activists, and the associated consumer boycott of Shell service stations, can be seen as acts that contest the distribution of legal places that define Shell as a spatial unity. In particular, the occupation and boycott call into question the commonality that Shell claims for its space. In effect, by occupying the buoy, the activists evoke a way of emplacing Shell's activities in a global distribution of places that is— literally—*outside* the interests furthered by the way in which Shell's activities distribute and use places. The buoy, when occupied, evokes a *strange* ought-place, an ought-place which has no place in the spatial unity Shell claims for itself, yet which ought to in some way—or so the activists claim. In this fundamental sense, the contrast between inside and outside is no less constitutive of a multinational than it is of a world polity.[9]

---

[8] Jean-Philippe Robé, "Multinational Enterprises: The Constitution of a Pluralistic Legal Order," in Gunther Teubner (ed.), *Global Law Without a State* (Aldershot: Dartmouth, 1997), 45.

[9] See the "Brent Spar" entry at http://en.wikipedia.org/wiki/Brent_Spar_oil_rig (accessed on 29 July 2009). Notice that the Brent Spar actions also contest the subjective boundaries that define who counts as an interested party to the collective (e.g., the recurrent question concerning shareholders and stakeholders), the material boundaries that determine

To repeat the basic insight articulated above, while the fixed territorial borders of nation states, and therewith the distinction between domestic and foreign places, is certainly contingent, the distinction between inside and outside is constitutive of legal orders when viewed as the distinction between, respectively, familiar and strange places. It is in this sense that all forms of global law are spatially bounded, no less than, say, nation-states, nomadic peoples and 'overlapping' legal orders. The closure of the 'meaning boundaries' of legal orders (Teubner) is also always a spatial closure. In the absence of the distinction between inside and outside, in this strong sense, no space can be a *legal* space.

Let me conclude this conceptual unpacking of collective self-legislation with four remarks. (1) Legal boundaries have lost none of their relevance for postnational legal orders, which must be bounded in the four ways noted hitherto if we are to meaningfully speak about them as *legal orders*. Although this idea calls for further research, the real difference between national and many postnational legal orders concerns the extent to which, and the ways in which, they institutionalise political reflexivity and legal boundaries. This means that the institutional rigidity of political reflexivity co-varies with the variable institutional rigidity of legal boundaries. Membership is particularly perspicuous in this respect: the boundaries of membership are rendered thematic in the process by which a collective institutionalises the question concerning who is an interested party to political reflexivity.[10] (2) In so far as reflexively structured legal orders are bounded in these four ways, every act of collective self-legislation posits all four boundaries *each time that it takes place*. What usually happens, however, is that because these acts tend to privilege one kind of boundary, as when determining the content or scope of a right, they *co*-posit the other boundaries in a way that is largely implicit and taken for granted. (3) The *practical* point of setting legal boundaries is to introduce what Charles Taylor calls a "qualitative distinction," and Bernhard Waldenfels a "preference in the difference": inside is preferred to outside; members to non-members; the history of a collective to other temporalities; and the rights and obligations made available by a legal order to other schedules of rights and obligations.[11] (4) Crucially, each of these four kinds of

---

what rights accrue to individuals (e.g., profits for shareholders in light of social costs generated by the firm's activities), and the temporal boundaries that define Shell as a collective project (e.g., the tension between the pursuit of profit over time and environmental concerns). In this sense, "private" self-regulation never has been nor can be insulated from politics. Evidently, a comparable analysis could be made of action taken against Shell's activities in the Niger Delta.

[10] For a nuanced taxonomy of political reflexivity in postnational legal orders, see Neil Walker, "Taking Constitutionalism Beyond the State" *Political Studies* 56 (2008):519–43.

[11] See Charles Taylor, *Philosophical Papers* (Cambridge: Cambridge University Press, 1985), 2:234. See also Bernhard Waldenfels, *Vielstimmigkeit der Rede: Studien zur Phäno-menologie des Fremden* (Frankfurt: Suhrkamp, 1999), 4:197, and Waldenfels 1994, 202–10.

boundaries delimits behaviour in terms of the distinction between the *legal and the illegal*, whereby legality is preferred to illegality. Thus behaviour is legal or illegal when someone is emplaced or misplaced; acts in timely or untimely fashion; exercises rights and fulfils obligations as established by the law—or not; or is the subject of rights and/or obligations when he or she ought or ought not to be. To posit the four boundaries of legal orders is to posit the master preferential distinction between legality and illegality—and vice versa.

Legal Unity and Political Plurality

These considerations cast new light on the problem of pluralism in law and politics. Teubner points out that the process by which the nation-state's legal boundaries forfeit at least some of their traction on human behaviour marks the passage from a monistic understanding of social life to the consolidation of legal pluralism. If the thought patterns that underpinned the nation-state sought to protect the integrity of its legal boundaries, often at the cost of diversity, the advent of postnationalism opens up the possibility of a pluralistic law less mindful of securing legal boundaries and more respectful of difference. Rather than either directly supporting or rejecting this assessment of contemporary developments, I want to probe a second fundamental issue it calls forth: How do legal boundaries relate to unity and plurality?

To begin with, the relation between legal boundaries and unity lies at the heart of political reflexivity. What holds for a collective self in general also holds for the collective self in reflexively structured legal orders in particular: "Its unity is a web of interrelationships between agents and nothing more" (Van Roermund 2006, 243). Now, as I have been at pains to argue, to regulate interpersonal relations is to posit the fourfold boundaries of legal order, indicating who ought to do what, where and when. So, the unity of a collective self manifests itself in the multitude of individual acts which fulfil these fourfold reciprocal expectations. Succinctly, the unity of a collective self manifests itself in an interlocking web of *legal* behaviour.

To render the relation between legal boundaries and unity more concrete, consider trespassing: someone enters a place where he or she ought not to be. In such cases, a distribution of ought-places lights up as a *whole*, because it becomes apparent that the misplaced person ought to be in any one of *those* ought-places, rather than in *this* one. Acts that trespass spatial boundaries render conspicuous the familiar unity of a totality of legal places as assigning a certain place to an individual (or debarring him or her from that place), which the individual does *not* (or does) occupy. Trespassing also renders conspicuous the collective as a *whole*—a self—because the illegal act is inconsistent with the web of mutual expectations concerning who ought to be where. This web of mutual expectations becomes more or less explicit, and is *reaffirmed* as a unity, in acts that qualify trespassing as illegal. In other words, by qualifying an act as trespass, a legal official claims that it cannot be attributed to the group, as authorised by it: "not in our name." The unity implied in the political use of the indexical "we" is both rendered thematic and confirmed when an act is qualified as illegal: "We cannot authorise this act as having taken place in our own interest." *Illegal boundary crossings reveal*, ex negativo, *the correlation between the unity of a legal space and the unity of a collective self.*

Although this example could be expanded to include analyses of the temporal, material and subjective boundaries of legal orders, it suffices to illustrate the general relation between legal boundaries and unity. But what about plurality? A first point to bear in mind is that what is most fundamentally at stake in plurality is not merely the coexistence of a manifold of legal orders but rather that these orders can—and often do— *interfere* with each other. As Neil Walker puts it, there is an "exponential increase in the density of trans-boundary relations and in the incidence of boundary disputes in the new post-Keynesian-Westphalian arenas of global law" (2008, 375). In turn, boundary disputes between legal orders are but one manifestation of the more general problem of political plurality: in its dealings with legal boundaries, human behaviour is the locus of conflicting normative claims. In other words, in general politics is the site of plurality because human behaviour does not only fall snugly on either side of the divide between legality and illegality; it also can call into question the ways in which legal orders draw the distinction between legality and illegality. This political manifestation of plurality, as noted at the outset, is *a-legality*. By the same token, a-legality is the primordial experience in which a legal order manifests itself as bounded. This means that behaviour can manifest itself as *a-civic*, to the extent that it challenges the distinction between membership and non-membership; as *a-nomic*, when it questions the schedule of rights made available by the legal order; as *a-topic*, if it contests the distinction between inside and outside; and as *a-chronic*, in so far as it interrupts the temporal unity of past, present, and future that a collective calls its own history. What, then, is the nature of political plurality, as it announces itself in a-legal behaviour?

Consider, again, the example of trespassing. Suppose that trespassing occurs when a group of homeless persons illegally occupy a privately owned apartment building, demanding that the government alleviate their plight. By illegally occupying the building, the homeless do more than trespass a spatial boundary; they also transgress it. In a word, they engage in *a*-legal behaviour, inveighing against the established distinction between legality and illegality as concerns who ought to be where. In particular, their transgression of a spatial boundary renders conspicuous a distribution of places as a region that makes no place for them— although it ought to, in some way. So, when illegally occupying the building, the homeless call into question where one *ought* to be, reminding the collective that the distinction between the public and the private is public. And they do this by entering a place *here*, in the distribution of places made available by the legal order, and linking this place to an *elsewhere*, in the sense of a place made available by another distribution of ought-places that, they claim, should be the collective's own space. Paradoxically, by *entering* the building the homeless are *leaving* it; they are going outside the distribution of places in which it is emplaced.

In short, a-legal crossings do two things. They reveal the spatial boundaries that join places within a single legal space as *separating* this distribution of places from an outside, in the form of a strange or outlandish place. And they show those boundaries as also *joining* the familiar inside to a strange outside, to the extent that the strange place can appear as a place that ought, in some way, to be included in the distribution of places "we" call our own. The experience of a boundary that separates and joins a familiar inside and a strange outside is, spatially speaking, the primordial experience of *political plurality*.

This spatial experience of political plurality has its correlate in terms of the collective self. As concerns legal space, the unity of a collective self manifests itself in shared expectations entertained by individuals concerning who ought to be where, and in the acts that fulfil these expectations. In the same way, the qualification of an act as trespassing renders conspicuous and reaffirms a collective as a whole: "not in our name." The situation is in a sense identical, yet entirely different, when spatial boundaries are transgressed. In our example, the homeless, when occupying the building, also claim: "not in our name." But here the claim is a counter-claim: the homeless deny that expectations about who should be where ought to be shared, that is, they contest the alleged commonality of the interest that denies them a place of their own. Hence they attempt to *interrupt* the attribution of legal boundaries to a collective self. Whereas illegality arrests attribution of an act to a collective because "we" did not authorise it in our own interest, a-legality moves to arrest attribution of the act by contesting not only what distribution of places joins us as a "we" but also that "we" are a unity. The transgression of spatial boundaries shows that acts of *self*-inclusion are also, to a lesser or greater extent, always acts of *self*-exclusion. As a consequence, what had been *familiar* behaviour, in the sense of behaviour that meets shared expectations about who ought to be where, gives way to *strangeness*, understood as the disruption of those expectations. A-legality throws joint expectations out of joint. What "we" *ought* to do, as members of a collective who circulate in a distribution of places, loses its straightforwardness, giving way, to a lesser or greater degree, to disorientation that is interpersonal as much as it is spatial. The ensuing experience of interpersonal strangeness is, with respect to collective selfhood, the primordial experience of *political plurality*. Hence *a-legal boundary cross-*

ings reveal the correlation between the fragmentation of a legal space and the fragmentation of a collective self.[12]

To be sure, this highly abridged—and partial—phenomenology of how legal boundaries relate to unity and plurality raises further questions about the distinction between (il)legality and a-legality. But before turning to these questions, some additional considerations are required about the compass and implications of the foregoing analysis.

Although the example described would be most easily recognised as coming about in a state legal order, it could just as readily illustrate a-legality in a world state, assuming that the world state were to embrace capitalism. For the act of the homeless does not contest the distinction between foreign and domestic places; it contests the way in which the collective distinguishes between public and private places, as well as the understanding of collective selfhood implied therewith. Analogous considerations hold for global forms of "private" self-regulation, as shown by the description of the Brent Spar actions. In so far as all reflexively structured legal orders, even those that have movable spatial boundaries, must organise the fourfold boundaries of human behaviour in *some* way, if they are at all to be legal orders, they are exposed not only to illegal behaviour but also to acts that contest those boundaries as such: a-legality.

These examples of a-legality bring into play, additionally, the tension between law as an *actual* or posited distribution of ought-places and *possible* law—an alternative way of ordering legal space. A-legality marks the experience in which possibility, in the form of alternative ways of drawing legal boundaries, announces itself to a collective. Precisely to the extent that it succeeds in intimating a place as a possible *ought*-place, a-legality depletes, as it were, the "ought"-character of a posited distribution of legal places, revealing this distribution as contingent. This depletion of the binding character of legal boundaries is, evidently, a condition for the transformation of a legal order, that is, for resetting the subjective, material, temporal, and spatial boundaries of (il)legality. At least two aspects of how a-legality reveals legal possibilities can be distinguished, in this respect. On the one hand, a-legality can reveal

---

[12] Readers versed in phenomenology will recognize a certain structural analogy between this analysis and Heidegger's description of the workplace, in which the interruption of work exemplifies the conditions governing the appearance of the world as world and its relatedness to *Dasein*. See Martin Heidegger, *Being and Time*, tr. John Macquarrie and Edward Robinson (Oxford: Blackwell, 1962), §§ 14–24. My analysis is also connected to Husserl's discussion of the distinction between "home world" (*Heimwelt*) and "alien world" (*Fremdwelt*) developed in his posthumous work, *Zur Phänomenologie der Intersubjektivität:Texte aus dem Nachlass* (The Hague: Nijhoff, 1973). In fact, one of my long-term projects is to graft analytical insights about collective intentionality and action onto phenomenological explorations of the concept of world in view of outlining a full-blown theory of politico-legal worlds (in the plural).

alternatives that are more or less determinate, more or less indicative of the transformation that ought to take place. On the other, a-legality can be more or less radical, depending on the extent to which the members of a collective can view the possibilities opened up by a-legality as *their own* (joint) possibilities. In terms of the joining and separating function of spatial boundaries, this means that the less an alternative ought-place manifests itself as an ought-place the members of a collective can view as their own, the more a contested boundary manifests itself as *separating* a familiar inside from a strange outside. Conversely, the more an alternative distribution of ought-places appears as one of the collective's own possibilities, the more a contested spatial boundary appears as *joining* a familiar inside to a strange outside.

To conclude this section, the foregoing considerations on the relation between a-legality and the realm of legal possibility are important on at least two counts. First, they dispel the misunderstanding that the contrast between a-legality and (il)legality renders the boundaries of a legal order impervious to change, that it hypostatizes legal boundaries. Inasmuch as a-legality evinces the domain of possibility, its introduction into a theory of legal boundaries amounts to a robust rejection of a positivistic understanding of legal order, whether national or postnational. Second, the notion of a-legality serves notice that the emergence of postnational legal orders, in particular of "global" law, does not efface the fundamental problem confronting *all* reflexively structured legal orders. In effect, if postnational legal orders are necessarily bounded, even if not necessarily in the same way as national or international law, then authorities in postnational legal orders also must deal with the problem of establishing, ever anew, *what counts as legal unity in response to challenges arising from political plurality*. In particular, by showing that all and sundry global legal orders are spatially bounded, an account of the a-topic features of human behaviour contributes to repoliticise the spatiality of global legal orders, calling attention to their spatial boundaries as the object of contestation.

Question and Response

We are now poised to enter the third and decisive stage of our enquiry. A first stage was concerned to show, against the de-localisation thesis, that no legal order is conceivable unless it is bounded spatially, in the same way that it cannot but be bounded subjectively, materially, and temporally. The de-territorialisation of law in postnationalism leads to new forms of emplacement, not to "dis-emplacement." A second stage sought to reorient the discussion about unity and plurality. It reveals that it would be reductive to view postnationalism as the era of "legal pluralism," in the sense that whereas state and international law exhausted the scope of positive law (or so it was assumed), we now witness a plethora of more or less autonomous cross-border legal orders that regulate specific kinds of human activity. While correct as far as it goes, legal pluralism so described presupposes a more fundamental issue about plurality, namely, the political plurality that manifests itself through a-legality, that is, through the contestation of the subjective, material, temporal, and spatial unity of legal orders.

When refocused in this way, the question about the fourfold boundaries of postnational legal orders joins up with the question concerning legal order and rationality. It is surely no coincidence that Jürgen Habermas links rationality to the problem of boundaries in general. As a desideratum, rationality is "the injunction to complete inclusion" (Habermas 2001, 148). On this reading, the internal *telos* of rational human activity is to achieve unity in the sense of *all-inclusiveness*. This injunction does not mean that legal boundaries disappear; as noted, law is inconceivable in the absence of the fourfold boundaries of human behaviour. It means that, in response to a-legal behaviour, legal boundaries ought to—hence *can*—be redrawn in such a way that the unity of the apposite order progressively includes what it hitherto excluded. In Habermas's view, legal boundaries are temporary and defeasible in such a way that political plurality can be progressively reduced to legal unity, even if an all-inclusive legal order must be indefinitely postponed in historical time. It is this assumption about the relation between political plurality and legal unity that I now want to critically scrutinize.

To this effect, we must shift our attention away from a static analysis, centred on the question "How do legal boundaries relate to unity and plurality?" and towards a dynamic mode of inquiry, focused on the following question: "How do acts of setting legal boundaries relate to unity and plurality?" This shift also allows us to further canvass the distinction between (il)legality and a-legality. This new exploration takes its point of departure in the thesis that although legislative acts can only qualify behaviour as (il)legal, that is, must posit the law as a unity, acts of setting boundaries always settle whether and how what calls for legal qualification is a-legal, that is, which kinds of political plurality a legal order can deal with.

To begin with, lawmaking is *responsive* to something that demands a normative, no less than a factual, qualification. Or, as Peter Fitzpatrick puts it, law is "responsable."[13] Something demands legal qualification, in the broad sense of a determination of who ought to do what, where and when. As such, legislation responds to a *question* about legal boundaries, hence to a question about the unity of a legal order. But the distinction between the trespass and transgression of spatial boundaries, discussed in the previous section, requires introducing a correlative distinction with

[13] Peter Fitzpatrick, *Modernism and the Grounds of Law* (Cambridge: Cambridge University Press, 2001), 76.

respect to questions about legal boundaries. First, lawmaking is responsive because, at every turn, human behaviour renders legal boundaries
questionable; if nothing else, it must be established whether behaviour is
legal or illegal—*derivative questionability*, as I would call it. But, secondly,
lawmaking is responsive in a strong sense of the term because a-legal
behaviour betrays the irreducible contingency of legal boundaries—
primordial questionability, as I would call it. Indeed, legal boundaries
are contingent in light of the fact that the unity of a collective is always a
represented unity.[14] Because there is no direct access to the unity of a
collective, legislative acts never only enforce the distinction between
legality and illegality, and hence never only enforce the unity of a legal
order. The legal qualification of human behaviour also always involves an
appraisal of what *counts* as (il)legality; it is also always an act that
constitutes the boundaries, hence the unity, of a legal order. More
precisely, boundary enforcement and constitution are always interconnected, in such a way that although one or the other is more prominent,
neither is ever given in pure form. On this reading of responsiveness, to
legislate is to have to deal, in one way or another, with the primordial
questionability of legal boundaries, as revealed through a-legal behaviour. In turn, to deal with this primordial questionability means, for a
manifold of individuals, having to determine time and again, with respect
to what demands legal qualification, *whether* they are (to become) a unity
and *what* defines them as a unity, that is, which interlocking webs of
expectations concerning the who, what, where, and when of human
behaviour are their own possibilities.

   Now, it is tempting to immediately map lawmaking as boundary
enforcement and as boundary constitution onto the distinction between,
respectively, (il)legality and a-legality, and this in such a way that
questions dictate responses. On the one hand, legislation can *enforce*
the boundaries of a legal order in response to *(il)legal* acts. Because a
group of individuals enter a place where they ought not to be, their act is
qualified as trespass, thereby announcing that a spatial boundary has
been breached because an individual should have been in any of those
places rather than in this one. *That* we are a unity and *what* shared
expectations about who ought to be where define us as a unity are
assumptions deemed to be more or less unproblematic in legislation that
enforces legal boundaries: "not in our name." In other words, boundary
enforcement takes for granted and confirms the distinction between
legality and illegality, as posited in existent legal boundaries. On the
other hand, lawmaking can *constitute* the boundaries of legal order in
response to *a-legal* acts. Because the homeless contest the commonality of
the distribution of places "we" call our own legal space, officials take

---

[14] See Bert van Roermund, *Law, Narrative and Reality: An Essay in Intercepting Politics*
(Dordrecht: Kluwer, 1997), 152–63.

measures to alleviate their plight, providing them, say, with government funded housing. These measures posit (anew) what are to be our mutual expectations about who ought to be where, that is, the mutual expectations that define us as a collective self. The transgression of the distinction between legality and illegality, elicited by a-legal challenges to legal boundaries, is responded to by acts that posit that distinction anew, thereby restoring the unity disrupted by the counter-claim: "not in our name."

Yet no simple sequence goes from illegal behaviour to boundary enforcement, on the one hand, or from a-legal behaviour to boundary constitution, on the other. Indeed, there is an irreducible hiatus between the questionability of legal boundaries and the responsiveness of law-making. This hiatus has two aspects. On the one hand, what demands legal qualification *precedes* the law, not merely temporally but most fundamentally because human behaviour never entirely fits legal expectations. By transgressing the spatial boundary that separates the private apartment building from public spaces, the homeless illustrate a general feature of human behaviour, namely, that it is always at least minimally a-legal because it in some way upsets the anticipations of legality/illegality encoded in legal norms. This "precedence" indicates that the meaning of human behaviour can never simply be a legal construct. To this extent, questions do precede responses. On the other hand, the responsiveness of legislation is never merely subordinate to what calls for legal qualification, never a fixed reaction to a pre-coded stimulus. Returning to our example, the legal meaning of the homeless persons' act is not settled prior to its qualification by authorities, and never entirely settled as either legal or illegal: legislation is responsive because it establishes retroactively *whether and how* behaviour is a-legal. Consequently, the sequence going from (il)legality to boundary enforcement and from a-legality to boundary constitution is paired to the inverted sequence: behaviour *becomes* (il)legal, albeit provisionally, when legislation enforces boundaries, for example when authorities evict the homeless, and a-legal when legislation constitutes boundaries, for example when authorities arrange social housing for the homeless, ensuring that they have a place of their own. To this extent, responses precede questions.[15]

There is a further implication of this strong sense of responsiveness that requires our further attention. In effect, to a lesser or greater extent *responses frame questions in ways that render them amenable to a response.* The interpretation of behaviour as a-legal is bound up with an authoritative assessment about which normative possibilities are the collective's *own* possibilities. This is because this appraisement determines the range

---

[15] My treatment of "precedence" and "retroactivity" draws on what Waldenfels calls, respectively, the *Vorgängigkeit* of questions and the *Nachträglichkeit* of responsiveness. See Waldenfels 1994.

of the collective's responses to what challenges its alleged unity. So legislative acts do not only establish whether an act is a-legal; most fundamentally, they also establish through their responses what kinds of a-legality a collective can deal with. To revisit the example about the homeless persons who illegally occupy a privately owned apartment building, an official response could not simply waive the fact that their occupation is illegal. It would have to signal, in one way or another, that the homeless have trespassed on private property, while seeking to ease their destitution. But even if the sanction that accrues to illegality is commuted or otherwise mitigated, and some form of durable housing is arranged for the homeless, does the legal response to the occupation address the challenge raised by the homeless in their *own terms* when, for example, they claim that the root of their plight is the collective's egregious commitment to private property? Would not social housing provided by the collective remain within the pale of—and even en-trench—what they inveigh: its capitalistic legal order?

Pettit's inquiry into collective selfhood and identity over time obliquely exposes what is at stake in the responsive framing of questions by collectives: "[A] group will be unable to present itself as an effective promoter of its purpose if it routinely seeks to establish consistency and coherence in the cases envisaged by renouncing one or other of its past commitments; if it never allows its present judgment to be dictated by past judgments, there will be no possibility of taking the pronouncements of such an inconstant entity seriously."[16] Pettit notes that if a group is to be a constant entity that can be taken seriously, it must stick, by and large, to its prior commitments, commitments that restrict the range of responsive options available to the group when affronting new challenges. Absent this relative constancy over time, there could be no collective *self-*legislation or collective identity over time as "intertemporal responsa-bility," as one might put it. Thus far Pettit. Yet, this insight, which already bespeaks the responsive framing of questions, can be honed still further: *the commitment to a common purpose that determines whether a collective can be "taken seriously" also determines which contestations of that commitment can be "taken seriously" by the collective.* Every reflexively structured legal order hides a blind spot that bursts the reciprocity of the hoary principle of (constitutional) dialogue: *audi alteram partem.*

This blind spot concerns not only the content of reflexively structured legal orders but also political reflexivity itself as a principle of legal

---

[16] Pettit 2001, 112. This idea stands very close to Ricœur's description of selfhood as a form of identity characterized by commitment over time, the paradigm of which is a promise: "Keeping one's promise . . . appear[s] to stand as a challenge to time, a denial of change: even if my desire were to change, even if I were to change my opinion or my inclination, 'I will hold firm.'" Paul Ricœur, *Oneself as Another*, tr. Kathleen Blamely (Chicago: Chicago University Press, 1992), 124.

ordering. A case in point is radical forms of environmental politics that forswear anthropocentrism. Invoking Rawls, Pettit argues that such cases call for pragmatism, and urges "those who are committed to various political causes" to "articulate the concerns they want the state to take up in terms which others can understand and internalize. Unless the devotees of a cause are prepared to do this, they cannot *reasonably* expect their fellow citizens to *listen*, let alone to go along."[17] Yet, surely Pettit's exhortation falls prey to a *petitio principii:* only those arguments that postulate the rationality of anthropocentrism count as "reasonable" and worthy of being "listened" to, which is precisely what radical environmental politics contests. Does the confrontation between the votaries of radical environmental politics and their fellow citizens presuppose "symmetry conditions" such that, provided they are sincere, the former cannot but acknowledge that their position must bow to "the force of the better argument"?[18]

Analogous considerations apply to the relation between religion and politics. The separation between state and religion is usually premised on the view that religion, which is said to belong to the private sphere, is—or should be kept—distinct from the public domain of the state and its legal institutions. This tenet takes for granted that religion is a *cultural* manifestation—a human achievement—and religious plurality an instance of "multiculturalism." This elementary—in the sense of foundational—assumption neutralises the radical challenge posed by individuals and groups who spurn viewing their religion as a cultural achievement because, for them, it is the word of God, or, to be more precise, the *law* of God. As my colleague, David Janssens, once put it to me, "By including religion as culture, the modern principle of collective self-legislation excludes religion as law."[19]

In such situations, legal orders reveal and presuppose differences that are not merely "preferential." The primordial questionability of a legal order can only be responded to by levelling these situations down to an entirely derivative form of questionability—or so authorities claim. At this point, a-legality manifests itself, to borrow Emilios Christodoulidis's trenchant expression, as the "objection that cannot be heard."[20]

---

[17] Philip Pettit, *Republicanism: A Theory of Freedom and Government* (Oxford: Oxford University Press, 1997), 136 (emphasis added).

[18] Habermas 1981, 25. Although they appeal to quite different conceptual frameworks, both Pettit and Habermas endorse a discursive approach to (practical) rationality.

[19] For an acute study on political theology, see David Janssens, *Between Athens and Jerusalem: Philosophy, Prophecy, and Politics in Leo Strauss's Early Thought* (Albany: State University of New York Press, 2008).

[20] Emilios Christodoulidis, "The Objection That Cannot Be Heard: Communication and Legitimacy in the Courtroom," in Antony Duff et al. (eds.), *The Trial on Trial* (Oxford: Hart, 2004), 179–202.

In short, legislative acts display a *finite* responsiveness to what challenges legal boundaries, which means that they frame human behaviour in such a way that it provokes the collective self with a *finite* questionability. This insight by no means precludes a variable measure of legal inclusiveness in response to political plurality. Nor does it gainsay that—in hindsight, and for the time being—a legal response can be more or less *fitting*. The cautionary point is, rather, that one does not grasp the specific way in which legal responsiveness is finite by asserting that legal orders cannot include without also excluding. This, in effect, is the position taken by Habermas when noting that "[a]ny political community that wants to understand itself as a democracy must at least distinguish between members and non-members" (2001, 107). I would add that any democratically organised political community would also, and necessarily, have to posit material, temporal, and spatial boundaries. But Habermas's concession to closure is less dramatic than what meets the eye. For it is consistent with the idea that even though legal orders must be bounded, they can become ever more inclusive by progressively integrating what they had previously excluded. Indeed, Habermas spells out the normative lodestar of cosmopolitanism as follows: "[S]olidarity with the other as one of us refers to the flexible 'we' of a community that resists all substantial determinations and *extends its permeable boundaries ever further*" (2005, xxxv–xxxvi; emphasis added). The metaphor that comes to mind, when attempting to capture the meaning of this cosmopolitan interpretation of rationality in law and politics, is a process of ever-expanding concentric circles. Yet this is a weak sense of finitude. It is certainly a form of finitude, to the extent that it recognises that political communities—even democratic political communities—entail a closure. But it is a weak form of finitude, because it implies the possibility, at least in principle, of realising an *all-inclusive* legal order. This means that although the full integration of political plurality in the unity of an all-inclusive legal order may have to be indefinitely postponed in historical time, any given episode of political plurality—of a-legal behaviour—is *provisional* because it can be brought into the fold of a more encompassing legal unity: "the other as one of us."

The sense of finitude I want to defend is stronger than this because it implies that, to a lesser or greater extent, *legal responsiveness excludes what it comes to include*. A-legality reveals possibilities that are, to a lesser or greater extent, possibilities as a legal collective's own possibilities; but this is also to say that a-legality confronts a collective with possibilities that escape it to a greater or lesser extent—possibilities that are not its own. The metaphor suggested by this strong interpretation of finitude is not the process of ever-expanding concentric circles, in which the other is increasingly recognised as "one of us." It is rather the metaphor of *variable intertwinements*: the experience of familiarity *and* irreducible strangeness; of recognition *and* non-recognition; of possibilities that appear as our own joint possibilities *and* others that are not. Crucially, when I say that legal orders intertwine, I mean that there is no common core all of these orders share or could share, no common normative standard for universal reciprocity in an all-inclusive legal order. Yet the metaphor also evinces why a theory of legal boundaries can defend radical political plurality without simply having to endorse massive incommensurability. *Intertwinement speaks to interference and interconnection without an environing normative framework.* It is in this strong sense, I claim, that the responsiveness of legal orders to a-legality is finite—that is, that political plurality is irreducible to legal unity.

Human Rights and the Dialectic of Cosmopolitanism

A fundamental objection suggests itself to this strong interpretation of the thesis that political plurality cannot be fully accommodated within the unity of a legal order. Even if it is recognised that any and every legal order is exposed to more or less radical forms of political contestation, does the recognition of political plurality not demand postulating a higher-level unity in the form of *human rights* as the shared and all-encompassing measure of legality that allows for arbitrating between conflicting normative claims? How can the normative conflicts arising from a-legal behaviour be meaningfully settled unless those conflicts are governed by the mutual recognition that, prior to all conflict, human rights are the legal manifestation of our common humanity? In short, do the boundaries of political pluralism not point to an all-inclusive order of human rights that must be presupposed by all parties in conflict if meaningful reference is to be made to (il)*legality* and to a-*legality*?

Habermas can be read as defending this idea in three essays, the first of which was published on the occasion of the bicentennial of Kant's famous essay "On Perpetual Peace." In this essay, Habermas offers the blueprint of a world polity in the form of "cosmopolitan law" (*Weltbürgerrecht*). After making the case that Kant's "federation of peoples" (*Völkerbund*) cannot safeguard the legal status and enforceability of the states' commitment to realising world peace, Habermas champions the foundation of a polity along the lines of what Kant called a "state of peoples" (*Völkerstaat*). This state sets aside the sovereignty of its member states in view of creating a world community of equal and free citizens: "The point of cosmopolitan law is, rather, that it bypasses the collective subjects of international law and directly establishes the legal status of the individual subjects by granting them unmediated membership in the association of free and equal world citizens" (Habermas 2005, 181). But the snag is that human rights, in the framework of Kant's federation of people, are unenforceable moral rights. Thus, to attain world peace through cosmopolitan law, Habermas rejects the distinction between human rights as moral rights and human rights as fundamental legal rights, audaciously proclaiming that "[h]uman rights are juridical *by their very nature*. What lends them the appearance of moral rights is ... their mode of validity, which points beyond the legal orders of nation-states" (2005, 190). The foundation of a world polity would secure their status as enforceable, subjective rights, and would assure all individuals membership in a world polity as free and equal citizens.

In two later essays, Habermas backs off somewhat from his initial plea for what seems to be a world federal state, defending instead a more nuanced version of multi-level governance. In substance, he argues in favour of a "world organization that can enforce peace and the implementation of human rights," leaving some issues—primarily economic and environmental—in the hands of regional polities such as the E.U. and other issues—cultural and the like—to individual nation-states.[21] The reason for sharply distinguishing between a world polity limited to securing peace and human rights, on the one hand, and regional and national polities, on the other, is that the former must be "distinguished from state-organized communities by the principle of complete inclusion—it may exclude nobody, because it cannot permit any social boundaries between inside and outside." And he adds: "This ethical-political self-understanding of citizens of a particular democratic life is missing in the inclusive community of world citizens" (2001, 107). The picture that arises is, therefore, of a world polity set up in three "layers" of reflexively structured legal orders: national, regional, and global. Whereas the material sphere of validity of the latter would be limited to enforcing human rights and securing world peace, its spatial, temporal, and subjective spheres of validity would be unlimited, as human rights are valid everywhere, "everywhen," and for everyone. In Habermas's words, "The normative model for a community that exists without any possible exclusions is the universe of moral persons—Kant's 'kingdom of ends.' It is thus no coincidence that 'human rights,' i.e. legal norms with an exclusively moral content, make up the entire normative framework for a cosmopolitan community" (Habermas 2001, 108). In Habermas's view, a world polity in the form of a legal order with a strictly moral content *would realise legal inclusion without exclusion*. Or, more precisely, if there is exclusion, it occurs only because those who breach human rights betray their own humanity, thereby excluding *themselves* from the all-inclusive legal community of world citizens.

Moreover, in so far as the implementation and enforcement of human rights trumps all other legislation, the validity of the legal boundaries of national and regional polities is subordinated to a universally valid and reflexively structured global legal order. By these lights, the legal boundaries of national and regional polities are the manifestation of

---

[21] Jürgen Habermas, *The Divided West*, tr. Ciaran Cronin (Cambridge: Polity Press, 2006), 136.

parochialism, which must give way, when legal rights with a strictly moral content are at stake, to the "injunction of complete inclusiveness." And to the extent that properly *human* rights articulate the concept of law as the set of rights whereby individuals coordinate their external freedom in relations of reciprocity, the all-inclusiveness of a human rights order comes first—teleologically speaking, albeit not chronologically.

To assess this thesis, we do well to reflect upon the most general conditions under which a multi-level world polity, as Habermas envisages it, could organise itself as a *legal* order. Patently, the three-step passage from nation-state to regional polity to world polity intends to mark the transition from substantive to formal legal unity. "If the international community limits itself to securing peace and protecting human rights, the requisite solidarity among world citizens need not reach the level of the implicit consensus on thick 'ethical' valuations and practices that is necessary for supporting a common political culture and form of life among fellow-nationals" (2005, 143; translation altered). Habermas is persuaded that "a coincidence in the moral wherewithal concerning massive human rights abuses and evident breaches of the prohibition of military attacks" would suffice (2005, 143).

When pondering Habermas's proposal, the first question that crops up is whether it takes us beyond the current status quo concerning Security Council resolutions. But this objection is too easy, and does not go to the heart of the matter. A more pointed question is, for example, whether agreement about what counts as *massive* human rights abuses does not already require quite a "thick" set of shared values. For example, can the E.U. and its member states be sure that African countries would not insist on viewing the E.U.'s Common Agricultural Policy, given its devastating effects on agriculture in these countries, as continued, flagrant, and massive human rights abuse? Can the industrialised Western nations and emergent nations, such as Brazil, China, and India, be sure that the environmental consequences of their economic activity would not count, in the eyes of those poor countries that are most threatened by such consequences, as massive human rights abuses that call for immediate and harsh intervention by the world polity? Even if this hurdle could be overcome, it remains the case that constitutions, when they posit human rights as fundamental legal rights, also establish the possibility of *limiting* the scope of those rights, to balance individual freedom and the common interest. Could it be otherwise with a world polity, even when dedicated to matters of peace and global security? Would not the possibility of legislating limitations to the scope of human rights in a world polity already presuppose a more or less determinate global common interest?

While it would be possible to continue elaborating on these examples, they suffice to call attention to the key problem confronting Habermas's move to secure world peace through the enactment and enforcement of human rights as legal rights. On the one hand, because their referent is the humanity of individual human beings, human rights betoken an order that is valid at all times, in all places, and for all individuals, an all-inclusive legal order. On the other hand, the moment human rights are posited as fundamental legal rights, they are inevitably linked to a *bounded* common interest. To posit and articulate human rights in a legal order is to *determine* the concept of humanity for legal purposes, to *limit* that which is germane from a politico-legal perspective as constituting *our* "common humanity." And this entails a preferential differentiation concerning relevant and irrelevant interests, with a view to fixing what defines *us*, the members of a global polity, as human beings. This preferential differentiation calls forth the possibility of irreducible conflict about what constitutes the humanity of human beings. This became pertinent to Amnesty International, for example, when outraged social sectors excoriated it for betraying the human right to life when it finally jumped off the fence and took a stand on the issue of abortion.[22] So, to return to Habermas's formulation, the problem with postulating an all-inclusive legal order of human rights, whether actual or realisable, is that there are no "*legal* norms with an exclusively moral content" (emphasis added). There can be no passage from human rights qua moral rights, to human rights qua legal rights, unless a manifold of individuals are deemed to take up the first-person plural perspective of a "we."[23] And this means taking up the perspective whence a collective determines—limits—who ought to do what, where and when. Accordingly, the institutionalisation of human rights as legal rights would not evade the conditions that spawn political plurality—*radical* political plurality. Put bluntly, legal determinations of humanity will not bring a-legality under normative control. Humanity is not a genus in the Aristotelian sense of the word, nor are legal orders, including regimes of human rights, its species: genus plus specific difference. To invoke humanity in the law is to evoke "family resemblances."[24]

I should note that the foregoing analysis is most emphatically *not* an argument against positing human rights as fundamental legal rights, any less than against human rights as such. Nor am I suggesting that human rights do not have an important role to play in helping to settle normative

---

[22] See, for example, the LifeSiteNews site: http://www.lifesitenews.com/ldn/2007/aug/07082001.html (accessed on 29 July 2009).

[23] Van Roermund makes a related point when noting that human rights are constitutively "selfish." See his "Migrants, Humans and Human Rights: The Right to Move as the Right to Stay," in Hans Lindahl (ed.), *A Right to Inclusion and Exclusion? Normative Fault Lines of the EU's Area of Freedom, Security and Justice* (Oxford: Hart, 2009), 161–82.

[24] For a critical analysis of the irresolvable dilemmas that confront Seyla Benhabib's attempt to mediate between positive law and human rights in her cosmopolitan approach to immigration, and an alternative reading of Hannah Arendt's famous reference to a "right to have rights," see my "In Between: Immigration, Distributive Justice, and Political Dialogue," *Contemporary Political Theory* 4 (2009): 415–34.

conflicts. And it certainly is not my intention to scoff at the model of global governance propounded by a thinker who has had the courage to make concrete institutional suggestions—something philosophers only do at their own peril—in an effort to find a way out of our contemporary predicament. My sole concern is to establish whether human rights, when posited as fundamental legal rights, will do the job Habermas expects them to fulfil, namely, to include without excluding. The answer is no.

Not only does the proposal to mediate political plurality by means of a global, legally valid schedule of human rights fail, it also points to the danger that lurks in cosmopolitanism, its lofty and beneficent intentions notwithstanding. Indeed, as Jeremy Waldron points out, cosmopolitanism is characterised by its insistence that "nothing human [is] alien,"[25] where "alien" or strange amounts to the strong sense of a-legality discussed heretofore. Because this strong form of a-legality will not disappear—not even with a worldwide catalogue of legally binding human rights—Waldron's formula is vulnerable to a political inversion he certainly does not want to endorse: *what is alien is inhuman*. Once this inversion has been embraced by authorities, why should they restrain themselves when responding to strong forms of a-legality? Why not simply obliterate those who so ostensibly have placed *themselves* beyond the pale of "our common humanity"? As is well known, Theodor Adorno and Max Horkheimer were concerned to reveal the "dialectic of Enlightenment," in which the self-affirmation of humanity by means of modern instrumental rationality led to its opposite: human self-destruction and the destruction of nature. Habermas's philosophical defence of Enlightenment can be seen as an attempt to overcome this dialectic by subordinating instrumental reason to a discursively enriched notion of practical reason.[26] Ironically, the inversion of Waldron's formula reveals that the dialectic of Enlightenment that Habermas had hoped to overcome is ensconced in the latter's philosophical project—this in the form of a "dialectic of cosmopolitanism."

Bidding Farewell to Communitarianism and Cosmopolitanism

This chapter took its point of departure in a critical examination of the prevailing assumption that legal boundaries—spatial boundaries in particular—are becoming increasingly irrelevant in the era of postnationalism. While the boundaries of the nation-state are certainly forfeiting some of their hold on human behaviour, political reflexivity shows that postnational legal orders are simply not legal orders unless they can *in some way* draw the spatial, temporal, material, and subjective boundaries

---

[25] Jeremy Waldron, "What Is Cosmopolitan?" *Journal of Political Philosophy* 8 (2000): 227–43, here 243.

[26] Theodor W. Adorno and Max Horkheimer, *Dialectic of Enlightenment*, tr. John Cumming (London: Verso, 1997). See also Habermas 1981, 366–402.

that make it possible to qualify human behaviour as legal or illegal. In other words, reflexively constituted legal orders, whether national or postnational, must be presented as legal unities. Hence the empirical fact that postnationalism attests to a proliferation of legal orders that bursts the neat divide between municipal and international law does not, in itself, transform the basic problem concerning legal boundaries. Indeed, because boundaries are the necessary condition of legal order, and therewith of legal unity, they also spawn the possibility of political plurality, manifested in behaviour that resists accommodation on either side of the distinction between legality and illegality, as drawn by an order of positive law.

The fundamental question about legal boundaries is, therefore, not whether they are waning but whether political plurality can be progressively integrated, at least in principle, in a higher-order legal unity. If so, then any given legal boundary is provisional and open to reformulation in a way that can assure the inclusion of what contests it—the "reducibility thesis," as one might call it. As we have seen, Habermas eloquently espouses this thesis when describing what he takes to be the normative lodestar of the postnational constellation: "Solidarity with the other as one of us refers to the flexible 'we' of a community that resists all substantial determinations and extends its permeable boundaries ever further." Here, he stands shoulder to shoulder with all theories of recognition that lead back to Hegel. Recalling Hegel's polemic with Kant concerning the "thing-in-itself," Gadamer notes that "what makes a limit a limit always also includes knowledge of what is on both sides of it. It is the dialectic of the limit to exist only by being superseded."[27] Although Gadamer draws on Hegel's thesis as a thesis about the limits of thinking, this passage ably captures the fundamental assumption about the meaning and functions of legal boundaries that animates Habermas's "theory of communicative action" and, say, Taylor's "politics of recognition."[28] In these and related political theories, the "dialectic of the limit" appears as the vehicle that allows us to become, albeit in a future that must be indefinitely postponed, what we already are *in posse*, if not *in esse*: one humanity under one law.

---

[27] Hans-Georg Gadamer, *Truth and Method*, tr. Joel Weinsheimer and D. G. Marshall (London: Sheed and Ward, 1993), 343.

[28] "[W]hat is preventing us from understanding the other initially is precisely the implicit and hence unwitting hold on us of our own too narrow horizon, the undisputed terms in which we understand our lives. The attempt to understand leads, if successful, to a 'fusion of horizons,' a broader set of basic terms in which the other's way of being can figure undistortively as one possibility among many. . . . Put baldly, teleologically, we are meant to understand each other. This mutual understanding is growth, completion." Taylor 2001, 91. Notice the analogy with Habermas's strong thesis about communication: "Reaching understanding is the inherent telos of human speech." Habermas 1981, 287.

The strength of the reducibility thesis resides in its eschewing the communitarian move to set up a simple disjunction between the two functions of boundaries: inclusion and exclusion. In effect, communitarian defences of political pluralism usually rest on the assumption that boundaries include those who belong to the collective and exclude its others.[29] The reducibility thesis will have no truck with this assumption, arguing that legal boundaries *include by excluding*. For only to the extent that legal orders in some way include what they have excluded can legal orders at all *respond* to a-legality, that is, to the primordial questionability of legal order. Legal boundaries would not be "porous" or "permeable," hence amenable to transformation, unless what a legal order has excluded is, in some normative sense, included therein. The subordination of exclusion to inclusion defines the concept of postnationalism advocated by the aforementioned authors, and many others in their wake, and allows them to view postnationalism as the harbinger of cosmopolitanism. In what is effectively an extended paraphrase of Waldron's dictum, Taylor describes cosmopolitanism as "the idea of humanity as something to be realized not in each individual human being but rather in communion between all humans . . . the fullness of humanity comes not from the adding of differences but from the exchange and communion between them. Human beings achieve fullness not separately but together" (2001, 90). Notice how the final sentence inverts the communitarian position: whereas the latter defends plurality because legal boundaries separate, cosmopolitanism advocates human unity because legal boundaries join.

Although cosmopolitanism's claim that legal boundaries include by excluding is correct as far as it goes, it takes the sting out of a-legality, making of it an occasion for and the celebration of an ever-greater legal inclusiveness. By contrast, a strong form of political plurality, one that does not simply fall back on communitarianism, emerges when we acknowledge that *legal boundaries not only include by excluding but also always exclude by including*. This, you will remember, is the upshot of the finite responsiveness and finite questionability of legal orders. A-legality retains its sting when it is acknowledged that although the boundaries of legal orders can be redefined to a certain extent, political pluralism is irreducible to an all-encompassing legal unity, in the strong sense noted above. In so far as lawmaking excludes by including, legal boundaries are not only provisional; they are *definitive* in the form of those aspects of a-legal behaviour that resist inclusion in a given legal order and its variable but finite possibilities.[30] Returning to the metaphors introduced at the

---

[29] This assumption also underpins Schmitt's thesis that "[t]he political world is a pluriverse, not a universe." See Carl Schmitt, *The Concept of the Political*, tr. George Schwabb (New Brunswick, N.J.: Rutgers University Press, 1976), 53.

[30] I am close here to Rudi Visker, who, in a relentless debate with Levinas, argues that unresponsiveness is a condition for responsiveness. See Visker, *The Inhuman Condition: Looking for Difference After Levinas and Heidegger* (Dordrecht: Kluwer, 2004).

end of the foregoing section, that legal boundaries include by excluding and also always exclude by including suggests that boundaries are the condition for variable intertwinements, not for an expanding series of concentric circles.

This insight demands that we part ways with the cosmopolitan vision of one humanity under one law, even if a world polity, democratic or otherwise, were ever to be founded. The variable intertwinement of legal orders with that which contests them means that all legal determinations of "our common humanity" not only join but also separate us— irreducibly. Although this insight raises a host of new and fundamental questions, it suggests that an inquiry into the possibility of an ethical dimension in legal responsiveness must take its point of departure in the acknowledgment that *the human can be irreducibly alien*, in the strong sense of a-legality noted above. Coming to terms with a-legality and the question of legal boundaries requires, I conjecture, neither the particularistic "ethics" of communitarianism nor the universalistic "morality" of cosmopolitanism but rather an ethics whereby acts of setting legal boundaries acknowledge, albeit indirectly, that they exclude what they include.

How does this train of thought impinge on postnationalism? Walker has noted that with the de-territorialisation of law, the "state-sovereigntist 'order of orders' or metaprinciple of authority, has been threatened in its position of pre-eminence" (2008, 376). He goes on to describe several such metaprinciples, which vie to become the new "order of orders" that could supersede and substitute for the "order of orders" that held sway in the era of nationalism. But according supremacy to any of these principles would, in fact, repeat the basic strategy of the municipal/international law paradigm, namely, postulating a form of legal unity that domesticates political plurality. Walker boldly arrests this strategy, asserting that postnationalism can best be characterised as a "disorder of orders," in which none of these principles succeeds in gaining ascendancy over the others, even though they can display a measure of mutual accommodation (2008, 392).

The account I have offered of a-legality and the question of legal boundaries shows a certain convergence with Walker's interpretation of postnationalism as a "disorder of orders." Indeed, the leitmotiv of the foregoing pages is that there is no all-encompassing measure of (il)legality that could guarantee an orderly encounter between what calls for legal qualification and the legal qualification thereof. Instead, this encounter attests to a hiatus that opens up between the questionability of legal boundaries and the responsiveness of lawmaking. This hiatus is an opening that renders possible all forms of legal openness and closure. It is not the ground of a legal order, and certainly not the ground shared by a plurality of legal orders, but rather an abyss—an *Abgrund*, as Heidegger might put it. I would argue that to interpret postnational politics as a "disorder of orders" is to understand it as deferring to an opening which no "order of orders" can bring under normative control, and which precedes and makes possible all claims to, and contestations of, legal unity, global or otherwise. Might this deference countenance the view that postnationalism is, or at least heralds, a new way of dealing with a-legality and the question of legal boundaries? Might "variable intertwinements" be its guiding metaphor? If postnationalism is indeed the "age of pluralism," as many insist, then this is so only by dint of bidding farewell to communitarianism and cosmopolitanism, and by acknowledging that legal boundaries are irreducibly in-between.

Acknowledgments

This chapter is a revised version of my inaugural lecture as chair of legal philosophy at Tilburg, and it was first published (in slightly different form) in the *Modern Law Review* 73, no. 1 (January 2010): 30–56. I am extremely grateful for comments on the first version made on diverse occasions by Hauke Brunkhorst, Emilios Cristodoulidis, Simon Critchley, Raf Geenens, Mireille Hildebrandt, Bonnie Honig, David Janssens, Bart van Klink, Martin Loughlin, Nanda Oudejans, Stanley Paulson, Gunther Teubner, Ronald Tinnevelt, Jim Tully, Wouter Veraart, Johan van der Walt, Neil Walker, and MLR's two anonymous referees. I am particularly indebted to Bert van Roermund, the former chair of legal philosophy at Tilburg, whose philosophical acumen has been a source of great inspiration to me.

References

Habermas, Jürgen. 1981. *The Theory of Communicative Action*. Volume 1. Translated by Thomas McCarthy. Boston: Beacon Press.
———. 2001. *The Postnational Constellation*. Translated by Max Pensky. Cambridge: Polity Press.
———. 2005. *The Inclusion of the Other: Studies in Political Theory*. Translated by Ciaran Cronin and P. de Greiff. Cambridge: Polity Press.
Pettit, Philip. 2001. *A Theory of Freedom: From the Psychology to the Politics of Agency*. Cambridge: Polity Press.
Taylor, Charles. 2001. "A Tension in Modern Democracy." In Aryeh Botwinick and William E. Connolly (eds.), *Democracy and Vision: Sheldon Wolin and the Vicissitudes of the Political*, 79–95. Princeton: Princeton University Press.
Teubner, Gunther. 1997a. "Foreword: Legal Regimes of Global Non-State Actors." In Gunther Teubner (ed.), *Global Law Without a State*, xiii–xvii. Aldershot: Dartmouth.

———. 1997b. "'Global Bukowina': Legal Pluralism in the World Society." In Gunther Teubner (ed.), *Global Law Without a State*, 3–28. Aldershot: Dartmouth.

van Roermund, Bert. 2006. "First-Person Plural Legislature: Political Reflexivity and Representation." *Philosophical Explorations* 3:235–50.

Waldenfels, Bernhard. 1994. *Antwortregister*. Frankfurt: Suhrkamp.

Walker, Neil. 2008. "Beyond Boundary Disputes and Basic Grids: Mapping the Global Disorder of Normative Orders." *International Journal of Constitutional Law* 6:373–96.

9

THE CONFLICTING LOYALTIES OF STATISM AND GLOBALISM:
CAN GLOBAL DEMOCRACY RESOLVE THE LIBERAL CONUNDRUM?

DEEN CHATTERJEE

1. Introduction

Mathias Risse conducts a thought experiment to demonstrate the initial plausibility of the assumption that the "earth belongs to humanity in common"—an assumption that is at the core of some versions of liberal cosmopolitanism. He writes: "Let us suppose for the sake of argument that the population of the United States shrinks to two, but that these two can control access into the country through sophisticated electronic border-surveillance mechanisms. Suppose, too, that nothing changes in the rest of the world. I would argue (and I think most would agree) that under such conditions these two citizens should allow for immigration based on the fact that they are grossly underusing the territory under their control" (Risse 2008, 25). Risse then wonders what sort of considerations can override the compelling moral intuition of this "common-ownership" assumption and provide moral legitimacy to the exclusive control of this imaginary space to these two citizens. For Risse, claims of culture fail to provide moral reason for exclusion. He notes: "A culture shared only by two people occupying a vast territory ... might be eminently worth preserving, but such occupancy would not count as appropriate use from the common-ownership standpoint. The burden of proof is on those who wish to overrule implications of the common-ownership standpoint by granting certain cultures more resources than proportionally they ought to have" (33). This and similar considerations prompt him to conclude that the exclusionary nature of immigration policies "fundamentally challenge those who see themselves in the liberal camp" (26).

The immigration dilemma for liberalism is indicative of a larger conundrum at the normative foundation of liberal political philosophy. Liberalism as a political ideology is committed to the universal moral equality of persons, yet the liberal polity is based on the idea of exclusive political membership of free citizens within state borders. The cosmopolitan ideal of liberal universalism seems to be at odds with liberalism's insistence on national borders for liberal democratic communities, creating disparate standards of distributive justice for members and outsiders.[1]

Political realists as well as the vast majority of people believe that ties of community—political, social, and cultural—create special duties of obligation that point toward conational partiality. Any global impartiality would run counter to this commonly held bias toward moral closeness. The liberal's dilemma over the question of cosmopolitan justice would seem to be an extension of this broader conundrum of conflicting loyalties of statism and globalism. The challenge for liberalism, then, seems to be to show how the practices of exclusive membership embody the principle of moral equality. How can the same liberals who denounce moral arbitrariness as fundamentally illiberal still claim that national boundaries make a moral difference? Can the liberal ideology offer a principled moral defense of conational partiality that would trump global impartiality?

2. Claims of Culture: Three Views

Three noted political theorists of our time, Michael Walzer, David Miller, and John Rawls, famously claim that obligations of egalitarian distributive justice apply only within political communities (Walzer 1983; D. Miller 1995, 2004; Rawls 1999). While dismissing cosmopolitan liberalism as unrealistic, morally problematic, or perhaps conceptually flawed, they base their claim for conational partiality on the idea of community membership. Walzer argues that social justice should be understood in terms of "a bounded world" (31), based on its history, culture, and membership. Distributive justice is local— not cosmopolitan—because its viability is determined by the standards internal to the shared understanding of a community. Miller contends that because all political communities are culturally unique, no universal principle of redistribution of resources from rich to poor nations will work. Rawls too (unlike in his earlier robust egalitarianism) is more mindful of cultural pluralism in accommodating decent but hierarchical societies in the society of peoples, and he sees a rather limited scope for international obligation, downplaying the demands of human rights in catering to the distant needy.

But what is the moral significance of Walzer's "bounded world," Miller's "culturally distinct communities" (2004, 125), and Rawls's "overlapping consensus" (172–74)—the key ideas these theorists employ in deciding on the priority of domestic need over global concern? In other words, what is the moral justification these concepts provide for confining the obligation of egalitarian justice to conationals, leaving room for only a limited obligation to ensure a certain threshold of human well-being in

---

[1] All liberal political philosophers from Kant to Rawls have had their ideas construed in a state-centric global order.

poor countries or endorsing only a "duty of assistance" to societies that lack the resources to achieve a well-ordered society? Community membership, cultural uniqueness, and collective consensus refer to contingent matters, but do they provide an inherent normative justification for principled discrimination between insiders and outsiders? As scholars have pointed out, the reason a cosmopolitan norm is not yet a reality is because it does not correspond to people's desire to connect themselves beyond their small units; but if and when people's felt identities and their objects of loyalty expand to coincide with the global domain, political globalization may go hand in hand with economic globalization (Arneson 2004; Oldenquist 2008). In other words, consensus, cultural uniqueness, or collective practices can change depending on contingent factors and should not be the criterion for moral justification.[2]

The problem of distance in morality is primarily about boundaries, which poses a seeming conundrum for the liberals committed to the moral equality of persons. Boundaries demarcate not only physical, political, and cultural space but also the moral space of exclusion and inclusion determining the limit and extent of our moral concern. The question of arbitrariness arises when political and cultural spaces are allowed to decide on the limit and extent of moral space. In other words, unless one spells out the moral reach of political and cultural concerns, one doesn't provide moral reasons for distinct principles of equality favoring conationals over noncompatriots.

3. Coercion

Some liberal theorists attempt to proceed beyond the claims of culture in defending the idea that a globally impartial liberal theory is not incompatible with distinct principles of equality within the national context. They do not disavow global impartiality. In fact, for them, global impartiality is an important feature of liberalism. But they look for a principled defense of conational partiality by seeking a legitimate, impartial ground for partiality toward one's fellow citizens, with the aim of showing that the seeming exception on the home front is not really a deviation from the liberal's global equality principle. For these liberal theorists, national borders matter morally, more so than the cosmopolitans are willing to admit, but for them this is compatible with the obligations of global impartiality and human rights. I examine here the claims of two such theorists—Richard Miller and Michael Blake.

Patriotic bias, for Richard Miller, can be impartially justified on the basis of the duties generated in a political community. In balancing national concerns and international needs in the political sphere, Miller spells out the difference between world community and a liberal political community, pointing out the alternative kinds of obligations they gen-

---

[2]   Macedo 2007 offers a similar argument. See also Macleod 2005.

erate. Citizens in a liberal democratic polity have a special role in coercively imposing rules of self-development and loyalty on one another, thereby playing a dual role of being the authors and the subjects of those coercive laws that operate in a political culture of trust and mutuality. This creates special duties and concern toward fellow citizens while generating a less demanding obligation toward foreigners because of much weaker considerations of coercion and loyalty that exist in the global community. As Miller argues, equal respect for all humans needn't mean equal concern for all (R. Miller 2004, 2005).

My aim here is to decide whether Richard Miller's reason for patriotic bias is sufficiently justified on normative grounds or whether it is based on morally arbitrary reasons. Since Blake's idea of special recognition of egalitarian justice among fellow citizens in a democratic polity is similar to Miller's in relevant respects, I'll first sketch Blake's position before commenting on both Miller and Blake together.

Blake makes a distinction between absolute deprivation and relative deprivation, arguing that although the rich countries have an obligation to ameliorate absolute deprivation in the world, their obligation does not extend beyond a certain threshold, whereas relative deprivation at home creates a more urgent obligation to respond to citizens' basic needs. In other words, we have special obligations to our own poor, even when they are better off than the poor foreigners (Blake 2002). Unlike Walzer, David Miller, and Rawls, who draw a similar conclusion based on their respective ideas of community membership and shared values, Blake brings in the imperatives of shared citizenship. Not unlike Richard Miller, Blake makes his case on the notion of direct institutional coercion that violates citizens' autonomy but that derives its justification from the hypothetical consent of all reasonable people to such an arrangement. Self-governance in a democratic polity creates shared obligations that are collectively binding, unlike obligations with outsiders with whom we do not have such binding contracts. This is the reason for egalitarian duties within a democratic state that forms the basis for conational partiality. This, for Blake, is still compatible with global impartiality.[3]

Blake's argument raises several debatable issues, some of which are also evident in Richard Miller's position. One may wonder whether *direct* institutional coercion, such as the same system of coercive property law, makes a significant moral difference compared to *indirect* institutional coercion in the global order. One may wonder, too, whether Blake has a sound notion of individual autonomy or of institutional coercion when he says that citizens' autonomy is violated by the normal functioning of

---

[3] Blake doesn't call it partiality; for him, what we take to be (conational) partiality, as he understands it, is not really (justified) partiality but rather a variation of the global impartiality principle, minus its cosmopolitan prescription for justice.

democratic institutions (can't we say that it is not coercion but constraints that democratic institutions exercise over citizens' conduct that promote cooperation, leading to Pareto optimality, which in turn contributes to individual autonomy?).[4] And one may wonder whether it is human agency based on choice and responsibility, rather than state coercion, that is more fundamentally linked to the questions of inequality and, thus, to justice.[5] Some of these issues come up in my discussion below as I proceed to show that Blake's argument does not give him what he wants. Blake doesn't provide a principled moral defense of a distinct principle of equality for fellow citizens in a liberal polity. If I am right, this critique would also apply to Richard Miller's position, as both Blake's and Miller's reasons are similar in relevant respects.

In an article published a year later than the one discussed above, Blake claims that liberals should not be restricted by the constraints of reciprocity or tolerance in their dealings with an illiberal world; instead, they should try to seek and promote liberal values abroad without any compromise (Blake 2003). If liberals need to limit their moral commitments in the international realm, that should be due only to practical concerns such as stability, harmony, and cost, and should not entail abandoning liberal commitment to individual dignity at home and abroad. The implication of Blake's position seems to be that because the world desperately needs both stability and human dignity, liberals can have it both ways by being practical yet remaining steadfastly committed to their liberal values. Blake questions Rawls's abandoning of robust egalitarianism in the global society of peoples in order to achieve consensus through a narrow construal of rights. This is very different from the Blake in his earlier article, who was sympathetic to Rawls for his view of limited duty to assist the foreign poor not because of constraints of practicality but because of what Blake thought was Rawls's principled cut-off point brought about by his noncosmopolitan commitment to international justice.

The liberal conundrum seems to be a moral conundrum. It asks: Why should domestic justice be construed in such a way that, in principle, it would have a higher egalitarian standard than justice in the international arena? But if practical concerns (such as cost, proximity, and other contingent factors) demand that fellow citizens' needs be given priority over similar or more pressing concerns of the foreign needy—though this disparity based on practicality need not hold true in all cases in our globally interconnected and interdependent world—then such concerns would not be a principled deviation from the global equality principle that would require a distinct standard of equality for conationals. This

---

[4] Macedo, while agreeing with Blake in general, disagrees with Blake's emphasis on the notion of coercion in the idea of autonomy (Macedo 2007).

[5] Landesman 2008 comments on this point.

would thereby conform to Blake's urging in his later article that liberals should, as a matter of principle, hold on to their liberal egalitarianism both at home and abroad.

So, Blake should have relied on pragmatic concerns in his earlier article and desisted from giving a principled moral justification of distinct distributive justice in the national context. After all, why should Blake's reason—the absence of mutually binding coercion laws for individuals outside national boundaries—be normatively relevant for distributive equality within state borders when such borders and the exclusionary scheme they project are themselves contingent and morally arbitrary? Blake takes for granted the existence of states and builds his normative justification on that empirical premise. The premise itself, however, needs to be normatively justified. Consider again the thought experiment that Risse offers, in which he starts with the assumption that the earth belongs to humanity in common. In that case, the burden of proof would rest on those who would offer a statist justification for a distinct principle of moral equality based on boundaries. It seems to me that one can raise the same concern with regard to Richard Miller's defense of patriotic bias. The locus of the concern is the justifiability of the connection between Blake's and Richard Miller's normative reasons for distributive equality among citizens and the contingency of common coercive laws. In a different world void of the modern state system, Blake and Miller would lack the needed empirical basis for their normative claim; in fact, in such a world, their claim for a distinct egalitarian principle for conationals would be redundant. The moral of the story is this: It is the normative ideal of egalitarian justice that should decide the scope of the political and institutional jurisdiction, not the other way around.

4. Reciprocity

In a recent article, Andrea Sangiovanni critiques Blake for failing to show how his normative reason is connected to his empirical assumption. But to make his case Sangiovanni takes a route different from the one I mentioned above. He claims that the normative ideal of distributive equality is a requirement of reciprocity, not state coercion. He does a thought experiment to show that the idea of coercion is "of only contingent . . . concern to a theory of distributive equality" (2007, 12). He postulates the possibility of a functioning state based on solidarity and reciprocity where the coercive power of the state is absent due to some national calamity, but where Blake's normative claims are operative nonetheless (11).

Sangiovanni notes that reciprocity presupposes a relational view of distributive justice, not a cosmopolitan one that is nonrelational and based on the demand of moral personhood independent of institutional and cooperative affiliations. And because reciprocity requires an institu-

tional model of political governance—not an abstract globalist cosmopolitan directive—special demand of egalitarian justice, for Sangiovanni,
applies only among fellow citizens. Thus, he tries to ground the argument
from moral arbitrariness of state boundaries in the normative ideal of
reciprocity.

Several factors are worth noting here. According to Sangiovanni, citizens
and residents provide the needed financial and sociological support to
sustain the state system through "contributions paid in the coin of
compliance, trust, resources, and participation" (20–21). For him, the global
order is quite different. Though there are elements of trust, compliance, and
participation in the global system, the range is comparatively narrow, and
without states the global order doesn't even have the needed regulatory
mechanism to sustain its basic structure. Sangiovanni proceeds to explain
how these facts are relevant to a conception of global justice. Specifically, he
tries to show how "reciprocity in the mutual provision of the basic collective
goods necessary for acting on a plan of life conditions the content, scope,
and justification of distributive equality" (22).

This is a rather tall order. Basically, Sangiovanni explains why a statist
view is better poised to account for distributive equality than a globalist
view is. In the imaginary example of a divided world where two states
exist totally independent of each other but one state is much more
prosperous than the other, the residents of the less affluent state cannot
reasonably press a claim for resource transfer from the prosperous state
on the basis of "bad brute luck." Moral arbitrariness, by itself, is not
"sufficient to generate a prima facie claim against anyone, anywhere to
compensation" (25). Special provisions against such inequalities, for
Sangiovanni, apply only "among those who share in the maintenance
and reproduction of the state" (29). He gives several examples of the
reciprocity-based interpretation of the argument from moral arbitrariness
to show that "there are no egalitarian social movements that have based
their struggle against injustice solely on being the victims of bad brute
luck" (30). To proceed from moral arbitrariness to specific principles of
distributive equality via the parameters of reciprocity operative in the
conception of society as a fair unit of cooperation, Sangiovanni turns to
the idea of justice as fairness in Rawls's *Theory of Justice*. Based on these
considerations, Sangiovanni concludes that though there is a system of
reciprocity and shared participation in the global order, inequality among
fellow citizens is more troubling than inequality between residents of
different states because fellow citizens "depend on, contribute, and are
subject to the same system of legal and political institutions" that make
up their own state (32).

Sangiovanni's argument raises several issues. Like Blake, Sangiovanni
rests his normative claim of a distinct principle of egalitarian justice on
the contingency of state boundaries. But he tries to show why the needed
connection between such contingency and distributive equality via the

ideal of reciprocity makes more sense. If he is right about the idea of reciprocity providing the normative justification of equality, then for him a globalist, noninstitutional demand of egalitarian justice would not do. For him, such a demand would be question-begging (37).

I believe the idea of reciprocity is a promising conceptual tool in understanding the obligation of egalitarian justice, but I see no reason why it needs to be both a necessary and a sufficient condition of egalitarian justice. That is, I don't see how reciprocity by itself can override Risse's compelling moral intuition of the common-ownership assumption I cited earlier. Sangiovanni does not specify what concrete forms of association operative in a state system but lacking in the emerging global order are necessary to generate duties of reciprocity that would by themselves be sufficient to provide moral legitimacy to the exclusive control of grossly disproportionate amounts of resources by a relatively few people. The burden of proof would seem to be on those who wish to overrule implications of the common-ownership standpoint by granting certain states more resources than proportionally they ought to have, simply in the name of reciprocity among fellow citizens. We seem to need something more than just reciprocity to account for this disparity. Likewise, it is not clear how reciprocity by itself can have enough traction in deciding on the emerging global issues that transcend state borders. For instance, how can the existing state system, in the name of reciprocity among its citizens, be sufficiently responsive to the challenges of cosmopolitan justice that underscore the importance of the emerging international solidarity, the increasingly vocal demands of the global human rights culture, or the global environmental perils? These transnational movements have emerged, at least in part, in response to the perceived inequity in the statist interpretation of distributive justice, so a reinforced defense of the existing state system may seem to be a circular move.

In response to the challenges of the nonrelational cosmopolitan interpretation of distributive justice, Sangiovanni remarks: "It is not clear why relational views should have the burden of proof" (36). He is partially correct in wondering why. In the imaginary example of a divided world where states have been absolutely independent of and disconnected from each other, it would indeed be odd if citizens of a less affluent state were to make a claim of justice, based on the moral arbitrariness of their bad luck, to the newly discovered citizens of a more affluent state. In such a case, the burden of proof would indeed be on the nonrelational globalist interpretation of egalitarian justice to show why such a claim of justice is not odd. But abstract cosmopolitanism of the nonrelational type is very rare these days. Today's cosmopolitan egalitarians tend to be adherents of "situated cosmopolitanism." They wonder whether a distinct principle of egalitarian distributive justice can be predicated on the contingency of national boundaries in a densely populated, interconnected, and interdependent world. For them, the burden of proof would fall on a relational view of justice based on the claims of sufficiency of reciprocity in generating egalitarian justice only among fellow citizens.

But does reciprocity obtain only among fellow citizens of a state? Sangiovanni concedes that the reciprocity-based institutional arrangement need not presuppose the need for state boundaries. Reciprocity is open to other institutional arrangements that may eventually evolve. Hence, Sangiovanni admits that he doesn't need to justify the existence of the state system. He points out, however, that given the world we live in, states are the best—perhaps the only—agents for making the required type of reciprocity a reality. If some other nonstatist institutional arrangement evolves that would deliver reciprocity better than a state system, then Sangiovanni is open to that idea. He cites the prospect of a peaceful world state, though he acknowledges that that it is a rather far-fetched idea at this stage of human existence.

What Sangiovanni does not cite or venture to examine is the prospect of a sufficiently rearranged and reformed global political and economic order that would generate duties of reciprocity globally. A global state is an unrealistic and undesirable prospect for many obvious reasons, as Sangiovanni rightly notes, but can't there be intermediate sorts of international governance and cooperation that may suffice to generate duties of reciprocity at the global level? It is not enough to base the prospects for egalitarian justice in our global world on the existing state system in the name of reciprocity, because that would simply validate the entrenched inequity in the current order.

A relational interpretation of egalitarianism based on the normative implications of reciprocity is a good beginning. Both the statist and the globalist interpretations of justice can concur with this. But the challenge is to push for an equitable global order based on appropriate political and economic reforms to make viable the ideals of human rights and democratic political participation. Just as a nonrelational, noninstitutional globalist demand of egalitarian justice would not do, and just as Sangiovanni is right to claim that such a demand would be question-begging, likewise, to leave the claims of justice on the existing arrangements of inequitable state systems is also question-begging, because, as noted earlier of Blake, it is the normative ideal of justice that should decide the scope of the political and institutional jurisdiction, not the other way round. Reciprocity is one important factor in this equation, not everything. A democratic realignment in the global order, extending the reach of reciprocity to the widest possible range, should also be included as an important consideration.

5. Conclusion

So it seems that the dilemma of whether statism trumps globalism is a false dilemma. It is not a case of only one or the other. The two are on the same curve, though they may be poles apart. Cosmopolitan liberals would be quite at home with the idea of a relational interpretation of justice in today's interdependent world. But for them justice cannot be limited by a preexisting system if the system clashes with our considered judgment of what is just.

The prospect of a democratic world order should be the challenge for both the statists and the globalists in their quest for justice. The idea is not all that premature, contrary to Sangiovanni's assertion. Global trends indicate that the process of moving in the direction of a democratic global order is already under way. The global recognition of endemic poverty and of systemic inequity as serious human rights concerns has put pressure on individual countries to implement internal democratic reforms and has made vivid the need for more just and effective international institutional directives. The demands of the developing countries at various world summits for democratic reform of the international global order are becoming progressively vocal. Likewise, global socioeconomic issues are increasingly dominating the agenda of the rich countries at their G-8 meetings. Today's entrenched global order affects all nations, especially the poor ones, and thus indirectly their citizens. It is well documented that the pervasive failure of the state to respond to its citizens' broader human needs is linked to the inequity in the global order itself.

Accordingly, the challenge for a liberal theorist should be to try to devise an institutional strategy for a democratic global system and supplement it with a suitably modified cosmopolitan theory. Cosmopolitanism needs to be reframed by being person-centered in an indirect way, via the institutional mediation of a global democratic order based on reciprocity. It is the task of an empirically informed liberal theory to conceptualize how to institutionalize the democratic norms of equality and fair political participation in the global system. At the least, it would call for an institutional rearrangement in the international order that would be democratically responsive and reflect the fluid dynamics of collaboration and interdependence in today's global world.

The prospect of a world state is indeed far-fetched, but reciprocity among states in a global democracy—that is, in a global democratic order—is a viable option. So, statism and globalism need not pose an irreconcilable dilemma within liberalism; in fact, they can be brought together through the common project of global democracy. If equality as a demand of justice requires a relational interpretation, then global democracy can be the direction for both a statist and a cosmopolitan liberal. Accordingly, the two camps present a case not of conflicting loyalties but of multiple loyalties. Claims of statism may sometimes compete with wider objects of loyalty such as globalism, but "nested multiple loyalties" is a challenge that people negotiate all the time.[6]

Acknowledgments

I wish to thank Ronald Tinnevelt, the editors of *Metaphilosophy*, and an anonymous reader for their valuable comments on an earlier draft of the chapter.

References

Arneson, Richard J. 2004. "Moral Limits on the Demands of Beneficence?" In *The Ethics of Assistance: Morality and the Distant Needy*, edited by Deen K. Chatterjee, 33–58. Cambridge: Cambridge University Press.

Blake, Michael. 2002. "Distributive Justice, State Coercion, and Autonomy." *Philosophy and Public Affairs* 31, no. 3:257–96.

———. 2003. "Reciprocity, Stability, and Intervention: The Ethics of Disequilibrium." In *Ethics and Foreign Intervention*, edited by Deen K. Chatterjee and Don E. Scheid, 53–71. Cambridge: Cambridge University Press.

Landesman, Bruce. 2008. "Global Economic Justice, Partiality, and Coercion." In *Coercion and the State*, edited by David Reidy and Walter Riker, 225–38. Dordrecht: Springer.

Macedo, Stephen. 2007. "The Moral Dilemma of U.S. Immigration Policy: Open Borders Versus Social Justice?" In *Debating Immigration*, edited by Carol M. Swaine, 63–84. Cambridge: Cambridge University Press.

Macleod, Alistair. 2005. "The Structure of Arguments for Human Rights." In *Universal Human Rights*, edited by David Reidy and Mortimer Sellers, 17–63. Lanham, Md.: Rowman and Littlefield.

Miller, David. 1995. *On Nationality*. Oxford: Oxford University Press.

———. 2004. "National Responsibility and International Justice." In *The Ethics of Assistance: Morality and the Distant Needy*, edited by Deen K. Chatterjee, 123–46. Cambridge: Cambridge University Press.

Miller, Richard W. 2004. "Moral Closeness and World Community." In *The Ethics of Assistance: Morality and the Distant Needy*, edited by Deen K. Chatterjee, 101–22. Cambridge: Cambridge University Press.

———. 2005. "Cosmopolitan Respect and Patriotic Concern." In *The Political Philosophy of Cosmopolitanism*, edited by Gillian Brock and Harry Brighouse, 127–47. Cambridge: Cambridge University Press.

Oldenquist, Andrew. 2008. "Varieties of Nationalism." In *Democracy in a Global World*, edited by Deen K. Chatterjee, 147–60. Lanham, Md.: Rowman and Littlefield.

---

[6] I borrow the term from Oldenquist (2008, 160).

Rawls, John. 1999. *The Law of Peoples*. Cambridge, Mass.: Harvard University Press.

Risse, Mathias. 2008. "On the Morality of Immigration." *Ethics and International Affairs* 22, no. 1:25–33.

Sangiovanni, Andrea. 2007. "Global Justice, Reciprocity, and the State." *Philosophy and Public Affairs* 35, no. 1:3–39.

Walzer, Michael. 1983. *Spheres of Justice: A Defense of Pluralism and Equality*. New York: Basic Books.

10

UNIVERSAL HUMAN RIGHTS AS A SHARED POLITICAL IDENTITY:
IMPOSSIBLE? NECESSARY? SUFFICIENT?

ANDREAS FØLLESDAL

Human rights scholars may worry about the present popularity of human rights talk. This is not only because of the growing mismatch between strong vocal support for human rights and weak adherence to the same norms on the ground. Another ground for worry is that human rights seem to be regarded as the appropriate solution to more and more problems. Does this popularity come at the expense of intellectual stringency about the proper function—or functions—of human rights?

One of several suggested roles for human rights is as part of citizens' "common political identity" in a stable legitimate political order—be it at the national or regional levels—or even for a future, legitimate global political order. Thus Charles Beitz observes that "[t]o whatever extent contemporary international political life can be said to have a 'sense of justice,' its language is the language of human rights" (Beitz 2001, 269). What are we to make of such proposals? Should human rights be part of—or even *exhaust*—the values or norms that democratic citizens must share, if their democratic institutions are to survive over time? Beitz's apparently affirmative answer is not obvious; even the thoughtful Jürgen Habermas and David Miller beg to disagree. These disagreements seem to stem from competing views of the role that a common political identity plays.

The present reflections address one aspect of this issue—namely, the claim that the requisite common political identity must be *unique* to members of the political order, to the intended exclusion of outsiders. Hence wariness about human rights in this role, since they by now are so broadly shared—at least nominally. I shall deny this assumption: the function of a common political identity does not require it to be unique to members. Thus a shared commitment to human rights norms may well be part of the requisite political identity.

Section 1 presents an account of the role of a common identity based on the need for trust among citizens, drawn from the debates about a European Union whose decision-making procedures require more trust when they move from unanimity to majoritarian rule. Section 2 identifies some components of such a common identity suited to secure trust, where human rights norms provide one of several parts. Section 3 considers criticisms drawn from David Miller's defense of national identity and from Jürgen Habermas and Jacques Derrida's conception of a European identity. All three endorse what I deny: that citizens of a sustainable democracy need a shared sense of community or "common identity" based on features that are uniquely theirs, to the exclusion of foreigners. I deny that the requisite trust among citizens requires an exclusionary conception of a common identity or community.

Two practical upshots of these reflections about the mechanisms for trustworthiness are cautiously optimistic on behalf of human rights and democracy. First, some of the pessimism regarding a more well-functioning democracy at the E.U. level is premature, since the requisite common grounds need not be exclusive. Secondly, debates about the feasibility and desirability of democratic arrangements of even more global scope may proceed unabated—while an "exclusionary" account of political identity might call this off, since there would be no one left to exclude from a global democratic order.

Note that this argument does not remove other, perhaps more serious and thought-provoking objections to democratic arrangements above the nation-state. They range from the view that international organizations might not really need much more in the way of democratic legitimacy (Moravcsik 2004), to various "impossibility theorems," such as Robert Dahl's perceptive concerns that democratic polities, delegation, and accountability mechanisms will lose their democratic quality if they overextend (Dahl 1999).

1. A Sense of Community and the Need for Trust

It seems an article of faith that citizens of a sustainable, fair, and democratic political order must share an "effectual sense of community" (MacCormick 1997; Weiler 1996; Gould 2004). In the setting of the European Union, the lack of some such sense of community has long been noted by politicians and academics alike (Føllesdal 2001b). Some scholars venture that Union citizenship was introduced precisely in an attempt to alleviate this absence, to create a closer bond between Europeans and the Union institutions (Closa 1992; Shaw 1997; Weiler 1996). That a sustainable legitimate political order requires mutual trust cannot be overstated. Citizens and officials must have reasons to expect that most others will comply with common laws and regulations, and that when asked to create new institutions and rules, they will all be guided by a common commitment to maintaining a fair political order.

In the European Union this need for trust and a sense of community or common identity has gradually grown with an expanded portfolio of increasingly controversial tasks, from securing peace to securing macro-economic stability. Changes in decision-making procedures to allow increased use of majority and qualified majority rule have rendered citizens more vulnerable to Europeans of other member states. Those who find themselves outvoted must trust the majority to temper their decisions by concern for their plight—for example, by the majority "identifying with" the minority. And the winning majority must trust the "losers" to comply with these decisions, even those counter to the losers' best judgments, for the sake of the common good and out of respect for the majoritarian decision-making procedures thought to best secure it (cf. Etzioni 2007, 31–33).

I submit that a common political identity can bolster trustworthiness under such circumstances, and thus facilitate the endurance of legitimate institutions. This is necessary to ensure that political institutions, authorities, policies, and decisions, if normatively legitimate, enjoy general compliance and adapt as necessary over time (Choudhry 2001).

To justify this claim, and to see why such a shared, trust-building creating of identity need not be unique among citizens to the exclusion of outsiders, let us start by considering the several ways in which institutions may render citizens and authorities trustworthy (Goodin 1992; Levi 1998; Braithwaite and Levi 1998). The forms of trust of particular concern to us are those required among people who are "contingent compliers" in what are known as "assurance games."

Contingent compliers are prepared to comply with common, fair rules as long as they believe that others do so as well—for instance, out of a sense of justice. They may be motivated by what John Rawls called a duty of justice: "They will comply with fair practices that exist and apply to them when they believe that the relevant others likewise do their part" (Rawls 1971, 336; see Scanlon 1998). A contingent complier thus decides to comply and cooperate with officials' decisions if: (a) she perceives government as trustworthy in making and enforcing normatively legitimate policies; *and* (b) she has confidence that other actors, officials and citizens, will do their part. Institutions, and a common political identity maintained by them, can provide important forms of assurance among contingent compliers on both of these counts. First, institutions may monitor legislation and policies, as well as others' compliance with them. Such monitoring may suffice to reduce the rate of non-compliance. Institutions may also shift the incentives of actors—for instance, by sanctions—to reduce the likelihood of non-compliance by officials and citizens. Institutions may also reduce the costs of failed trust. Thus, the members of a minority can be assured by human rights restrictions on the scope of legal political decisions that their vital interests will not suffer unduly from majoritarian decisions. Furthermore, institutions may socialize individuals to be contingent compliers and hence do their share in common projects. Such socialization to a common political identity may happen through public education as well as through political parties that shape the range of possible policy platforms (Føllesdal and Hix 2006; Etzioni 2007).

Note that these functions do not require that the common identity be unique to the members of that political order. That other persons elsewhere have similar values, norms, and beliefs need not detract from the trust-building contribution of a common political identity. To promote general compliance among citizens and reduce the sources of mistrust among them does not seem require that they be different from others. To be sure, there is a need to identify and sanction non-compliers or free riders, but the need for trust neither requires such persons nor requires that there are others, outsiders, who do not share the values, norms, or beliefs of the citizenry.

2. Components of Common Identity

What would the content of a common political identity have to be if its role is to ensure stability in this sense of general compliance by contingent compliers with existing, normatively legitimate institutions? What values, norms, and beliefs do citizens need to accept or support in order to give each other reason to believe in general compliance with legitimate institutions and authorities—be they domestic, European, or global? I submit that citizens must be habituated to at least three sets of commitments.

2.1 Normative Principles of Legitimacy

First, they must accept and act on principles of legitimacy for the political institutions and the constitutional norms. This may be similar to what Habermas calls "constitutional patriotism" (Habermas 1998). Normative principles of legitimacy for national, regional, or global polities contribute to stability in several ways. Principles provide critical standards to assess—and possibly confirm—existing, concrete institutions. Such public standards allow critical discussion of whether an existing order merits compliance by contingent compliers, and facilitate diagnoses of where improvements are needed. In the European Union, some of the values and objectives of the Lisbon Treaty aspire to such standards (European Council 2007). They include human rights, democracy, the rule of law, pluralism, tolerance, justice, gender equality, solidarity and non-discrimination, social justice and protection, and subsidiarity. The intellectual and political challenge is obviously not to list these values, norms, and principles but rather to specify and order them in a defensible way.

One apparent objection to this claim is that there is broad disagreement about conceptions of equality, justice, and human rights—not least within federations, and globally. Andrew Mason concludes from this fact of disagreement that shared reasons are unnecessary, since different conceptions of these principles do not hinder compliance. Citizens may value the same institutions, but for reasons drawn from contested conceptions of the ideals of equality, justice, or freedom (Mason 1999,

281). I submit, however, that the fact of such disagreement indicates that future compliance is not secure—it will depend on whether the various conceptions will support future compliance under new circumstances. In the absence of publicly shared principles, individuals are therefore less able to appear trustworthy, and this may threaten long-term general compliance.

2.2 Conceptions of Citizens and of the Political Order

Secondly, beyond constitutional patriotism, citizens must share fragments of a justification of such principles of legitimacy. To illustrate: one justification might consist of a conception of the proper roles of individuals, including their responsibilities as citizens, and an understanding of the objectives of the political order. One exemplar of this is Rawls's well-known conception of society as a system of co-operation among individuals, regarded for such purposes as free and equal participants. That particular conception is even on its own terms insufficient or inappropriate for regional or global political orders, characterized as having at best non-centralized political authority (cf. Rawls 1999).

In the multi-polar European political order this would include conceptions both of the role of member state and of the Union institutions; similarly, perhaps, in a (quasi-) federal global political order. A Rawls-inspired response might hold that such orders must also be perceived by citizens as a complex system of co-operation that expresses the inhabitants' standing as political equals. Such non-unitary political orders would need standards for the proper allocation of political authority between sub-units and the common political bodies. One candidate might be a defensible specification of a "principle of subsidiarity," one version of which is found in a protocol to the Lisbon Treaty (European Council 2007, 150–52; cf. Føllesdal 1998).

Why is a shared commitment to the grounds for common principles necessary or desirable? One important reason is that such shared grounds help settle disagreements about principles and institutions and their interpretation, not least about when the institutions should be changed. Consider how in the European Union disagreements about the appropriate division of powers between member states and Community institutions are a recurrent source of mistrust within and among the member states. Citizens suspect their politicians and other politicians, and politicians suspect their civil servants, of inappropriately supranational loyalties, induced by "two-level diplomacy," group think, and loyalty shifts (Trondal and Veggeland 2003). A shared conception of the proper roles of member states and the E.U. institutions can reduce such disagreements, bolster trustworthiness, and reduce mistrust.

One objection to accounts such as this is that they fail to show what reason individuals have to comply with their own government. Since many constitutions satisfy my preferred principles and conceptions of the person, why—on this view—do I have a moral duty to comply with my *own* authorities, rather than simply with those that are the most just? This has given rise to worries that constitutional patriotism seems to provide citizens with insufficient bonds and allegiance to their own political institutions at the national, Union, or global level (Kymlicka and Norman 1994).

In response, I submit that we must look more closely at the political virtues and duties of citizens in a political order. Such virtues, on Rawls's account, include "toleration and mutual respect, and a sense of fairness and civility" (Rawls 1971, 122). In particular—and central to the present account that focuses on contingent compliers—citizens have, and should be brought to have, a sense of justice. That is: an effective desire to comply with existing, fair rules and to give one another that to which they are entitled, "predicated on the belief that others will do their part" (Rawls 1971, 336, 505, 567). I submit that this duty of justice helps justify the ties to one's own political order, given that this order is legitimate and generally complied with by others.

Through the duty of justice, citizens have political obligations to just institutions that exist and apply to them. Those who accept this abstract duty must abide by the requirements that particular institutions lay down, as long as these institutions satisfy the normative principles and claim to regulate their actions. Some of these institutions are typically specified in written or unwritten constitutions—for example, of one's member state and those of larger regional or world political orders. The duty of justice also requires citizens to comply with the results of these institutions, namely, particular laws and political practices, in so far as they are legitimate.

2.3 Acquaintance with Local Norms, Cultural Practices, and Others' Institutions

A third commitment among contingent compliers is that citizens of democracies are, and must be known to be, somewhat familiar with the institutions, the public political culture, and the other cultural practices that flourish in their own state and at the regional and global levels. There are several reasons to require such *familiarity*—though not full compliance by each person.

The central concern is that proposed common legal institutions and policies may conflict with normatively unobjectionable existing social practices and local institutions. More responsive or creative legislation and policies can often avoid or reduce such conflicts, and such accommodation seems required for responsible democratic rule. In large and multi-level political orders citizens may thus have an obligation to consider how centralized decisions by majority rule may impact on particular segments of the population and within each sub-unit. Citizens should therefore have some knowledge of the main cultures that have adherents in the political community, so they can be brought to understand whether the proposals will respect these cultures to a sufficient degree. For instance, within the European Union, citizens need a sound understanding of at least the major religious, intellectual, and philosophical traditions. Only then can citizens pay due respect to the expectations of adherents to those traditions while they exercise political power.

This duty undoubtedly puts burdens on citizens, but note, first, that such knowledge does not require that citizens generally have to be committed to permanently maintaining the various cultural practices and institutions. Secondly, I submit that this obligation may largely be honoured indirectly, by political parties and media. Furthermore, the burden can be alleviated by a principle such as subsidiarity that would limit the occasions for centralized decision making and restrict the scope of parties affected by common decisions (Føllesdal 1998, 2001a).

Familiarity with the various social cultures and traditions also helps ensure a general appreciation among citizens that the requisite shared values have indeed been secured by citizens within the existing political order, through various institutions and practices. Such knowledge of local practices is helpful in times when institutional creativity is needed, in order to explore how the same values and norms are best secured in new circumstances. This awareness also helps the public understand how common institutions and history have endorsed these conceptions, values, and norms. For instance, welfare arrangements by voluntary organizations and states, taxation for humanitarian purposes, and other forms of solidarity remind all that the will to pitch in for the common good is broadly shared. By recalling and always reclaiming such values and ideals, citizens remind each other that they are citizens with an overriding sense of justice. Such a historical perspective reminds citizens that they have indeed been trustworthy and fair. This may help give each citizen reason to comply, in the confirmed belief that others have done and will do their share.

2.4 No Need for a Common Political Identity Unique to Citizens

I have sketched three main components of a common political identity that helps serve to provide assurance among contingent compliers that they will comply in the future. They must be committed to principles of legitimacy and to conceptions of citizens and of the political order; and they must be somewhat acquainted with the world views, practices, and legal institutions of other citizens within the political order.

Note that this common political identity does not require that the components be endorsed only by citizens, not by others. Nor is it important that others, such as non-citizens, hold other norms, values, or beliefs. The concern is only to provide citizens with reasons to believe that other citizens will honour what is expected of them. Whether non-citizens have similar reasons to honour expectations that hold for them is irrelevant for this objective.

This distinguishes this account from two other theories that call for a "common identity" in response to the needs for trust within democratic arrangements.[1] Indeed, David Miller and Jürgen Habermas agree on little else with regard to the conditions for and prospects for a European identity and a legitimate European integration. Miller in particular is highly sceptical of the prospects of maintaining pan-European welfare regimes, owing to the lack of a substantive national identity among Europeans. In contrast, Habermas hopes that such an identity can be constructed, a construction he explicitly sought to contribute to an article co-written with Jacques Derrida.

What unites the three is the belief that the common identity needed— in Europe, and presumably in democratic political orders everywhere—must be unique: it must set members apart from non-members.

3. Objections Considered

3.1 David Miller

David Miller's account of citizenship also focuses on the role of trust, assurance, and stability. He defends the need for a shared national identity with substantive norms, beliefs, or commitment. This identity serves to set members off from other peoples: "The people who compose a nation must believe that there is something distinctive about themselves that marks them off from other nations, over and above the fact of sharing common institutions. This need not be one specific trait or quality, but can be a range of characteristics which are generally shared by the members of nation A and serve to differentiate them from outsiders" (Miller 2000, 30–31). Miller holds that such a national identity is required to maintain trust, especially for solidaristic arrangements characteristic of European welfare states.

---

[1] Amitai Etzioni has recently argued for the need for particularistic values among Europeans, in addition to some that are universal, such as human rights (Etzioni 2007, 33–34). Unlike Habermas and Miller, Etzioni does not argue that these values must be shared only by Europeans. Some of these arguments are presented and further developed in Føllesdal, 2009.

I shall suggest that the argument for an exclusionary national identity has flaws, so the need for trust and trustworthiness among citizens does not require them to seek values or norms that are unique to their own community (cf. Føllesdal 2000). Miller's main argument is that "a viable political community requires mutual trust, trust depends on communal ties, and nationality is uniquely appropriate here as a form of common identity" (Miller 1994, 143). Miller is correct about the need for citizens to share some public, common value platform. But it is not clear why these communities must build on "natural" divisions that "must correspond to what are taken to be real differences between peoples" (Miller 1994, 140). Miller also fails to explain why a unique "national identity" with a broad range of shared social norms is the *only* appropriate candidate for such an identity. What he has in mind is "a set of understandings about the nature of a political community, its principles and institutions, its social norms, and so forth" (Miller 1995, 158). But he fails to explain which social norms should be shared, why these should be exclusionary, and why these elements are needed in order to maintain trust.

Miller is pessimistic about any commonalities that can serve such purposes among Europeans. There are no obvious and attractive values accepted only by Europeans yet acceptable as legitimate common grounds. On my alternative account, the search for unique values or norms is misguided: they are not required for mutual trust in the future compliance of others.

3.2 Jürgen Habermas

The call by Habermas and Derrida for a common, unique European identity likewise seems based on the need for trust, especially the extensive need for trust within majoritarian democratic institutions. They look for "historical experiences, traditions, and achievements offering European citizens the consciousness of a political fate that has been shared together, and *that can be shaped together*" (Habermas and Derrida 2003, 293). This approach seems appropriate and plausible. However, Habermas and Derrida dismiss some values and norms central to Europeans, because these are by now broadly shared also elsewhere:

> Haven't the most important historical achievements of Europe lost their identity-creating power exactly because of their worldwide success? And what is to hold together a region characterised like no other by continuing rivalry between self-confident nations?
>
> Christianity and capitalism, natural science and technology, Roman law and the Code Napoleon, the bourgeois-urban way of life, democracy and human rights, which spread the secularization of state and society over other continents, no longer form its unique possessions. (Habermas and Derrida 2003, 294)

So Habermas and Derrida look elsewhere. Their findings are hardly successful, or so I shall suggest—but on my alternative account this is of little importance. They should instead not be so quick to dismiss the components of a political identity that are not unique to Europeans.

The reason for this dismissal may stem from Habermas's account of the role of a shared political identity (Føllesdal 2009; cf. Choudry 2001, 393; and Laborde 2002). His concern seems to be that constitutional principles lack driving force on their own: constitutional patriotism "is not enough" (Canovan 2000). Citizens need a "motivational anchorage" that the nation's unique historical experience can best provide (Habermas 1992, 16). Existing institutions and political practices are instrumentally valuable in this regard, since they motivate us to abide by and promote the constitutional principles. Norms or practices that are not unique to Europe cannot serve this motivational role. Democracy and human rights are unsuited for this purpose, since they "no longer form [Europe's] unique possessions" (Habermas and Derrida 2003, 294).

Habermas's nominees include the French Revolution, scepticism about market efficiency, trust in state capacity, caution about the role of the state vis-à-vis religion, and the welfare models now secured by European states.

Two general observations are appropriate. First, there is much to criticize with regard to the historical accuracy and normative significance of these claims (Føllesdal 2009). Put briefly:

(1) Trust in the state's ability to organize and govern varies much more among Europeans—and among non-Europeans—than seems compatible with Habermas's concern for a unique and shared attitude among Europeans. Crucially, surveys such as the European Values Study and the World Values Survey show that citizens of European and other states have markedly different levels of trust in their own governments, varying across states and political affinities (Norris 1999).

(2) One of the central challenges facing the European Union is clearly the relationship between church and state in Europe. But this issue is hardly settled in the way claimed by Habermas: religious leaders often endorse politically contested positions. Consider the role of the Catholic Church in Irish politics, or against liberalization of abortion legislation, or in support of Polish resistance against communism. Recall church support for Dutch welfare arrangements or church protests against equal rights for homosexuals. Habermas cannot imagine that European politicians would start the day with public prayer or would see their decisions tied to a religious mission—he presumably wants to contrast their lack of public display of religious belief with President George W. Bush's

display. But this distinction is open to challenge. Consider the many Christian Democrats who fight, and fought, for a supranational European Union: Jean Monnet, Robert Schuman, Alcide de Gasperi, and Konrad Adenauer were all deeply affected by Catholic social thought, and they no doubt saw the European project as one required by their God.

(3)   Likewise, it seems difficult to identify a shared and uniquely European welfare state model whose arrangements and ideals are distinct from those of Japan, New Zealand, the United States, and other states—*and* a model that Europeans will agree is worth establishing and keeping.

The point here is not that these norms or practices are not of great value but that the empirical claims are not correct, or that they are not unique to Europe. For Habermas and Derrida there would be bleak prospects for a European common identity, and hence for a stable, legitimate and democratic European Union.

The second observation is that Habermas and Derrida's search for unique values seems unnecessary, on the account offered above. An immediate challenge is then to address the motivational challenge that critics pose to Habermas's constitutional patriotism. Can individuals be motivated by such inherently "abstract" motivations and an abstract sense of solidarity or reciprocity based on universalistic principles of social justice, contingent compliance, and a sense of justice? (Preuss 1995, 275.) If principles of human rights and democracy are not themselves enough to motivate people, what does my alternative offer as a supplement?

In response, I submit that the three components of a common political identity sketched above do include motivational drivers. In particular, the motivation stems not only from principles of legitimacy but also from the duty of justice. Recall that this duty "requires us to support and to comply with just institutions that exist and apply to us" (Rawls 1971, 115). Stated thus, this no doubt appears to be a somewhat "impersonal" motivation: the interest in doing our moral duty. But this duty also accounts for individuals' political allegiance towards their own political institutions—and their obligations to fellow citizens, as indicated above. Citizens must be committed not only to abstract principles but also to particular institutions (as specified in constitutions) and their results, namely, concrete laws and political practices.

The account sketched above thus also offers an account of why existing institutions and the political culture have value that is not merely instrumental, and of why it matters, normatively, that they are *ours*. To justify political obligation, we draw on the duty of justice and not only appeal only to "abstract principles" but also show that a particular, legitimate set of institutions does in fact exist. That is: the institutions' rules are publicly known, they are generally complied with by other citizens and authorities, *and* they apply to us.

One relevant premise is, thus, that these institutions and practices are indeed ours—that they apply to us. To act on this general, abstract sense of justice is thus to act in our day-to-day lives towards other particular individuals in accordance with the particular legitimate expectations they have about our behaviour here and now. I submit that to seek to honour others' trust in us in these day-to-day settings is a principle of action, based on a sense of justice, that does motivate many. Thus formulated, it also seems clear that the practices and expectations that citizens share must somehow exclude someone.

Conclusion

I have sought to argue against the view that citizens in a stable democracy, at the national, regional, or global level, must share an exclusionary political identity—that is, that they must share values, norms, or beliefs that are uniquely theirs to the exclusion of others. If that view were correct, we would have reason in principle to suspect that a European—not to mention an all-encompassing global—democracy could not be sustained. I have argued against arguments in favour of this position by David Miller and Jürgen Habermas, and there are several implications of the alternative I have defended.

First, some of the pessimism regarding a more well-functioning democracy at the E.U. level is premature. Second, discussions about the feasibility and desirability of democracy on an even more global scale should not dwindle. Thirdly, human rights norms may well be part of—though not all of—a common political identity suited to build trust among members of a political order. Fourthly, political theorists may want to move beyond alleged conflicts between liberalism and communitarianism, between abstract principles and particularistic commitments (Føllesdal 2009). To act on an "abstract" duty of justice is to honour in our daily lives the particular legitimate expectations of those around us. In a globalized world, where many common institutions have consequences that cut across state borders, many of the expectations at stake are likewise global. I have suggested that a conception of global citizenship may draw upon commitments to the human rights of these many others who invisible to us participate in upholding our common institutions. The fact that human rights norms are more generally accepted does not detract from their value as part of a possible conception of global or regional citizenship. To the contrary: in so far as human rights norms are shared, they can contribute to the trust we need, as contingent compliers motivated by a sense of justice, to honor the legitimate expectations of each other as political equals (Føllesdal 1990).

Acknowledgments

This chapter has benefitted from several exchanges, including at a EURESCO Conference in Italy, June 2003; the University of Minho, October 2005; the ECPR General Conference in Budapest, September 2005; the conference entitled "Multiculturalism and Nationalism in a World of Immigration," Copenhagen, May 2006; and the conference entitled "Les citoyennetés à l'ère de la mondialisation," University of Montreal, April 3–4, 2008, including prepared comments by Jean-Philippe Therien. I am grateful to the Mossavar-Rahmani Center for Business and Government and the Ash Institute for Democratic Governance and Innovation, both at the Kennedy School of Harvard University; the European Union's Integrated Project on New Modes of Governance (NEWGOV); and the Norwegian Centre of Excellence on the Study of Mind in Nature (CSMN).

References

Beitz, Charles R. 2001. "Human Rights as a Common Concern." *American Political Science Review* 95, no. 2 (May): 269–82.

Braithwaite, Valerie, and Margaret Levi. 1998. *Trust and Governance.* New York: Russell Sage.

Canovan, Margaret. 2000. "Patriotism Is Not Enough." *British Journal of Political Science* 30, no. 3 (July): 413–32.

Choudhry, Sujit. 2001. "Citizenship and Federations: Some Preliminary Reflections." In *The Federal Vision: Legitimacy and Levels of Governance in the US and the EU*, edited by K. Nicolaidis and R. Howse, 377–402. Oxford: Oxford University Press.

Closa, Carlos. 1992. "The Concept of Citizenship in the Treaty on European Union." *Common Market Law Review* 29:1137–169.

Dahl, Robert A. 1999. "Can International Organizations Be Democratic? A Skeptic's View." In *Democracy's Edges*, edited by I. Shapiro and C. Hacker-Cordon, 19–36. Cambridge: Cambridge University Press.

Etzioni, Amitai. 2007. "The Community Deficit." *Journal of Common Market Studies* 45, no. 1:23–42.

European Council. 2007. "Treaty of Lisbon Amending the Treaty on European Union and the Treaty Establishing the European Community," signed at Lisbon, 13 December 2007. *Official Journal of the European Union* 50 (2007/C 306/01).

Føllesdal, Andreas. 1998. "Subsidiarity." *Journal of Political Philosophy* 6, no. 2:231–59.

———. 2000. "The Future Soul of Europe: Nationalism or Just Patriotism? On David Miller's Defence of Nationality." *Journal of Peace Research* 37, no. 4:503–18.

———. 2001a. "Federal Inequality Among Equals: A Contractualist Defense." *Metaphilosophy* 32, nos. 1–2 (January):236–55.

———. 2001b. "Union Citizenship: Unpacking the Beast of Burden." *Law and Philosophy* 20, no. 3:313–43.

———. 2009. "If There Is No Common and Unique European Identity, Should We Create One?" In *Nationalism and Multiculturalism in a World of Immigration*, edited by Nils Holtug, Kasper Lippert-Rasmussen, and Sune Laegaard, 194–227. Basingstoke: Palgrave.

Føllesdal, Andreas, and Simon Hix. 2006. "Why There Is a Democratic Deficit in the EU: A Response to Majone and Moravcsik." *Journal of Common Market Studies* 44, no. 3:533–62.

Goodin, Robert E. 1992. *Green Political Theory*. Cambridge: Polity.

Gould, Carol C. 2004. *Globalizing Democracy and Human Rights*. Cambridge: Cambridge University Press.

Habermas, Jürgen. 1992. "Citizenship and National Identity: Some Reflections on the Future of Europe." *Praxis International* 12, no. 1:1–19.

———. 1998. "Struggles for Recognition in the Democratic Constitutional State." In *The Inclusion of the Other: Studies in Political Theory*. Cambridge, Mass.: MIT Press.

Habermas, Jürgen, and Jacques Derrida. 2003. "February 15, or What Binds Europeans Together: A Plea for Common Foreign Policy, Beginning in the Core of Europe." *Constellations* 10, no. 3 (October): 291–97.

Kymlicka, Will, and Wayne Norman. 1994. "Return of the Citizen: A Survey of Recent Work on Citizenship Theory." *Ethics* 104, no. 2 (January): 352–81.

Laborde, Cecile. 2002. "From Constitutional to Civic Patriotism." *British Journal of Political Science* 32, no. 4:591–612.

Levi, Margaret. 1998. *Consent, Dissent, and Patriotism*. New York: Cambridge University Press.

MacCormick, Neil. 1997. "Democracy, Subsidiarity, and Citizenship in the 'European Commonwealth'." *Law and Philosophy* 16, no. 4:331–56.

Mason, Andrew. 1999. "Political Community, Liberal-Nationalism, and the Ethics of Assimilation." *Ethics* 109, no. 2:261–86.

Miller, David. 1994. "The Nation-State: A Modest Defence." In *Political Restructuring in Europe: Ethical Perspectives*, edited by C. Brown, 137–62. London: Routledge.

———. 1995. *On Nationality*. Oxford: Oxford University Press.

———. 2000. "In Defense of Nationality." In *Citizenship and National Identity*, 24–40. Cambridge: Polity.

Moravcsik, Andrew. 2004. "Is There a 'Democratic Deficit' in World Politics? A Framework for Analysis." *Government and Opposition* 39, no. 2:336–63.

Norris, Pippa. 1999. *Critical Citizens: Global Support for Democratic Government*. Oxford: Oxford University Press.

Preuss, Ulrich K. 1995. "Problems of a Concept of European Citizenship." *European Law Journal* 1, no. 3:267–81.

Rawls, John. 1971. *A Theory of Justice*. Cambridge, Mass.: Harvard University Press.

———. 1999. *The Law of Peoples*. Cambridge, Mass.: Harvard University Press.

Scanlon, Thomas M. 1998. *What We Owe to Each Other*. Cambridge, Mass.: Harvard University Press.

Shaw, Jo. 1997. "Citizenship of the Union: Towards Post-National Citizenship?" Harvard Jean Monnet Chair Paper 6/97. At http://www.jeanmonnetprogram.org/papers/97/97-06-.html

Trondal, Jarle, and Frode Veggeland. 2003. "Access, Voice and Loyalty: The Representation of Domestic Civil Servants in the EU Committees." *Journal of European Public Policy* 10, no. 1:59–77.

Weiler, J. H. H. 1996. "The Selling of Europe: The Discourse of European Citizenship in the IGC 1996." Harvard Jean Monnet Working Paper 3/96. At http://www.jeanmonnetprogram.org/papers/96/9603.html

11

MOTIVATING THE GLOBAL DEMOS

DANIEL WEINSTOCK

Introduction

According to a fairly standard line of argument that has been mounted in recent years against global democracy, democracy is only possible within the context of a cohesive national community. Various reasons are commonly adduced to buttress this claim. First, it is often said, democracies function best when their citizens are united around a set of shared values of the kind that national communities instantiate. Second, democracy requires debate and deliberation, and these in turn are only possible given a shared language. Citizens need to talk to one another, and for this a common vernacular is needed. But a shared language is according to some theorists also required in another sense: the debates and deliberations that make up the bread and butter of democratic life require shared meanings and interpretations, not just shared words. Third, the life of a democratic community is one in which people will often be called upon to make sacrifices for one another, most notably through the taxes that they pay in order to fund institutions ensuring common welfare (Miller 1995, 2000, 2007; Kymlicka 2001).

Much of my work on global justice has sought to debunk various strands of this line of argument. I have argued in the past that it is based on an unduly nostalgic view of democracy according to which democratic institutions are justified by their allowing citizens to instantiate a robust conception of democratic agency, rather than by their more workaday ability to secure the realization of citizens' basic interests (Weinstock 2006a). I have also argued that shared democratic institutions do not only *reflect* the democratic will of an antecedently existing political community. Such institutions can also *create* community by engendering habits of cooperation and shared membership. There is thus greater plasticity in people's capacity for communal affiliation than nationalist democratic theorists have allowed (Weinstock 1999, 2001a). I have argued, finally, that it is a mistake about the nature of democracy to suppose that it presupposes or requires value consensus. Indeed, democracy is all about getting along together in the absence of such consensus (Weinstock 2001b).

I want in this chapter to develop a different yet largely complementary line of argument. I want to argue that nationalist democratic theorists overestimate the degree to which members of national communities agree to the sacrifices that life in a modern democracy involves out of *fellow feeling*. Coercion and self-interest play an ineliminable role in getting citizens in a democracy to "do the right thing." Actions that might at first glance be seen to betoken spontaneous communal feeling are actually engineered by institutional design. Rather than seeing themselves as having to overcome a disadvantage relative to theorists of the democratic nation-state in having to resort to artifice to motivate political morality, global democrats can learn from the practice of national democracies that have also had to channel self-interest in the direction of the collective good through the use of incentives of various kinds.

I will proceed as follows. First, I will spell out in greater detail why I think that partisans of global democracy have in recent philosophical debates conceded far too much ground to nationalist democrats on the issue of what one might term the motivational requirements of solidarity. Second, following arguments first developed by Robert Goodin, I will suggest some strategies for channelling self-interest towards the cause of communal solidarity, first developed in the context of democratic nation-states, but for which analogues might be found on the global scale. Finally, I will address the related question of the moral limits that exist in the global democrat's use of moral argument for the purposes of "global community building," which is analogous to the inquiry that one may launch into the moral constraints that would-be nation builders should observe in their campaigns to form national communities. What will result, I hope, is the beginning of a "toolbox" for the construction of a global democratic polity, one which can avail itself of many of the same tools as nation builders have made use of at least since the nineteenth century.

On the "Naturalness" of National Partiality

I want in this first section to argue that it is a fundamental error committed by both parties to the debate about the possibility of global democracy that cosmopolitans and nationalists stand motivationally on different sides of the natural/artificial divide. According to this view, national partiality comes naturally to humans, whereas cosmopolitanism does violence to their natures, no matter what the independent truth of the cosmopolitan position might be (Miller 1993; Kymlicka 2001). When the well-off members of a society pay taxes, for example, they do so on this view because they share an identity with their co-nationals. They are connected to them by fellow feeling. To the extent that cosmopolitanism requires the transfer of resources to distant others, it cannot tap into the same fund of feeling, and thus the whole cosmopolitan project understood as a political project rather than as a mere theory has trouble getting off the ground. The project therefore requires making motivational peace with nationalism, either by defining cosmopolitanism in a way that makes place for nationalism or by trying to exploit nationalism as a springboard for broader solidarity (Tan 2005; Lenard 2006).

This view, which, I repeat, is largely common ground between nationalists and at least some cosmopolitans, does not withstand a moment's critical scrutiny. Two considerations seem to me to dispose of this truism.

First, we actually know very little about how disposed people are to redistributing resources towards their less well-off co-nationals. This is because in every modern state redistributive obligations are backed up by the coercive power of the state. The state does not suggest to people that they might want to consider parting with some of their riches so as to come to the assistance of the less well-off and to create welfare institutions from which all might benefit. Rather, it forces people to pay taxes, does it at rates over which people have no say (except to the limited extent that they can vote for political parties that have different—although rarely radically different—views on the issue). And it attempts to track down tax cheats and to punish them. It might be that were this entire coercive apparatus lifted, and a system of voluntary contribution put in its place, the numbers would not change dramatically. Then again, it might not be. As it stands, we will never know. What we know is that most people pay their taxes in a context in which not to do so attracts significant legal penalties. We simply do not have enough evidence to support the ambitious claim that co-nationals are naturally disposed to share with one another in ways that people from different countries are not.

A response is available to the nationalist, however. The tax laws and their associated coercive apparatus, the reply would go, are at least in democratic societies the result of the exercise of a people's democratic will. Democracies have by and large chosen through democratic mechanisms to bind themselves to practices of national solidarity. Now, people know themselves well enough to realize that when tax time rolls around, they will not always be motivationally up to their highest aspirations. There will be rival motivations that might at that point hold sway. Tax laws and associated penalties reflect a kind of second-order moral commitment. The reply might be stated as follows: "We believe we ought to share with one another, but know that when the time comes to act on this belief we might backslide, and so we put in place self-binding mechanisms through which we force ourselves to act on our higher moral inclinations. Now note," the reply would go, "that we do not choose to enact such mechanisms in order to commit ourselves to coming to the aid of people in other countries, or if we do so, it is to a significantly lesser degree. This suggests that there is a naturalness to national solidarity that does not exist in the transnational case."

The cosmopolitan's response to this line of argument should be clear. The institutionalized commitment of citizens through their tax laws to their fellow nationals may also be an artifact of the nation-state system. That is, these laws do not emanate organically from a democratic public contemplating all possible modes of resource distribution as equipossible. Rather, they have had the agenda set for them by democratic *states* that have viewed it as their moral mission to institutionalize moral solidarity at the national level. It is difficult to use the moral attitudes that people who have been socialized in all kinds of ways, both grandiose and banal (Billig 1995), to give greater weight to the needs and interests of their fellow nationals as evidence that they could not, absent such socialization, be anything but nationalistic in their moral feelings.

But is there not something natural about the connection of states and nations? Do states not act as they do because they reflect some pre-existing collective "we" longing for political self-expression? This brings us to the second reason to reject the claim of "naturalness" made on behalf of nations by nationalists. The nations that exist today are the result, rather than the pre-condition, of the states formed in the Westphalian world. Most successful states have had to undergo a phase of nation *building* in order to create identities capable of sustaining institutions of solidarity without recourse to illiberal and undemocratic means. Social scientists and historians studying the emergence of national identities are almost unanimous in rejecting "primordialism," which is the view that nations pre-exist states, which are then seen as expressions of an antecedent national identity. The Westphalian order resulted from geostrategic considerations more than it did from some pressing need felt by nations to break free of political structures that did not adequately reflect the division of Europe into distinct nations. Nations were then largely constructed through a range of deliberate state policies in order to satisfy the political and economic needs of newly created states. Nations, in other words, are artifices (Anderson 2006; Bell 2001).

Now, to point this out is not to belittle their importance or to suggest that they are somehow morally suspect (Rawls 1999). It *is* to say that nations cannot claim the kind of naturalness that would allow nationalists to assert that there exists the kind of ontological divide between national and cosmopolitan contexts that subtends the motivational argument. It is also to claim that there is no reason *a priori* to think that cosmopolitans could not avail themselves of institutional mechanisms and devices to "motivate the global demos" in much the same way that nationalists historically have.

Thus, the defensiveness that has been evinced by some cosmopolitans when the issue of moral/political motivation is raised is groundless, or at the very least it cannot be grounded in the way that nationalists have tended to do it, by pointing at the greater "naturalness" of national identity and of the obligations that flow from it. Nation-states provide citizens with powerful nonmoral incentives to comply with the obligations of justice that they have towards their countrymen. What's more, the political identities that can be mobilized as a motivational basis for redistribution are in all but the rarest cases the results of deliberate nation-building strategies that have succeeded in creating a sense of shared political belonging out of (in some cases) quite unpromising raw materials.

What artifices have theorists and politicians at the national level availed themselves of in order to foster a sense of community among individuals standing under common political institutions? A full inventory would be a topic for a long book rather than a short chapter. I want in the following section much more modestly to provide an account of suggestions made in an early book by Robert Goodin, in order to see whether any of the devices he describes can find analogues on the global scene.

What Cosmopolitans Might Learn from Nationalist Community Building

In a book published in 1992 entitled *Motivating Political Morality*, Goodin argued that there are many institutional and psychological mechanisms that can be used in order to establish support for morally defensible policies. Very briefly stated, he argued that self-interest can be marshalled in order to establish support for policies that embody the principle of reciprocity. We have non-moral reason to do unto others as we would have them do unto us when there is reason to think that others will actually be in a position to do unto us what we have done unto them. Prudence dictates morality, in other words, when we find ourselves in the Hobbesian situation in which no agent possesses a significant threat advantage over others (Goodin 1992).

Of course, the Hobbesian situation does not always obtain. The real world is one of huge differentials in terms of money, power, and influence, even when we limit our purview to affluent societies. But we can as it were bootstrap ourselves into the Hobbesian situation through various institutional means that either provide the economically or socially disadvantaged with political clout or increase the uncertainty under which all parties labour (say, by extending the temporal horizon over which political decisions range), or again that neutralize power differentials by requiring of individuals that they provide impartially acceptable reasons for their political behaviour. Democracy and the extension of the democratic franchise, constitutionalism, and institutions that increase accountability and transparency in the political decision-making process are in Goodin's view interpretable as institutional mechanisms that place us artificially in a Hobbesian situation, and that thus induce support for reciprocity-based policies, where the concern is that moral motives might at the moment of decision prove ineffective as compared to more narrowly self-centered ones.

A significant difference between the kinds of cases discussed by Goodin and those that concern us in the context of this collection of chapters is of course that he is thinking primarily of ways in which durable support for morally defensible policies can be achieved within the context of existing states. One can, for example, well imagine myriad ways in which the electoral system can be used in order to level the playing field by giving democratic power to individuals and groups who lack economic and social clout. Beyond the mere extension of the franchise to qualified individuals previously excluded for arbitrary reasons, there are any number of institutional devices that can be used to offset politically the impact of economic power and social status (Guinier 1995). States have many institutional mechanisms at their disposal with which to "engineer" Hobbesian situations where none spontaneously emerges.

Does this mean that the kinds of institutional devices envisaged by Goodin to parlay people's self-interest into support for ethically defensible policies are unavailable to those who would advocate distributively just policies at the global level? There is clearly no agent at the global level comparable to the state that might create Hobbesian situations leading to people seeing their fates as bound up with each other's to a degree sufficient to motivate certain kinds of communal solidarity. Does the absence of such an agent mean that Goodin's observations are irrelevant to the global context? Not necessarily. The global context may *already* constitute a Hobbesian context of the kind that in Goodin's view tends to generate prudential grounds for basic moral dealings among persons.

The question thus arises whether there is a prudence-based argument that might show that we are already in a Hobbesian situation with the world's neediest populations, thus bypassing the need for the kinds of institutional artifices that are possible within the context of established political agents, most notably nation-states.

At first glance, this might seem a daunting task. It seems depressingly easy simply to forget about the needs and interests of the world's poorest populations. The differentials in power and wealth separating the populations of the world's richest and poorest countries are, to say the least, staggering, and there are no institutional levers to speak of that might be employed by the poor in order to induce reciprocal behaviour on the part of the rich.

Closer inspection reveals that there are in fact numerous prudence-based arguments that might be used by those who hope that a sense of community uniting the world's populations might come to emerge. In fact, some of the chief concerns of the citizens of well-to-do societies can quite plausibly be connected to the plight of the world's poorest populations. These concerns have to do with the spread of infectious disease, with the development of networks of global terrorists increasingly emboldened to carry out destructive actions in affluent countries, and with the degradation of the natural environment and the depletion of global natural resources (Kaul, Grunberg, and Stern 1999). There are, in other words, "global public goods"—that is, goods that the world's richest countries cannot obtain unless the needs of the global poor are catered to as well.

The link between poverty and infectious disease is probably clearest, and was dramatized in recent years by persistent fears of a bird-flu pandemic, in the case of infectious disease. To put the causal relation in its most basic form, there is a high correlation between poverty and poor hygienic conditions, and poor hygienic conditions are efficient breeding grounds for the proliferation of infectious diseases, including, in cases in which humans and animals live in close proximity with inadequate hygienic safeguards, of "virgin soil" viruses with which the immune systems of even the world's healthiest people might be unable to cope (Farmer 2001). Though the eradication of poverty, leading to the improvement of public health and hygiene conditions in the world's poorest countries, would clearly not spell an end to infectious disease, it would represent one of the most efficient means at our disposal to contain the spread of the deadliest viruses in as much as it would make the "species barrier" more robust.

It is striking just how little this causal connection has been exploited by promoters of a global justice agenda. Researchers attempting to define a range of global public goods represent a prominent exception (Chen, Evans, and Cash 1999). Though public fears over the spread of deadly viruses are, to put it mildly, highly mobilizable, the agenda in the fight against a global bird-flu pandemic has been defined by pharmaceutical companies that have convinced (gulled?) developed nations the world over into investing vast sums in stockpiling antiviral drugs of questionable efficacy, rather than tackling the problem at its root, in the poor public health conditions, born of poverty, that are acting like so many Petri dishes the world over. Clearly, there is a potentially very motivationally effective prudential argument connecting a public health priority in the world's richest countries with the alleviation of the squalid conditions in which a significant number of the world's population lives, an argument that has not been exploited to its fullest extent.

Another context within which we arguably find ourselves in a Hobbesian situation with respect to the world's poor countries has to do with the global environment. Fears about the degradation of the natural environment, about climate change, and about the depletion of the world's natural resources have moved to the top of the political agenda in the minds of many citizens of the world's richest countries. Public debate, crystallized by the Kyoto protocol, has tended to focus on the responsibilities that the rich countries of the world have to lessen their enormous environmental footprints. Without wanting in the slightest to underestimate the importance of measures that might be taken by rich northern countries to put their environmental houses in order, there has been a tendency, at least in public debate, to neglect the myriad connections between global poverty and environmental risk. It has been fairly well established that poverty and poor environmental practices co-exist in many countries in a vicious circle, the impacts of which are impossible to contain within national boundaries. Poverty creates a short-term incentive towards resource stripping, both at a macro-level (for example, as a matter of economic policy aimed at finding quick fixes to debt crises) and at a micro-level, leading communities to engage in practices that are in the long term detrimental, such as deforestation, in order to meet short-term needs. The desire to catch up with the rich countries of the north has, moreover, led countries in which poverty is endemic, such as China and India, to embark on development policies that are clearly unsustainable on the global scale. Here again it seems that the connection of an agenda that is very much at the forefront of the political agendas of rich countries might be usefully connected to the cause of global poverty alleviation (Caney 2008).

Finally, and perhaps most controversially, I will mention the connection between global economic injustice and the spread of terrorism. While it is true that the perpetrators of the most dramatic terrorist acts of recent years were not themselves drawn from the most indigent segments of the populations to which they belong, it is nonetheless the case that they presented themselves as acting on behalf of disenfranchised and economically marginalized populations, and against countries in Europe and North America that stand at the summit of the economic ladder. Though the purported link between global injustices and inequalities is under fire from many economists and political scientists, all the number crunching in the world cannot totally eradicate the suspicion that the anger and the desperation that seem to drive many terrorist organizations would not find fertile soil in the minds of as many people were economic opportunity more fairly distributed on the global level (Leblanc 2008).

Thus, it might very well be the case that there are prudence-based arguments to be made for a global egalitarian agenda that does not require the institutional bootstrapping described by Goodin in his book. Global poverty represents a threat for the citizens of the world's richest countries because it increases public health, environmental, and security risks to which these constituencies are keenly attuned. There are thus existing motivational hooks to which the cause of global demos building might be hitched, without the need for the kind of institutional engineering that according to Goodin is needed to bring the citizens of advanced nation-states into a Hobbesian situation.

Another way of putting the same point is this. According to what one might term a romantic conception of solidarity and community, individuals are disposed to act in a communal and solidaristic manner towards one another because they share an identity. Prominent among solidarity-promoting identities are *national* identities. According to what one might term a Hobbesian theory, we act in such manner with respect to individuals whose non-co-operation represents a threat for us. The first section of this chapter sought to show that the second theory is actually more plausible than the first. But even if the argument of that section were judged to be unsuccessful, the project of motivating the global demos could find support in the considerations adduced here, which suggest that with respect to some of the issues that are seen by them as being of gravest concern to them, citizens of the world's riches countries would stand to gain from seeing their lot as tied to that of the world's poor to a far greater degree than they currently do. Both theories point to complementary sources of communal affiliation, and builders of the global demos can avail themselves of the mechanisms that are at the center of the second.

Community Building Through Instrumental Appeals to Morality

I have up to now been considering a worst-case scenario from a motivational standpoint. The question I have been asking is: Is there a way of motivating a sense of global solidarity and community, absent any moral motivation on the part of those whose decisions will determine whether or not such policies get put in place? I have concluded that naked self-interest provides us with a number of motivational hooks for such solidarity.

But, of course, the pessimistic assumption under which I have been labouring thus far is probably too sombre. In this section I want to examine some of the moral quandaries that arise under the probably more realistic assumption that most people do feel that we have obligations with respect to the world's neediest people.

The point of departure of the remarks in this section rests upon a piece of armchair sociology, to be confirmed or refuted by the real kind: most people in developed countries feel that the condition of poverty in which a vast proportion of the world's population lives is a moral problem, one that generates moral obligations on their part. But they have no stable *theory* about what it is about poverty that raises the moral problem, what causal role we have in maintaining that poverty, and what the nature and the extent of our obligations are.

Consider a number of possibilities. These are all constructed out of materials culled from the works of prominent political philosophers, which will be immediately familiar to followers of recent debates around global justice.

1) The poverty under which many in the world live is caused in large part by corrupt governments and bad policy decisions taken in those countries. We are in no way responsible for the plight of these populations, nor are we connected with them

economically or politically in ways that would activate concerns of distributive justice within the context of a nation-state. Still, there is an obligation to help "burdened" societies reach a state in which they can begin to exercise political agency. There is also an obligation to act in the case of humanitarian crises, such as floods and famines (Rawls 1999; Miller 2007).

2) The density of trade and commerce that exists in the world today, and the fact that this activity takes place in the context of rules set by transnational institutions such as the World Bank, the World Trade Organization, and the International Monetary Fund, mean that there exists a global "basic structure," one within which it makes sense to speak of distributive justice and injustice on a par with the situation that obtains within nation-states (Caney 2005).

3) The poverty and suffering that characterize much of the world today are the result of human rights violations perpetrated by the rich countries of the world, via the rules governing the international economy that they impose upon the world's poorer countries (Pogge 2008). We have an obligation to desist from the perpetration of such violations of rights.

4) We have an obligation to distribute resources in a manner that maximizes the utility that can be derived from them. This means that inequality represents a moral problem independently of questions of responsibility for the creation of poverty. The rich of the world should address that problem by transferring resources to the poor up to the point where any further transfer would generate disutility on a par with the utility that it would generate (Singer 1972).

Followers of debates about global distributive justice would have no difficulty putting names to these statements even if I had presented them without attribution. Needless to say, they differ greatly on all the important philosophical issues. They would not agree on the kind of bad that poverty is, on the degree of responsibility borne by the world's richest countries in the creation of that poverty, or on the extent of the demandingness of the duty that we have with respect to the global poor.

That said, there is, from a policy perspective, probably a great deal of convergence between the positions just described. That is, they all agree that it would be a good thing if policy in rich countries gave greater importance to the interests of the poor. Even a holder of the least demanding view would probably see the paltry sums devoted to foreign aid as miserly, and their increase as admirable, even if such an increase were not an obligation of justice, *stricto sensu*. Politically feasible increases in development aid and poverty relief probably all fall within the range of obligation specified by each of these theories.

The question I want to raise is, What if it turns out that the theory that lies closest to moral truth on this issue is less motivationally efficacious than a more obviously wrong one? Are there limits, in other words, on the extent to which global community builders can make instrumental use of moral argument? This is an important question for the present inquiry because it touches on the moral limits that would-be global community builders should observe in exploiting the context created by the incompletely theorized moral concerns that many people have about the plight of the world's least fortunate populations. Should they use arguments that they view as philosophically lacking but motivationally efficacious?

There are, of course, analogous debates at the nation-state level. In a very important book, *Negotiating Nationalism*, Wayne Norman has considered the question of whether the susceptibility of people to nationalist arguments should be exploited for ethical ends. Norman asks himself whether arguments for policies towards which citizens might not be naturally disposed—policies of wealth redistribution, for example—should be argued for by making use of nationalist rhetoric ("Sharing is what our nation is *really* about"), or whether there are risks and moral obstacles to such instrumental uses of motivationally efficacious arguments that ought to stand in the way (Norman 2006).

Consider the following possibility, which has at least the air of psychological plausibility about it. It is difficult for people to accept responsibility for a wrong, especially in the absence of a smoking gun, when the causal chains connecting them to the wrong in question are not obvious. People by and large like feeling good about themselves, and if presented with an account of a harm that casts them in a bad light they may be inclined to attempt to deny the account that underpins their being cast in that manner, unless incontrovertible evidence of their complicity is presented to them (Unger 1996).

Or consider this: theories that present our obligations of redistribution towards the poor as being extensive might end up being motivationally disabling. Even those individuals who are antecedently disposed to viewing themselves as having responsibilities towards the world's poor may reach the conclusion that they could never live up to the level of obligation that these theories specify. Helping a little may on such a theory end up being morally only vanishingly better than not helping at all, so why bother? (Singer 1993) Consider on the other hand theories that cast our obligations as lying in the domain of the supererogatory. These theories tell the global rich that the poverty of much of the world's population, though tragic, is not something they should feel responsible for. Nor is there strictly anything wrong with their continuing to disregard their plight. According to such theories, aid, though not required, is admirable. Those who engage in it go above and beyond what morality and justice in the strict sense require. Or consider a view that would attempt to represent the bulk of our obligations as assimilable to the mere respect of beneficiaries, negative rights, such respect being at the core of a rather minimalist conception of morality to which most people might be expected to subscribe.

Now what if it were to turn out that theoretical accounts of the moral relationship between rich and poor countries that came closest to the truth were the ones that ascribed greatest responsibility to the governments and citizens of rich countries, and that imposed the most demanding obligations upon them, whereas the most motivationally efficacious theoretical accounts were the ones that presented the moral relationship as devoid of any dimension of responsibility, and as supererogatory rather than obligatory? What considerations might weigh for and against using the theory that stood the most chance of motivating ethical behaviour?

Let me rule out the extreme positions on either side of this debate, those that intuitively seem too permissive and too restrictive, respectively. A crude utilitarian, on the one hand, would be inclined to assess the worth of all arguments on purely instrumental grounds. Any form of deception would be justified if it generated morally desirable results. An orthodox Kantian would just as implausibly condemn any argument that led people to perform actions which conform to moral rules but the motive of which was morally lacking. Neither position need detain us in the present context. What philosophical guidance can we provide promoters of a global demos pondering the rightness of instrumental uses of moral arguments geared to motivating political community among the world's populations?

One could claim that there are many *reasonable* theories designed to make sense of our moral obligations towards the global poor.[1] The four theories sketched above would certainly fall into this category. They are still very much in play in the philosophical literature, and while authors who advocate one or the other of these theories often do so passionately, they do not go so far as to say that advocates of other theories are unreasonable or irrational. Clearly, they believe them to be *mistaken*, but this is not quite as strong a condemnation as is the claim that someone is being unreasonable. Crudely, the former is an epistemic judgment, while the latter connotes moral condemnation as well. When I say of someone that she is mistaken but not unreasonable, I am saying that I can see how, from her perspective, she might see things the way she does, and that I might see things in the same way were I in her shoes. When I say of someone that she is not only mistaken but unreasonable to boot, I am

---

[1] I am obviously aware of the philosophical controversies surrounding the notion of "reasonableness" as it has emerged in the literatures on political liberalism and on deliberative democracy. Considerations of space require that I forgo specification of the concept for present purposes. I have proffered my own conception in Weinstock 2006b.

saying that she should not hold the view that she does, even given her particular vantage point.

Arguments formulated on the basis of theories that fall within this set are clearly not open to the same moral condemnations as are arguments based on theories that fall outside the set. But it is one thing to say that *arguments* formulated in the terms of a reasonable theory are themselves reasonable, and quite another to say that an *individual* making use of reasonable theories, to which he does not himself subscribe, merely for the purposes of persuading is not acting duplicitously and thus immorally. Should we not limit ourselves to making public arguments on the basis of theories to which we actually subscribe?

A first consideration to be brought to bear in answering this question would emphasize the fact that the judgment that a theory is reasonable is actually a form of endorsement. To say that a reasonable person could endorse a theory is to say that under different circumstances (say, had the burdens of judgment applied to me in ways just slightly different from the ways in which they actually did), I might have been led to endorse it too.

A second, perhaps more controversial ingredient of a response would follow John Rawls in elevating reasonableness, as opposed to truth, to the position of primary epistemic value in a political context (Rawls 1992). Truth-claims foreclose political debate; they are thus problematic in a democratic context. Taking seriously the "political" turn in political philosophy pioneered by Rawls means accepting a certain epistemic humility. It means recognizing that reasonable people can continue to disagree, and that justified political positions will emerge from consensuses and compromises achieved among them, rather than through the imposition of one party's "true" position upon all others.

If we accept these two claims, the formulation of ethical arguments on the basis of reasonable theories to which one does not oneself subscribe takes on a slightly different colour. Rather than simple duplicity, it involves making arguments on the basis of considerations that are part of the pool of reasonable theories among which a political liberal will seek to construct an "overlapping consensus."

There are thus reasons that militate in favour of making arguments on the basis of theories to which one does not subscribe, so long as one views them as reasonable. Note that this argument has the advantage both of providing a plausible rationale for strategies of persuasion of this kind and of indicating clear limits to this permission. Clearly, even effective arguments grounded in unreasonable theories are on this view morally excluded.

There are important considerations on the other side of the moral ledger, however. Let me emphasize the following. If we attempt to mobilize public support for morally defensible policies on the wrong moral grounds, the grounds that we adduce in this specific context may come back to haunt us the next time an attempt is made to generate support for the right policies. That is, it may be that an appeal to the most easily mobilizable moral emotion will allow us to achieve a particular urgent end. The risk, however, is that the most natural implications of the principles we will have ended up inculcating will serve us ill in subsequent policy debates. Moral appeals that simply attempt to ignite people's moral sympathies by dramatizing the suffering of the global poor, and that attempt to make them feel good about themselves by sending charity, may prove more effective in the short term, but they do not form a citizenry reliably disposed to act in the right way in situations in which such appeals are unavailable—for example, because the moral stakes are not as dramatic, and therefore not as dramatizable.

So there are fairly weighty considerations available on both sides of the question of whether one ought to employ moral arguments that one thinks weaker but that one suspects might be more effective at motivating compliance with morally justified policies, the true justification of which is to be found on other grounds. I suspect that these considerations are sufficiently weighty to rule out the extreme (Kantian and unreconstructed utilitarian) positions according to which such appeals are either required or prohibited. Rather, the position towards which I am inclined is to the effect that such appeals are permissible within certain bounds. Those bounds include (at least) the requirement that the argument being put forward be possessed of philosophical plausibility, as evidenced at least by its continued presence as a live option in philosophical debates, as one that we will have to include in an eventual overlapping consensus or compromise concerning what we will take to be the truth about our moral obligations with respect to the world's poorest persons.

Conclusion

Let me briefly summarize the argument that has been developed in the past three sections. I have argued, first, that large-scale nations are the result of political artifice, from which believers in the possibility and desirability of a global demos can learn. Second, I have suggested that citizens of rich and of poor countries find themselves bound across a variety of contexts in a Hobbesian situation that provides the global rich with prudential reasons to view their fates as bound up with those of the global poor in ways that militate in favour of their seeing their fates as linked to the fates of the global poor. A first artifice that might then be employed by would-be global demos builders is to make those contexts plain, and to draw up policy proposals that speak to them. Third, I have suggested that though some philosophers may believe in theories accounting for the relationship between the global poor and the global rich that are least conducive to being used in campaigns of persuasion aimed at fostering global community, there are perhaps fewer obstacles than they may have supposed in making use of more "congenial" theories for persuasive purposes, so long as they are "reasonable."

The two parts of my arguments are intended as illustrations of a much broader research agenda. This agenda, which would require the collaboration of normative political theorists and of historians, would consist in a careful study of the tools that nation builders have made use of in their (largely successful) enterprise of creating a sense of community on the basis of what must at first glance seem like fairly unpromising materials. Those interested in the cosmopolitan agenda should give thought to ways in which such tools can be adapted to the global context. And since the nation builders of yore often made use of rather illiberal means, additional reflection must address the issue of the moral boundaries that should be respected in all attempts to foster the kind of sense of community on the global scale capable of underpinning democratic institutions.

My hunch is that what we would end up with is a rather messy set of disparate tools that do not necessarily refer back to some pleasing overarching theory of community building. Just as nation builders manifested a great deal of opportunism in mobilizing psychological and moral susceptibilities in the service of what they took to be the morally important task of nation building, so cosmopolitans will have to learn to employ a wide range of different kinds of arguments for the purpose of motivating the global demos.

Acknowledgments

Earlier versions of this chapter were presented at the Internationale Vereinigung für Rechts- und Sozialphilosophie congress in Kraków in August 2007 in a panel entitled "Global Justice," convened by Margaret Moore, and at a workshop entitled "Intentions and Motivations in International Relations," organized in May 2008 at the University of Montreal by Ryoa Chung. I wish to thank participants at both venues for helpful comments. Thanks also to Patti Lenard, who provided extensive written comments on an earlier draft.

References

Anderson, Benedict. 2006. *Imagined Communities*. 2nd edition. New York: Verso.

Bell, David A. 2001. *The Cult of the Nation in France*. Cambridge, Mass.: Harvard University Press.

Billig, Michael. 1995. *Banal Nationalism*. London: Sage.

Caney, Simon. 2005. "Global Interdependence and Distributive Justice." *Review of International Studies* 31, no. 2:389–99.

————. 2008. "Justice, Climate Change, and Motivation." Paper presented to the workshop entitled "Intentions and Motivations in International Relations," University of Montreal, May 2008.

Chen, Lincoln C., Tim G. Evans, and Richard A. Cash. 1999. "Health as a Global Public Good." In Kaul, Grunberg, and Stern 1999, 284–306.

Farmer, Paul. 2001. *Infections and Inequalities: The Modern Plagues.* Berkeley: University of California Press.

Goodin, Robert. 1992. *Motivating Political Morality.* Oxford: Basil Blackwell.

Guinier, Lani. 1995. *The Tyranny of the Majority.* New York: Free Press.

Kaul, Inge, Isabelle Grunberg, and Marc Stern (eds.). 1999. *Global Public Goods: International Cooperation in the 21st Century.* Oxford: Oxford University Press.

Kymlicka, Will. 2001. *Politics in the Vernacular.* Oxford: Oxford University Press.

Leblanc, Martin. 2008. "Éthique et violence politique: Repenser la réponse des démocraties libérales à la menace terroriste." Ph.D. thesis, Department of Philosophy, University of Montreal.

Lenard, Patti Tamara. 2006. "Motivating Cosmopolitanism? A Sceptical, but Not Pessimistic View." Paper presented at the American Political Science Association convention, Chicago, 2007.

Miller, David. 1993. "In Defence of Nationality." *Journal of Applied Philosophy* 10, no. 1:3–16.

————. 1995. *On Nationality.* Oxford: Oxford University Press.

————. 2000. *Citizenship and National Identity.* Oxford: Polity Press.

————. 2007. *National Responsibility and Global Justice.* Oxford: Oxford University Press.

Norman, Wayne. 2006. *Negotiating Nationalism.* Oxford: Oxford University Press.

Pogge, Thomas. 2008. *World Poverty and Human Rights.* 2nd edition. Oxford: Polity Press.

Rawls, John. 1992. *Political Liberalism.* New York: Columbia University Press.

————. 1999. *The Law of Peoples.* Cambridge, Mass.: Harvard University Press.

Singer, Peter. 1972. "Famine, Affluence and Morality." *Philosophy and Public Affairs* 1, no. 1:229–43.

————. 1993. *Practical Ethics.* Cambridge: Cambridge University Press.

Tan, Kok-Chor. 2005. "Cosmopolitan Impartiality and Patriotic Partiality." In Daniel Weinstock (ed.), *Global Justice, Global Institutions,* 165–92 (*Canadian Journal of Philosophy,* supplementary volume 31). Calgary: University of Calgary Press.

Unger, Peter. 1996. *Living High and Letting Die: Our Illusion of Innocence.* Oxford: Oxford University Press.

Weinstock, Daniel. 1999. "National Partiality: Confronting the Intuitions." *Monist* 82, no. 3:516–41.

———. 2001a. "Prospects for Transnational Citizenship and Democracy." *Ethics and International Affairs* 15, no. 2:53–66.

———. 2001b. "Saving Democracy from Deliberation." In Ronald Beiner and Wayne Norman (eds.), *Canadian Political Philosophy*, 78–92. Oxford: Oxford University Press.

———. 2006a. "The Real World of (Global) Democracy." *Journal of Social Philosophy* 37, no. 1:6–20.

———. 2006b. "A Neutral Conception of Reasonableness." *Episteme* 3, no. 3:234–47.

12

IS LIBERAL NATIONALISM INCOMPATIBLE WITH GLOBAL DEMOCRACY?

HELDER DE SCHUTTER AND RONALD TINNEVELT

1. Introduction

Processes of globalization have provoked a surge of normative analyses of forms of justice and democracy above the level of the nation-state. To counteract the negative effects of these processes, cosmopolitans such as Thomas Pogge, Charles Beitz, David Held, and Jürgen Habermas have defended global principles of distributive justice and/or a system of global governance.

Since the early 1990s, however, normative political theory has also witnessed a renewed normative defense of nationhood. This has led to the emergence of liberal nationalism. Liberal nationalists—such as Margaret Canovan, Chaim Gans, Will Kymlicka, David Miller, Margaret Moore, and Yael Tamir—are essentially committed to the belief that liberalism is compatible with a defense of the value of national identity and of national self-determination.

On the face of it, this is ironic: at a time when individuals and states are increasingly outgrowing the nation-state paradigm, some normative theorists are reemphasizing the importance of national belonging and nationally bounded political communities. It might seem, then, that enthusiasm for forms of global (or supranational) justice and democracy is fundamentally opposed to nationalist ideals and concerns about the value of national identity, and, vice versa, that liberal nationalism is inherently incompatible with global justice and democracy.

Proponents of this oppositional picture can be found both among nationalists and among cosmopolitans. Often the former are accused by the latter of being backward-looking romantic collectivists who nurse forlorn hopes of restoring an outdated Westphalian world order. Alternatively, proponents of global justice or democracy are often portrayed by nationalists as neoliberals striving for a new world order without any meaningful identities or attachment between people.

We do not share this highly oppositional picture. It does not do justice to either of the two positions. Nationalists are not necessarily conservative rejecters of global egalitarianism or transnational institutions like the European Union, and there is no reason why moral and political cosmopolitans could not endorse national identities or affirm the importance of national self-determination. We believe it is possible to come up with a conception of the importance of nationhood that does not preclude the legitimacy and desirability of supranational forms of justice and democracy. Developing this more *harmonic* picture of nationalist ideals and cosmopolitan visions is the aim of this chapter.

In particular, we focus here on the compatibility of liberal nationalism with forms of global *democracy*, leaving aside the issue of global distributive *justice* (such as questions about global egalitarianism).[1] So in what follows we develop a negative answer to the question, Is liberal nationalism incompatible with global democracy?[2]

We proceed as follows: we first clarify the terms of the discussion, defining both liberal nationalism and global democracy; we then systematically analyze whether any of the central tenets of liberal nationalism necessarily involve a rejection of global democracy, and work out a point-by-point rebuttal of the incompatibility thesis;[3] and finally we examine one possible objection to our thesis, based on the view that (national) identity requires exclusion.

We will not set out to justify independently either liberal nationalism or global democracy. For the purposes of this chapter, we take as given the existence both of liberal nationalism *and* of claims for forms of democracy beyond the nation. Our claim is simply that *if* you are a liberal nationalist, there is no internal theoretical necessity for you to reject global democratic commitments. For anyone who is committed to either liberal nationalism or global democracy, the results of this project, if successful, offer hope, since in each case they eliminate one crucial source of opposition to the defended cause.

2. Defining the Terms

2.1. What Is Liberal Nationalism?

Because an argument about the compatibility of liberal nationalism with global democracy will hinge on what we take those terms to mean, it is important to explain our understanding of them. What is liberal nation-

---

[1] For the compatibility of liberal nationalism with global distributive *justice*, see Tan 2004 and 2005.

[2] For an example of the *incompatibility* thesis of liberal nationalism and global democracy, see Brock 2002.

[3] We focus on liberal nationalism's compatibility with global democracy, not on how theories of global democracy are compatible with liberal nationalism. While both undertakings are logically equivalent, they involve different argumentative strategies. We focus on liberal nationalism internally, and show why none of its premises necessarily involves a rejection of global democracy.

alism? In general, liberal nationalism's main feature is that "it fosters national ideals without losing sight of other human values against which national ideals ought to be weighed" (Tamir 1993, 79). Thus understood, it is primarily a very moderate nationalism, a nationalism stripped of the illiberal tendencies it has acquired in the course of its history.

More specifically, liberal nationalism has, as its name suggests, a liberal and a nationalist component. Its basic aim is to show that both components can be reconciled. Nationalism need not be inherently illiberal, and liberalism does not have to be inherently antinationalist. Let's look at each feature in turn.

The *liberal* characteristic of liberal nationalism is exhibited by the belief that individual rights should not be overridden by group rights, as well as by the stipulation that nationalism has to be "moderate." Liberal nationalist policies are not aggressive toward other national identities and typically expose a "thin" or open conception of national identity. This thin view ensures that in principle everyone can join the nation. Liberal nationalism is thus very different from race-based and ethnicity- or descent-based forms of nationalism. It is essentially cultural and linguistic in nature (see, e.g., Kymlicka 1995 and 2001a).

The essence of the *nationalism* of liberal nationalism is the belief that national identities matter, that the state should protect and promote them, and that it is desirable that the boundaries of political units coincide with national (and linguistic) units.[4] Based on this, liberal nationalists argue that liberal democratic communities should be national communities. The reasons given for these conclusions all have to do with the furthering of important *goods* which are both liberal democratic in nature and which can best be provided in national units. The three most crucial goods are: identity, social justice, and deliberative democracy.

The *first* is the good of national identity. Liberal nationalists believe that national identity is valuable and that it should be politically protected. Different accounts have been given for why national identity matters. On the very influential account of Will Kymlicka, for instance, national identity matters because it is a precondition of the liberal ideal of autonomy. To be autonomous, individuals need a national, cultural, and linguistic background, which makes available a diversity of options and thus offers us a "context of choice" (Kymlicka 1995, 83).

That is the first reason why liberal nationalists believe that infusing nations with political self-determination is a valuable good: it is likely to foster the ability for people to have their interest in identity satisfied by having a separate political context within which the nation is central. Note that this does not necessarily lead to secession into fully independent

---

[4] Versions of this normative recommendation to (re)draw political boundaries around national units are defended in Gans 2003, Kymlicka 2001b, Miller 1995, Moore 2001a, and Tamir 1993.

separate nation-states. Although some liberal nationalists do believe full self-determination (and secession) to be the best possible outcome, both those who believe this and those who don't believe it explicitly endorse the idea of *multinational* states and adhere to a *federal* solution for realizing multinational justice.[5] More specifically, they often endorse federalism *because* they consider it to be a mechanism for recognizing claims to self-determination. Multinational federalism is then supported as a way of giving national groups the ability to exercise territorial self-determination (Kymlicka 2001a, 91–119, and 2001b, 249–75).

The *second* good is that of social or distributive justice.[6] Redistributive policies presuppose that people are willing to make sacrifices for "anonymous others whom we do not know, will probably never meet, and whose ethnic descent, religion and way of life differs from our own" (Kymlicka 2001a, 225). This kind of sacrifice requires a high level of trust—trust that sacrifices will be reciprocated. The principle of nationality (which sets out to draw political boundaries around national boundaries) and (liberal) nation-building can create such a common bond between individuals that will increase their willingness to make those sacrifices.

The *third* argument is that shared nationality is conducive to deliberative democracy. This is the case not only because deliberative forms of democracy presuppose that people can understand each other and because a shared nationality (including a shared language) enhances mutual understanding, but also because the success of democracy hinges to a large extent on the belief (or the trust) that others are genuinely willing to consider your own views, and that others will in the future also be willing to moderate their claims in order to reach common ground or consensus if you do so now (Kymlicka 2001a, 226–27, and 2001b, 266; Miller 1995, 96–98).

2.2. Global Democracy?

Within the current literature there is no generally accepted definition of global democracy. Although several justifications of the idea of democracy beyond national borders have been developed, their understandings of what democracy entails are quite distinct (see for instance McGrew 1999, 232, versus Gould 2004, 173). Therefore, in what follows we use a fairly broad working definition of (forms of) global democracy. We understand proposals for "forms of global democracy" to include all proposals for forms of democratic supranational decision-making—that

[5] For the first view, see Miller 1995, 82; for the second view, see Kymlicka 1995 and Tamir 1993.

[6] See Miller 1995, 83–85, 98; Kymlicka 2001a, 225–26; and Tamir 1993, 117–21. Here we use "social justice" and "distributive justice" interchangeably. Miller distinguishes both (see Miller 2007, 12–13).

is, decision-making *above* the level of the nation—as far as these endorse both (i) supranational institutions that make decision-making possible and (ii) the view that these institutions must be democratic—that is, these institutions should enable people to participate freely in the political process.

The *first*, institutional feature is included in the definition in order to oppose global democracy to a purely state-based system, whereby international negotiations or agreements between states occur without supranational institutions or organizations of any kind.[7] The *second*, democratic feature is included in order to oppose it to those views that argue for global political institutions, but that either see no need for holding these institutions democratically accountable or don't think they can be democratized.

This definition leaves two things open. First, it does not specify which specific form the democratization of these institutions should take. Possible forms of global democracy include "global social democracy" (Held 2004), "a world polity without a world state" (Habermas 2006), "a world parliament" (Monbiot 2003), a "world republic" (Höffe 1999), "democratic networks" (Gould 2004), "directly-deliberative polyarchy" (Cohen and Sabel 2003), "global federalism" (Marchetti 2008), and "consociational democracy" (Moore 2006).

This definition of global democracy also leaves open whether these supranational democratic institutions are really global in scope, since the definition encompasses all attempts, including subglobal ones, to realize forms of democracy above the level of the nation: this comprises supranational associations like the European Union as well as near-global or fully global institutions like the United Nations.

Thus understood, global democracy involves features of political cosmopolitanism. Political cosmopolitanism refers to the view that democratic supranational (ultimately global) institutions are legitimate and/or should be erected to cope with problems related to globalization. This view has to be carefully distinguished from cultural and moral cosmopolitanism. We understand cultural cosmopolitanism as the view that cultural identities are global in scope; we understand moral cosmopolitanism as a view about the global scope of our duties of (distributive) justice.

3. The Global Democratic Potentials of Liberal Nationalism's Main Tenets

Global democrats argue that nation-states can no longer be the sole units of liberal democratic decision-making. Instead, they believe that anyone who adheres to liberal democratic values should today be committed to

[7] This does not imply that such a system cannot be highly organized. Compare Walzer's definition of international hierarchy (Walzer 2003, 127–73).

realizing forms of democracy above the level of the nation-state. Now, all liberal nationalists are also liberal democrats. The question therefore emerges whether liberal nationalism can support attempts to realize democracy at supranational levels. To answer this question, let us analyze the three central tenets of liberal nationalism discussed above, and see if they involve a rejection of global democracy.

In doing so, we do not directly answer the question whether liberalism in itself is compatible with global democracy. That is, we do not look at whether the *liberal* dimensions of liberal nationalism (such as the focus on individual rights) are compatible with a defense of forms of global democracy. Instead, we are interested in what is distinctive to liberal nationalism, and we focus on the coherence of the liberal *nationalist* assumptions with the case for global democracy.

3.1. The Identity Argument

The identity argument is perhaps the most crucial argument for liberal nationalists. It states that liberal democratic political communities should promote national identities and should themselves be national in scope because of the value of national identity. Is a theory that focuses on the value of national identities incompatible with global democracy? We argue that there is nothing in the argument that people should have access to their national identity context that necessarily precludes participating in political contexts larger than the national culture itself.

We can see why this is the case by looking at the two conclusions that liberal nationalists draw from the value of cultural identity. The *first* states that because national cultures are valuable, political communities should actively set out to enable, protect, and promote national cultural contexts. This is a conclusion regarding the type of *policy* that political communities should adopt vis-à-vis national communities. While others might think that cultural and national identities should not be promoted by state policies, liberal nationalists believe that they should. Let's call this the *policy* conclusion. This conclusion can be distinguished from a second, *authority* conclusion. The authority conclusion does not involve the specific sort of policy that political communities should adopt but instead involves a view as to *who* should design this policy, who should have the authority to make the policies. While some may hold the view that national identities should have no bearing on state structures, liberal nationalists hold that, given the value of national identity, nations should be self-determining.

3.1.1. The Policy Conclusion

Does the policy conclusion conflict with forms of global democracy? It is hard to see how it could. Proposals for expanding the level of democracy do not in themselves involve content-based claims as to which policies would be legitimately decided upon in these supranational forums.[8] So supporters of forms of global democracy need not deny the argument that national identities are worthy of protection. The issue of the scope and appropriate level of decision-making is orthogonal to the issue of the promotion of national identity. Given, then, that the pursuit of global democracy does not in itself entail the abolition or downplaying of national identities, there is no inherent clash between liberal nationalism's commitment to safeguard national identities and forms of global democracy.

To put this differently, the policy version of liberal nationalism—the view that the nation is a protection-worthy source of identity—is merely opposed to cultural cosmopolitanism, the view that cultural identities are *global* instead of national in scope. It cannot in itself deny political cosmopolitanism, the view that democratic supranational institutions are legitimate and needed.

This line of reasoning may face the objection that while in theory there is no incompatibility between promoting national identities and forms of global democracy, in practice the latter will very likely lead to a rejection of the importance of promoting national identity. But this worry cannot be sustained by current supranational political practices. In today's globalizing world, the cultural identities of nations are often better promoted if these nations join supranational institutions than if they don't. For instance, the fate of small nations' identities in Europe is significantly strengthened symbolically by the European Union's official language policy. As a result of this policy, the official status of languages spoken by few, like Danish and Irish, is equal to the official status of languages spoken by many, like Italian and Spanish. The practical compatibility of global democracy and the protection of national cultures is also illustrated by the spirit behind initiatives like the Council of Europe's *Framework Convention for the Protection of National Minorities* (1995), which sets out to protect national minorities and create appropriate conditions enabling national minorities to preserve their culture and retain their identity.

Given such indications of the practical harmony of global democracy and national protection, it is not surprising that many small nations in the world have not opposed participation in larger political associations. Forms of supranational democracy are often felt not as an infringement of their sovereignty but as international recognition of their being a global conversation partner of equal standing.

Perhaps one might object that this may hold for small but not for more powerful nations, who may be thought to have much to lose from joining supranational institutions. However, even the national identity of larger European states can be strengthened by joining the European Union. The European media program subsidizes, for instance, French and German movies.

---

[8] We do not examine the difference between formal and substantial models of democracy.

But even *if* powerful nations ultimately see some of their power transferred to smaller nations (as a result of joining supranational democratic institutions or as a result of supranational policies that aim to protect national identities), this is a fact that liberal nationalists can accept. Liberal nationalism is not an expression of the self-interested desire to retain the power of particular nations; it is a political theory that sets out to defend the equal rights to national identity of all nations. In majority-minority disputes over political boundaries in multinational states, for instance, liberal nationalists typically defend the equal rights of national minorities.

3.1.2. The Authority Conclusion

What about the compatibility of the *authority* conclusion with forms of global democracy? The authority conclusion clearly presents—at least at first sight—a more serious challenge to the idea of supranational decision-making. This is the case because the authority conclusion is intended as a justification of national political units. It derives a reason for national self-determination out of the value of national identity. In endorsing this conclusion, liberal nationalists think it is legitimate and desirable for nations to be self-governing *as* nations. Forms of global democracy, however, include nonnational forms of self-determination and are thereby logically incompatible with those who wish to attribute *full* self-determination abilities to national groups. Therefore, a possible argument goes, support for global democracy cannot but end in disrespect for nations' desire for self-determination.

But this may be too quick. Note first that justifying forms of democracy above the nation is not at odds with granting nations *substantial* powers of self-determination. There are very few global democratic theorists who would argue that global democracy involves denying nations' rights to self-determination. Doing so would require such a theorist to work out a very extreme and unrealistic interpretation of supranational democracy where nation-states are abolished and where *all* political decision-making occurs at the global or transnational level. There is no reason why subscribing to the case for global democracy would require endorsing anything so drastic as a nonfederal world state. Any convincing case for global democracy will limit itself to *supplementing* rather than *replacing* national collective self-determination with supranational and potentially global levels of collective decision-making. National units, then, will retain significant political autonomy.[9]

---

[9] Given the nature of our argument (that it is possible for liberal nationalism to endorse forms of global democracy), to show why the extreme version of global democracy is unconvincing is not requisite. The point is simply that it is *possible* for liberal nationalists to endorse forms of global democracy, not that it is possible for them to endorse *any* such form.

Those skeptical of the compatibility thesis might still argue, however, that, surely, yielding some sovereignty to larger political associations will in some way compromise national self-determination, and thereby also liberal nationalism itself. Allowing for forms of global democracy, then, must necessarily be in tension with national self-determination and ultimately with the value of national identity itself.

There is indeed a tension here. But just as only extreme versions of global democracy would deny national self-determination, so only extreme versions of liberal nationalism would argue that the value of national identity implies *full* national self-determination—a form of self-determination where all decision-making whatsoever occurs at the national level. This extreme interpretation of the authority conclusion of liberal nationalism, however, is not convincing. This is the case because full national self-determination is inconsistent not only with supranational forms of decision-making but also with *subnational* decision-making. But subnational decision-making—for example, at the municipal or provincial level—is a universally approved democratic practice. It would be odd to demand that all decisions—including decisions on town hall renovations or particular street name changes—be made at the national level or to argue that such subnational decision-making impairs national identity. Given that subnational decision-making could hardly be understood as harmful to the value of national self-determination, a convincing interpretation of national self-determination cannot be one that is *full* as opposed to one that is (merely) *substantial*.

But there is a way for liberal nationalists to guard against this objection. Instead of "full *national* self-determination," which excludes all nonnational (including subnational) decision-making, the liberal nationalist might merely endorse "full *intranational* self-determination," a view which says that all decision-making should occur within democratic communities united by a national culture. Self-determination then merely needs to be exercised *within* the protective quilt of nationality; it shouldn't (always) encompass the *entire* quilt.[10] So the objection can be avoided. What, then, are the more challenging reasons for arguing against the authority argument, now understood as an argument grounded in the importance of full intranational instead of full national self-determination?

---

[10] One might object that intranational self-determination, defined as the idea that self-determination is legitimate so long as it occurs intranationally, is incompatible with some policies that liberal nationalists favor on the basis of the identity argument. Liberal nationalist theorists typically favor separate political contexts not only for nations smaller than states (such as the Catalans and the Scots) but also for nations larger than states (such as the German nation that encapsulated West and East Germany; see, e.g., Miller 1995, 188). But the liberal nationalist might avoid this objection by endorsing the "intranational if also national self-determination": the view that intranational units of self-determination are legitimate, but only when there is also a nationwide level of self-determination.

First, there are justice-based reasons why the value people experience in shaping the world together with their conationals can in many cases not imply full intranational self-determination. What, for instance, is the right solution for the problem of nonterritorially demarcated national minorities like the Dutch-speaking minority in Brussels? Granting them *full* self-determination would be unjust. It would allow one group to make decisions over matters (say, the maintenance of the road network) that concern and affect all the groups in the territory. What this implies is that the argument for self-determination cannot always be understood as a right to full self-determination.

Now, perhaps it is possible to apply a similar type of reasoning to the "interconnected threats and challenges" (Annan 2005) we face in a globalizing world. A clear example here is the case of environmental problems. Environmental problems often involve a situation analogous to the example just given about the presence of more than one group in one territory, where full self-determination for one group would impair the democratic rights of other groups. In today's world, environmental policies (or the lack of them) or practices often have effects on parts of the globe where the national group that is responsible for the effects does not live. This is one example where full self-determination for the group that causes harm to other groups far away is not consistent with the equal rights to self-determination of those other groups. The obvious solution for such a supranational problem is one where the affecting and the affected groups cede some sovereignty to a higher level and engage in a form of supranational decision-making, just as this is done in the nonterritorial multinational case.

The *second* argument focuses on the "moderate" feature of the nationalism that liberal nationalism presents. This moderation is reflected in the fact that the forms of identity recognition that liberal nationalism supports are nonaggressive and compatible with the recognition of the identity of other national groups. As a result, most if not all liberal nationalists explicitly endorse the idea of *multinational* states instead of merely promulgating the right to full independence for each nation (see Miller 1995; Gans 2004; Kymlicka 1995; Tamir 1993). But once liberal nationalists accept that nation-states are not the only way to realize the right to national self-determination (Tamir 1993, 75; see also 9 and 150–51), they have neither a good reason why self-determination should be *fully* (intra)national nor a principled argument against a vertical dispersion of sovereignty.

A final reason why full (intra)national self-determination is undesirable is more speculative, and directly relates to the value of identity. Recall that the authority argument for national political units is an argument grounded in the value of identity. It is because national cultural identities are valuable to us that national groups should be granted the necessary means to maintain their own liberal democratic polities.

Why are these cultural identities that justify self-determination *national* in scope? The standard answer liberal nationalism gives is that national cultures are the most salient forms of cultural identity in today's world. This is clearly an empirical argument. Now, while it is empirically true that national identities remain "strong and politically significant" (Miller 2007, 265) and perhaps even constitute the *primary* locus of people's cultural identity in the current world, this could change, and there is no *principled* objection to nonnational cultural identities (see also Miller 2003, 365, 366, 368). Moreover, identities are already changing. We are currently experiencing not only the (admittedly slow) formation of a global public sphere but also to some extent the emergence of (weak) supranational identities, such as a European identity in Europe, and also some forms of cultural cosmopolitanism. There is no principled objection to be found in the normative premises of liberal nationalism to recognizing such nonnational cultural identities alongside, and in a way similar to, the recognition of the value of national cultural identities.[11] If certain supranational identities exist, such as an overlapping cultural identity in multinational states, or if new cultural identities pop up, such as affiliations to a European cultural context, then the logic of the liberal nationalist argument suggests the importance of also valuing these—even if national cultural identities remain more salient. Thus, policies can be endorsed that recognize and grant rights to more than one cultural identity. Such policies give due recognition to the fact that—as a result of increased global and international processes—certain citizens may start to develop European or other supranational identities. This last reason why national self-determination is compatible with supranational forms of self-determination considers the existence of (limited) forms of cultural cosmopolitanism as a separate, if still weak, justification of the case for political cosmopolitanism (or global democracy).

3.2. The Social Justice Argument

The social justice argument stipulates that distributive justice requires the existence of a shared national culture that carries with it mutual trust, loyalty, and willingness to make sacrifices for anonymous others. We can be brief here. This is first and foremost an argument about the scope of distributive justice. It is not an argument about the appropriate level of democratic decision-making. Although the argument is potentially de-

---

[11] Something similar can be thought to justify the existence of dual self-determination in multinational states. In constellations where many members of a particular nation, say Quebec, experience dual identities—that is, they derive their identity both from a substate nation (Quebec) and from the statewide nation (Canada)—a federal political system may be a solution that does justice to both identities and recognizes them politically. Federal political systems divide powers between a federal government and two or more subunits, such that each level has sovereign authority over certain issues (see De Schutter 2007).

structive to the claim that liberal nationalism is compatible with support for global distributive justice, it does not affect the claim that liberal nationalism is compatible with forms of global democracy.[12]

3.3. The Deliberative Democracy Argument

The last argument that we need to discuss is the deliberative democracy argument. It may be useful to put this argument in logical form. Steps 3 to 5 capture the most crucial move of the argument:

1. Liberal democracy involves democracy.
2. The best form of democracy is deliberative democracy.
3. Deliberative democracy functions best when there is trust, responsibility, reciprocity, and shared identity among the citizenry.
4. In this world, trust, responsibility, reciprocity, and shared identity among the citizenry only exist within national communities.
5. Given 3 and 4, in this world, deliberative democracy works best in national communities.
6. Given 1, 2, and 5, liberal democratic political communities should ideally be national political communities.

Arguably, along with the authority version of the cultural identity argument, the democracy argument presents the most serious challenge to the thesis that liberal nationalism is compatible with forms of global democracy. This is the case because the argument reaches the conclusion that national self-determination is required on democratic grounds alone: it is because democracy involves the features described above that the preference is reached for national/political units. To what extent do these democratic grounds and the conclusion reached based on them imply that forms of democracy above the national unit are unsupportable?

In answering this question, we proceed in two steps. (i) The first step analyzes whether the democracy argument is a sound reason for rejecting forms of supranational democracy. (ii) The second step analyzes whether the democracy argument can be a sound reason for actively supporting the development of more robust forms of supranational democracy through supranational nation-building.

3.3.1. Multinational Federal States

The most crucial question we should ask is whether the argument that deliberative democracy works best in national communities (steps 3 to 5 above) necessarily implies a rejection of supranational forms of democ-

---

[12] Note that the fact that the compatibility issue discussed here can avoid having to deal with the social justice argument does not entail the view that global justice and global democracy are unrelated. Several global justice and global democracy theorists take the view that the two are not intrinsically unrelated.

racy. It is hard to see how that could be the case. It is one thing to say that democracy works best in nationally unified political units, and that therefore national democratic units are preferable to nonnational units. But it is quite another to claim that all nonnational democratic decision-making processes are therefore illegitimate or insupportable. In other words: the view that national units are preferable units for democracy does not entail that supranational units can never be supported. Sometimes good reasons may exist for pursuing supranational decision-making. While the democratic argument provides an important reason for realizing democracy in national units, there may be other arguments that go against the central preference for national decision-making.

Take again the example of multinational federal states. While in such cases the democratic argument could be invoked to argue that the substate nations are the primary and most appropriate units of democracy, the idea of a multinational state in itself entails the existence of at least some competences and decision-making at the federal level itself. Since most contemporary liberal nationalists normatively endorse the legitimacy of multinational federal states, they ipso facto endorse the legitimacy of some form of decision-making at the (supranational) federal level itself. So the fact that they can and do endorse the legitimacy of a federal level of decision-making and citizenship shows that the general preference for national political units can be overridden by other concerns.

Now, it may be argued that this federal decision-making is to be regarded as only a second-best option (see, e.g., Miller 2000, 89; Tamir 1993, 140–67). But that is exactly the point: the view that national political units are the ideal case does not rule out the possible legitimacy of supranational forms of democracy.

What this example of federal states shows is that in some cases the general preference for national citizenship can and should be qualified by a second-best preference for nonnational citizenship. This is the case when there are good reasons why it is "impossible to appeal to a shared national identity as a basis for citizenship" (Miller 2000, 89). Such good reasons can be found in multinational federal states (2000, 125–41).

Now, if this is the case, then nothing prevents liberal nationalists from thinking that current globalization-related processes present *other good reasons* to neutralize or at least qualify the general preference for national citizenship in a purely nation-based system. What might such reasons be? Simon Caney gives three reasons why supranational political institutions are required: ensuring compliance, solving collective action problems, and protecting liberty, because "supra-state political authorities can check the power of states and are more protective of liberty than a purely statist framework" (Caney 2005a, 159–60; see also 2005b, 41–46).

There may be other good reasons besides these for supranational institutions, and particular liberal nationalists may or may not be persuaded by them. But the point is that it is compatible with the democracy argument sometimes to qualify and override the general preference for national citizenship. While national units may be the most appropriate units for active citizenship, there may sometimes be reasons why it is not appropriate to restrict all decision-making to the national level.

The fact that the form of citizenship that will accompany nonnational decision-making is less than the ideal republican form of citizenship that most of us favor is perhaps a bullet we should sometimes be willing to bite. Interestingly, one thought that might motivate us here is the fact that in some cases people do seem to be able to adopt robust forms of citizenship at nonnational citizenship levels too. For instance, Kymlicka, who is in general a committed defender of national citizenship and skeptical about the prospects of direct supranational citizenship (see Kymlicka 2001a, 323–26), argues that "having a strong Canadian identity is not a precondition for citizens to cooperate in the functioning of pan-Canadian institutions. Indeed, there is interesting evidence that feelings of trust and legitimacy in Canadian institutions have remained strong in Quebec even when Canadian identity has diminished" (Kymlicka 2003, 380).

3.3.2. Supranational Nation-Building

In cases where it is thought that national citizenship has to be supplemented with some form of supranational citizenship, the democracy argument might also be read as supportive of attempts to strengthen supranational citizenship and to make it approach the more robust form of democracy and citizenship that is thought possible at the level of the nation.

Note that the reason why we should prefer national units on the democracy argument is different from the one given by the (authority version of the) identity argument. The identity argument aims to show why national units must be politically self-governing. In contrast, the democracy argument shows why politically self-governing units must be national. The democracy argument is not in itself an argument for why nations must be political communities. It reaches the argument for self-determining nations on the basis of the value of democracy alone. The democracy argument says that if we want deliberative democracy, we need trust and reciprocity, and these features are currently only found in nation-states.

This leaves open the theoretical possibility of setting out to create nations out of currently nonnational political units. This could be done by intensive forms of "supranational nation-building" aimed at bringing about the benefits that national citizenship currently enjoys, such as trust, responsibility, shared identity, and commonality.

This possible interpretation of the democracy principle need not conflict with the identity argument discussed above, as it is possible to have supranational nation-building alongside national nation-building. Evidence for such a possibility is given, again, by the existence of multinational federal states. Such states often have some forms of nation-building (including through national anthems, flags, or educational curriculum requirements) both at the federal and at the substate national level. And often their citizens have dual (or nested) identities.

But will supranational nation-building work? Will it be possible to create enough commonality and trust at supranational levels to enable some form of genuine republican and deliberative citizenship? Answering that question is difficult. One idea that might guide us here is that the creation of national identity itself has been possible too, which in important respects can be seen as a surprising achievement, brought into existence through extensive nation-building efforts.

Nationalism and nation-building can in important respects be seen as progressive historical forces insofar as they have been able to extend familial and parochial spheres of trust, commonality, reciprocity, and solidarity to the much bigger national sphere, which contains huge numbers of individuals who have never met and will never know each other personally. It is interesting to see that liberal nationalists approve of the historical emergence of national contexts that came into existence through active nation-building efforts. They support, for instance, the development that transformed peasants from southern France into French citizens.

If current globalization processes are believed to necessitate supranational forms of cooperation and decision-making, then there may be good reasons to make sure that these supranational levels are not detrimental to existing national identities—for instance, by making sure that they are democratically accountable and by protecting national choice contexts and national self-government. But there is no reason not to support supranational nation-building efforts—for instance, efforts to create some sense of commonality within the European Union so that French citizens might be motivated to perceive the Polish plumber as "one of us"—alongside national nation-building efforts to guarantee national identity.

The fact that supranational "nation-building" will be hard to achieve and even harder to be effective is of course no reason not to attempt it. On the face of it, the democracy argument leaves us with only three options: (i) we renounce all attempts at supranational decision-making, (ii) we bite the bullet and accept that our forms of supranational citizenship will at best be second-best, or (iii) we attempt to create a sufficient sense of trust and commonality among nonnationals at supranational levels.

It is perfectly possible for liberal nationalists to opt for (iii), and in the absence of its success to accept a version of (ii). Note that option (iii) operates in the wake of the democracy argument and is premised on the view that citizenship requires commonality and trust. It is possible to believe in the value of bounded citizenship and a democracy based on trust, yet still be committed to supranational citizenship. That is why even advocates of disaggregated citizenship like Selya Benhabib argue that citizens "need bounded communities . . . within which they can establish mechanisms of representation, accountability, participation and delibera-tion" (Benhabib 2006, 169).

At this point, it is perhaps useful to repeat that while we believe it is possible to reconcile liberal nationalism with global democracy, not all versions of liberal nationalism will be compatible with it. This is the case for those liberal nationalists who will be inclined to support option (i). The liberal nationalist most inclined to this version is David Miller. It is, therefore, instructive to take a closer look at his most compelling argument against supranational citizenship.

4. David Miller's Account

On Miller's account, "the practice of citizenship must . . . , for as far ahead as we can reasonably envisage, be confined within the boundaries of national political communities" (Miller 2000, 81). But why should this be the case? Primarily, according to Miller, because there is a difference between a thin, liberal version of citizenship and a more robust and much more preferable republican version. While liberal citizenship only in-volves a set of rights and corresponding obligations, republican citizen-ship also entails a strong sense of responsibility and commitment to the political community.

Miller particularly stresses the "collective action problem" of respon-sibility. The problem is that there is an obvious temptation to free-ride on the willingness of others to moderate their demands in the course of public deliberation. Whatever the others do (act responsibly or merely push their own interests), there is a temptation for each individual to not act responsibly. The solution to the collective action problem, says Miller, is trust and reciprocity. To act as a responsible citizen, one must have the reasonable assurance that the majority of one's fellow citizens will be doing the same. This is why the republican tradition placed so much emphasis on cultivating public virtue and why it was assumed that it required strong patriotic loyalty and nation-building efforts to inculcate this loyalty in people (2000, 86). It is also why, in the modern world, common nationality has been invoked to serve the purpose of generating the trust and loyalty that citizenship requires. National identities and nation-building are therefore crucial as catalysts of trust and responsibility.

These are the main reasons why Miller opposes efforts to expand our locus of national citizenship to include transnational forms of citizenship. At the transnational level there are no communal ties, no expectation of reciprocity, and no mutual trust. As a result there is no reason for members of that constituency to behave as responsible citizens. Transnational citizenship, in other words, can at best be thin and liberal (2000, 96).

So Miller will not buy the compatibility view we are proposing. He does not believe that even if supranational citizenship is thin, we might still think it is better than no supranational citizenship at all. And while he strongly supports nation-building insofar as it concerns the uniting of earlier identities into what we now call national identities, he does not consider the possibility of extending it to the supranational realm (2000, 86–87). "International peace, international justice and global environmental protection are very important objectives, and we must hope that republican citizens will choose to promote them externally. But this cannot be achieved by inventing in theory cosmopolitan forms of citizenship which undercut the basis of citizenship proper" (2000, 96). What can be said about this rejection from within the versions of liberal nationalism that we think *are* compatible with forms of global democracy? One thing to ask is whether Miller can really be so committed to understanding the urgency of supranational issues like international peace, international justice, and global environmental protection as he seems to suggest in the passage just quoted.

This question is relevant because Miller's argument for (uniquely) national political communities and national citizenship has at least one major drawback: it narrows the sphere of responsibility to the national sphere, which in itself inhibits responsible behavior in dealing with the globalization-related challenges that we are currently facing. The reason why Miller opposes supranational citizenship is that there will not be enough responsibility: citizens may be committed to certain cosmopolitan ideals, but given the absence of relations of reciprocity and mutual trust, there is no reason why citizens will be responsible citizens devoted to the common good. Such trust and reciprocity *can* be found at the national level. The conclusion is that therefore citizenship must be national.

But this line of reasoning bites its own tail. Surely the effect of relegating all forms of decision-making to the national level will have the effect of making responsibility at supranational levels even less likely than it is now. There will be even *fewer* reasons for citizens to incorporate the demands of those who are not conationals than in a cosmopolitan citizenship model or even than in the current world system, where there are many supranational institutions that are already in part democratically accountable. Relegating all citizenship to the national unit aggravates the problem of responsibility instead of solving it in any meaningful sense. Not only will citizens not have a good reason to make efforts to see the legitimacy of the views of transnational others and to moderate their own demands in order to reach a consensus, citizens will actually be motivated to moderate their claims *only* in the light of conationals' input into the deliberative democratic sphere.

The view of liberal nationalism that we have stressed is one where at least two other options are open: the option (ii) above that says nonrepublican forms of citizenship may nonetheless still be preferable to *no citizenship at all* at supranational levels, and the option (iii) above that says there is every reason to support attempts at creating republican forms of citizenship in these supranational democratic arenas.

It is hard to avoid the conclusion that one reason why Miller does not see the problems caused by the lack of responsibility at supranational levels is that he thinks that the challenges we face are not crucial enough. At one point, he argues that "if global warming accelerates to the point where the continuance of human life in anything like its present form becomes doubtful, people might be willing to sign a Hobbesian global contract giving a central authority the power to impose fierce environmental controls on all societies" (2007, 269). Ultimately, then, the likelihood of liberal nationalists' commitment to global democracy will depend predominantly on their assessment of globalization-related developments. As long as these are seen as not very urgent, then option (i) might indeed still be open to them. But even then there is no reason why they couldn't support options (ii) and (iii). While these options become all the more compelling once one is convinced of this urgency, if one isn't convinced, those options are still open. Our compatibility thesis is, therefore, not affected by the fact that some might indeed prefer option (i).

5. The Exclusion Problem

We have focused here on liberal nationalism's central tenets and examined whether they rule out the legitimacy of global democracy. Our claim has been that liberal nationalism, well understood, can encompass claims for supranational democracy.

A number of possible criticisms of this line of reasoning can be expected. Perhaps the most important charge might be that we have presented a too inclusive version of liberal nationalism. Doesn't the liberal nationalist view on national identity necessarily also imply exclusion—drawing boundaries between insiders and outsiders, between citizens and strangers? And does global democracy not logically exclude all forms of exclusion?

The answer to both questions is perhaps less evidently affirmative than one might think. Let's start with the first question, Doesn't identity entail exclusion on the liberal nationalist view? The first thing to note here is that while forming a group of insiders to the exclusion of outsiders is indeed crucial to many liberal nationalists, interestingly, it does not form the crux of their statements, and it is not portrayed as one of the central premises of liberal nationalism. Liberal nationalists, as has been clear from the three central tenets we have been considering so far, all focus on the importance of *identity*, of *commonality*. They argue that national units should be political units (and vice versa) because they are concerned about the value of *identity*, and because they are concerned about the social preconditions of social justice and democracy, which entail *sameness, trust*, and a sense of *commonality*. The focus is not on difference from others but on identity.

Perhaps one might object that identity with conationals logically entails difference and exclusion. The idea of identity itself, one might say, always includes exclusion of others against whom one can pit oneself. As Miller has put it, one aspect of national identity is that it is essential "that the people who compose the nation are believed to share certain traits that mark them off from other peoples . . . . When I say that national differences must be natural ones, I mean that the people who compose a nation must believe that there is something distinctive about themselves that marks them off from other nations, over and above the fact of sharing common institutions" (2000, 30). Now, even if this is true and taken to be crucial, it is not clear how this could be a counterargument against the compatibility thesis. The point about exclusion as presented in the quotation from Miller is one grounded in national identity. Liberal nationalists sympathetic to forms of supranational democracy, however, might grant this point but deny that it affects their commitment to supranational democracy. As we saw above, the discussion about the value of national identity as a *policy* conclusion is different from the issue about the level of political decision-making. Individuals may have particular, nonsupranational attachments. But that in itself is not a reason for limiting all forms of decision-making to the national unit. And even if exclusion, as a corollary of identity, is taken to be crucial to self-determination (and is thus taken to justify an *authority* conclusion), still this ought not to imply *full* (as opposed to substantial) self-determination.

So exclusion from the nation, understood as an extension of national identity, need not imply that supranational democracy is impossible. What, however, if the point about exclusion is taken to be one grounded not in identity but rather in the value of democratic self-determination? Habermas, for instance, has argued that "any political community that wants to understand itself as a democracy must at least distinguish between members and non-members. The self-referential concept of collective self-determination demarcates a logical space for democratically united citizens who are members of a particular community" (Habermas 2001, 107; cf. Benhabib 2004, 45; and Walzer 1983, 64). What does this imply for truly *global* democracy?

To answer this point, let's take up the second question: Does global democracy not entail the abolition of all forms of exclusion? Note first that there are many forms of global democracy as we have defined it that do not face this possible objection, since they are not truly global. The European Union, for instance, could still be excluding others: the non-Europeans. Rather, the objection faces the really all-encompassing global instantiation of global democracy. But even if exclusion is thought to be crucial, there is no reason to think of exclusion in a strictly spatial sense. A potential truly cosmopolitan citizenship could self-identify in a way that avoids the exclusion of spatial others. As Arash Abizadeh has put it,

"Difference and otherness can be constructed not just spatially, as it were, but also imaginatively and temporally" (Abizadeh 2005, 58). For instance, it could self-identify as a potential human rights–based community where all citizens are of equal moral worth, as opposed to an imaginary society where some citizens would have more rights than others. Apart from imaginary others, such a cosmopolitan citizenship could also ground its exclusion in historical others; say, as opposed to a world where the only citizenship was still national.[13]

Acknowledgments

This chapter was improved thanks to helpful comments from the participants and speakers at the workshop entitled "Global Democracy and Exclusion" organized as part of the XXIII World Conference of Philosophy of Law and Social Philosophy in Kraków in August 2007, as well as from Barbara Buckinx. We also wish to thank Otto Bohlmann for useful editorial suggestions.

References

Abizadeh, Arash. 2005. "Does Collective Identity Presuppose an Other? On the Alleged Incoherence of Global Solidarity." *American Political Science Review* 99, no. 1:45–60.
Annan, Kofi. 2005. *In Larger Freedom: Towards Development, Security and Human Rights for All*. New York: United Nations.
Brock, Gillian. 2002. "Cosmopolitan Democracy and Justice: Held Versus Kymlicka." *Studies in East European Thought* 54, no. 4:325–47.
Benhabib, Seyla. 2004. *The Rights of Others: Aliens, Residents and Citizens*. Cambridge: Cambridge University Press.
———. 2006. *Another Cosmopolitanism*. New York: Oxford University Press.
Caney, Simon. 2005a. *Justice Beyond Borders: A Global Political Theory*. Oxford: Oxford University Press.
———. 2005b. "Cosmopolitanism, Democracy and Distributive Justice." In *Global Justice, Global Institutions*, edited by Daniel Weinstock, 29–63. Calgary: University of Calgary Press.
Cohen, Joshua, and Charles Sabel. 1997. "Directly-Deliberative Polyarchy." *European Law Journal* 3:313–42.
De Schutter, Helder. 2007. "Nations Beyond Nationalism." *Inquiry* 50, no. 4:378–94.
Gans, Chaim. 2003. *The Limits of Nationalism*. Cambridge: Cambridge University Press.

---

[13] Habermas, for instance, does acknowledge the possibility of exclusion along temporal lines (Habermas 1998, 118).

Gould, Carol. 2004. *Globalizing Democracy and Human Rights*. Cambridge: Cambridge University Press.

Habermas, Jürgen. 1998. *The Inclusion of the Other: Studies in Political Theory*. Cambridge, Mass.: MIT Press.

———. 2001. *The Postnational Constellation: Political Essays*. Cambridge, Mass.: MIT Press.

———. 2006. *The Divided West*. Cambridge: Polity Press.

Held, David. 2004. *Global Covenant: The Social Democratic Alternative to the Washington Consensus*. Cambridge: Polity Press.

Höffe, Otfried 1999. *Demokratie im Zeitalter der Globalisierung*. Munich: Beck.

Kymlicka, Will. 1995. *Multicultural Citizenship: A Liberal Theory of Minority Rights*. Oxford: Oxford University Press.

———. 2001a. *Politics in the Vernacular: Nationalism, Multiculturalism, and Citizenship*. Oxford: Oxford University Press.

———. 2001b. "Territorial Boundaries: A Liberal Egalitarian Perspective." In *Boundaries and Justice: Diverse Ethical Perspectives*, edited by David Miller and Sohail H. Hashmi, 249–75. Princeton: Princeton University Press.

———. 2003. "Being Canadian." *Government and Opposition* 38, no. 3:357–85.

Marchetti, Raffaele. 2008. *Global Democracy: For and Against Ethical Theory, Institutional Design and Social Struggles*. New York: Routledge.

McGrew, Anthony. 2000. "Democracy Beyond Borders? Globalization and the Reconstruction of Democratic Theory and Practice." In *The Transformation of Democracy: Globalization and Territorial Democracy*, edited by Anthony McGrew, 231–66. Cambridge: Polity Press.

Miller, David. 1995. *On Nationality*. Oxford: Oxford University Press.

———. 2000. *Citizenship and National Identity*. Cambridge: Polity Press.

———. 2003. "A Response." In *Forms of Justice: Critical Perspectives on David Miller's Political Philosophy*, edited by Daniel Bell and Avner de-Shalit, 349–72. Lanham, Md.: Rowman and Littlefield, 2003.

———. 2007. *National Responsibilities and Global Justice*. Oxford: Oxford University Press.

Monbiot, George. 2003. *The Age of Consent: A Manifesto for a New World Order*. London: HarperCollins.

Moore, Margaret. 2001a. *The Ethics of Nationalism*. Oxford: Oxford University Press.

———. 2001b. "Normative Justification for Liberal Nationalism: Justice, Democracy and National Identity." *Nations and Nationalism* 7, no. 1:1–20.

———. 2006. "Globalization and Democratization: Institutional Design for Global Institutions." *Journal of Social Philosophy* 37, no. 1: 21–43.

Tamir, Yael. 1993. *Liberal Nationalism*. Princeton: Princeton University Press.
Tan, Kok-Chor. 2004. *Justice Without Borders*. Cambridge: Cambridge University Press.
———. 2005. "Boundary Making and Equal Concern." *Metaphilosophy* 36, nos. 1–2:50–67.
Walzer, Michael. 1983. *Spheres of Justice: A Defense of Pluralism and Equality*. New York: Basic Books.
———. 2003. *Arguing About War*. New Haven: Yale University Press.

13

IMMIGRATION, NATIONALISM, AND HUMAN RIGHTS

JOHN EXDELL

Liberal nationalists writing on the subject of immigration face a dilemma about the ethical basis for the authority to determine membership in a political community. Is the right to exclude inconsistent with the moral equality of persons and their commitment to universal human rights? Or is this authority inherent in the concept of a sovereign democracy, where citizens may determine who can participate in the common life constructed within its borders? As Phillip Cole puts it, "Can we draw a boundary that constitutes insiders and outsiders in a way that embodies the principles of equal respect and concern for humanity as such . . . that many regard as the central commitments of liberal theory?" (Cole 2001, 60). Answers to these questions have generated debate on the relationship between the impartiality warranted by universal human rights, on the one hand, and the special obligations that citizens owe to each other in a self-determining democracy, on the other.

A liberal nationalist position on immigration affirms the right to exclude. As I discuss it in this chapter, liberalism is nationalist in its theory of the state if it accepts the moral distinction between members and outsiders, and the preference that members generally give to each other over what they owe to humanity as such. Nationalism is liberal if it does not found a national identity on a shared conception of the good, or on the bond of common ethnicity and descent, but looks instead for a more abstract form of nationality on which to found a cohesive democracy (Kymlicka 2002, 261–68). Philosophers holding this view have argued that national identity is still essential for the reason that the redistributive solidarity essential for social justice within the state is threatened by the unlicensed entry of outsiders. Citizen-members must secure the bonds of mutual aid among themselves, and they cannot succeed if they open borders to the mass influx of nonmembers. Seen in this light, a human rights defense of open borders undermines liberal values within the nation-state and is therefore utopian.

I will challenge this empirical claim underpinning the liberal nationalist argument on immigration. I begin with a look at the solidarity argument defended by Michael Walzer and David Miller, and then present two views sympathetic to open borders in the work of Jürgen Habermas and

Carol Gould. I subsequently defend the Habermas-Gould position against the charge that it is utopian. In the United States redistributive solidarity will be strengthened, not reduced, by a surge of Latino and Latina immigrants. It follows that the appeals to social solidarity offer no principled justification for favoring democratic sovereignty over human rights in resolving the liberal dilemma over immigration policy.

1. Walzer and Miller: Nationalism and Solidarity

For Michael Walzer, appeals to human rights ask too much when they demand that we be concerned for the welfare of all persons equally. Human rights principles can perhaps effectively define limited duties of forbearance. But they will fail to motivate ordinary human beings to sacrifice as much for strangers as they will for their fellow nationals. It follows that members have reason to oppose an immigration policy that might deflect or betray the moral obligations they owe to each other. Justifying the right to exclude is therefore tied to a justification of the nation-state itself, understood as an institution in which its members exercise ruling authority for their mutual benefit. The state founded on democratic principles and encompassing the special positive duties citizens owe each other gets us as close as we can to the realization of a liberal conception of human equality.

From this vantage point borders are necessary to preserve nations, and in the modern world nations are the foundation for social justice, sustaining what Rawls called the "bonds of civic friendship" essential for successful liberal societies. Without a sense of nationality uniting them, those who live under state institutions will not constitute "a group of people committed to dividing, exchanging, and sharing social goods, first of all among themselves" (Walzer 1983, 31). As members of a nation we may exclude others "in accordance with our own understanding of what membership means in our community, and what sort of community we want to have" (32). Either a national community has a right to control membership on this basis or the logic of the global market will determine residency and shatter the sense of obligation to those with whom we live as members of the same country. It follows that "restraint of entry serves to defend the liberty and welfare ... of a group of people committed to one another and to their common life" (39).

Walzer's conception of nationality steps outside the liberal nationalist framework because it allows a nation to establish who belongs to it on the basis of race and ethnicity. If national identity ultimately rests on "a world of common meanings" uniting those who constitute a nation's community, we could not easily challenge racist self-understandings as a basis for excluding certain categories of "strangers" from membership in the nation (28, 32). Indeed, given his communitarian emphasis on the need for national cohesion enabled by a "sharing of sensibilities and intuitions," it is not surprising that Walzer affirms the legitimacy of "white Australia" policies that once denied indigenous peoples rights of citizenship and closed borders to immigrants from Asian lands (28, 46). If as a result of Australia's founding and subsequent political history whiteness became part of the national understanding, then the exclusion of nonwhites is reasonable. Walzer's position gives us no grounds to condemn racial or ethnic nationalisms—for example, those of Israel, whose citizens claim the right to decide how many Palestinians will inhabit the Jewish state—and in this respect it is not a liberal nationalist position.

David Miller agrees with Walzer's thesis that a defense of nationality must not ultimately appeal to universal principles that obligate all persons independently of their special relationship as members of a social group. Appeals to human rights or to abstract ideas of fairness in cooperative contexts are motivationally too weak to engender the strong duty of mutual aid we find among citizens of a nation. Such appeals will not generally move people to sacrifice very much for the good of those beyond their borders, or to those within who are not members of the nation. Nations are "communities of obligation, in the sense that their members recognize duties to meet the basic needs and protect the basic interests of other members" (Miller 1995, 83). Without a membership right to exclude outsiders the obligation of reciprocity and social justice cannot be sustained. The reason is that "a shared identity carries with it a shared loyalty, and this increases confidence that others will reciprocate one's own co-operative behavior" (92). Without trust it is much less likely that "individuals will give their support to schemes of social justice, particularly schemes involving redistribution to those not able to provide for their needs through market transactions" (93).

According to Miller, then, nationalism is justified by realism about the human capacity to be guided by abstract principles of human equality. Against Walzer's endorsement of white Australia, however, Miller denies that "nationalism is necessarily an illiberal force" that withholds "equal respect for the many different personal and group identities that would otherwise flourish in a modern plural society" (119). Those who equate the nation with existing ties of ethnicity, religion, or language and who cloak themselves in the ritual and symbols of the past are really defending subservience to a historically dominant group and its current leadership. The demand for solidarity is in effect a demand for submission. Excluding immigrants on the grounds that they do not already share these traditions cannot be justified on liberal premises. As long as an immigrant culture does not enter on a scale or in a manner that threatens to turn the state into a binational society, Walzer's communitarian argument fails. "Why," asks Miller, "should immigrants pose a threat to national identity once it is recognized that that identity is always in flux, and is molded by the various sub-cultures that exist within a national society?"

(128). Although a "well-functioning state rests upon a pre-political sense of common nationality," this does not demand that we preserve the "present sense of national identity and the authority of the institutions that now express it" (129). A nation "need not . . . select as new members only those who already share the existing national identity" (129). It is sufficient that immigrants "accept current political structures" and "engage in dialogue with the host community so that a new common identity can be forged" (129–30).

On the other hand, Miller fears national identities thinned "to the point where they cease to have any content that could compete with ethnic or other such cultural identities" (141). Hence he backs away from a "strictly political" definition of nationality that is nothing more than "allegiance to a set of institutions and their underlying principles" (141). In the United States, beyond their vow to uphold constitutional principles, immigrants are expected to accept more concrete ideas of common membership, including acceptance of a shared history, and "comprehensively respected symbols," such as the national flag (141–42). Miller envisions a process of mutual accommodation: "Existing national identities must be stripped of elements that are repugnant to the self-understanding of one or more component groups, while members of these groups must themselves be willing to embrace an inclusive nationality, and in the process to shed elements of *their* values which are at odds with its principle" (142). Thus Miller rejects also what he calls a "radical multiculturalist" policy that would enable an immigrant minority to preserve its culture through the practice of educational separatism (142). In the public schools, states may "take steps to ensure that the members of different ethnic group are inducted into national traditions and ways of thinking" (141–42). The argument Miller makes for these conclusions generally relies on claims about the conditions for social cohesion and the threat of disunity, many based on the American experience. I will challenge one of these assumptions later.

2. Habermas and Gould: Open Borders and Human Rights

Like Miller, Jürgen Habermas rejects Walzer's view "that the right of immigration is limited by the right of a political community . . . to secure the ethnic-cultural substance of the particular form of life" (Habermas 1998, 513). Civic solidarity need not be based upon the culture of a prepolitical community with a sense of shared destiny. On the contrary, to the extent that the modern state fully realizes its democratic potential, membership will be divorced from the solidarities of descent, language, and culture. This thinning of national identity advances humanity toward the values implicit in rational discourse itself, for example, the inclusion of all capable of speech, the refusal to suppress relevant argument, the supremacy of persuasion over force, and the condition that all affected by a norm must find it to be in their interests. Nevertheless, the political distinction between members and nonmembers is unavoidable: "Any political community that wants to understand itself as a democracy must at least distinguish between members and non-members. The self-referential concept of collective self-determination demarcates a logical space for democratically united citizens who are members of a particular political community" (Habermas 2001, 107).

By "members" we are to understand people who see themselves as having special obligations to each other that they do not share with outsiders. Thus the argument offered in this passage seems to go like this:

A. To be a democracy there must be a people whose members understand themselves to have collective autonomy, that is, a right to communal self-determination.
B. Those who claim this collective autonomy must constitute themselves as members of the community distinguishable from those who are not.
C. Therefore, democracy is possible only for a people who constitute themselves as members with special obligations to each other that they do not share with nonmembers.

A democratic political community, then, is "self-referential" in the sense that *its members* determine who qualify as members, that is, who are entitled to the special benefits of belonging, and who are obligated to sacrifice so that these benefits are enjoyed by all the others who belong to the political community. Only those whom we count as members of *our* democracy in this sense are thereby tied together by the special obligations and benefits of nationality.

We may wonder whether Habermas sees any moral basis for restricting the authority of a democratic state to determine who will be admitted as new members of the polity. Here he seems to dismiss human rights principles as lacking sufficient weight to bear this load in the nonideal world: "Even a worldwide consensus on human rights could not serve as the basis for a strong equivalent to the *civic* solidarity that emerged in the framework of the nation-state. Civic solidarity is rooted in particular collective identities; cosmopolitical solidarity has to support itself on the moral universalism of human rights alone" (2001, 108). Given his view of the self-constituting authority of the democratic state and the empirical weakness of human rights norms in the world as we know it, Habermas's view would seem to deny that human rights values can limit effectively the authority of citizens to determine who will become members of their territorial community. The "worldwide consensus on human rights" cannot match in motivational force the "civic solidarity" that ties together the current membership of the national territory. Of course, a policy of open borders could be created by a federation of countries—for example, the European Union—for the mutual advantage of member states, but no universal moral obligation compels it.

On this reading, Habermas in the end elevates democractic sovereignty over obligations to persons who are not recognized as members of the nation. Carol Gould's disagreement with this position motivates her argument for an alternative human rights framework that can help guide globalization processes "in more humanistic and justice-regarding ways" (Gould 2004, 2). I will focus on Gould's arguments that bear most directly on the topics of membership and immigration in response to the following two questions: When is it legitimate to limit democratic authority in the interests of justice? How can we reform global institutions in a way that enables the world's least advantaged to participate in decision-making which profoundly affects their basic well-being?

We get the wrong answers when we fail to begin with a well-grounded principle of human rights. Habermas's theory, argues Gould, is an example of this failure. It begins with the discourse principle institution-alized in the democratic constitution of the modern state. On this view, says Gould, human rights arise in the context of democratic procedures and have no independent universal efficacy, unless "through international agreements that would constitutionalize them on a global level" (30). Habermas, she thinks, cannot then explain the moral significance of human rights as "claims that people can make on each other independent of their nation-state" (30). His position privileges the democratic equality of citizens as members of the sovereign state over human equality and community among all persons. By the same token, Habermas's derivation of rights from democratic procedures weakens the moral gravity of urgent human rights claims. From the discourse principle we generate civil rights as the conditions for a fair democratic process, and from this we get economic, social, and cultural rights as conditions for the effective enjoyment of civil rights. Gould argues that this train of argument leaves economic-social-cultural rights "in a somewhat precarious position," likely to be neglected among the list of human rights demanding strong universal support (30). Also, the derivative justification of rights fails to provide "an independent criterion of justice" that enables us to show how "a democratic procedure, however justified, may still arrive at an unjust outcome" (32).

The moral import of human rights claims, Gould continues, is better explained when we derive them directly from "the critical or distinguish-ing feature of human action," which is *freedom*, understood as the exercise of a capacity of choice "in the realization of long-term projects … an activity of self-development or self-transformation as a process over time" (33). On the basis of their inherent agency all persons can claim a human right not only to negative freedom but also to the material and social conditions that enable self-transformative activity in the course of a life. This demand for "equal positive freedom" as a universal principle of justice is therefore "ingredient in our recognition of the other as human" (34).

Since individual agency is manifested also in cooperative contexts, says Gould, the right to positive freedom affirms "*democracy* as the equal right to participate in decision-making concerning the common activities in which individuals are engaged" (34–35). Democratic rights are then exercised in a sphere of social activity to which the principle of equal positive freedom directly applies (175). The human rights guarantees needed for both effective individual autonomy and democratic participation are paramount "where democratic decisions may violate one or another of them" (39). It is the role of a democratic constitution to institutionalize the normative priority of human rights as civil rights for citizens and of the state. But insofar as freedom is a *human* right, all persons must be protected against violations by their own state, by foreign states, or by supranational institutions in the globalized world.

Gould alerts us to the possible radical implications of her view, in contrast with Habermas, when she takes up "one of the many paradoxes of democracy" (174). The puzzle arises when we ask "who gets to make democratic decisions—the scope of the *demos*—inasmuch as the issue who gets to make democratic decisions cannot itself be settled democratically without an infinite regress" (174). That is, the individuals who collectively decide the question of membership must already identify each other as members. But with what authority do they draw the boundary around themselves to the exclusion of others? It cannot be on the basis of their preexisting right to self-determination, because that *assumes* an answer to the question of who is and who is not legitimately inside the self-determining group. One might think that if the founding membership of a democratic community is necessarily and legitimately decided by an act of self-creation for which there can be no prior authorization, then the group once founded has the authority to accept or reject new members and to guard its borders accordingly. There is no higher principle external to the value of democracy itself that can supersede the right of members to determine their membership.

For Gould this shows that "issues of membership in a *demos* (or citizenship), as well as the more general question of who has rights to participate in collective decision making, require an appeal to concepts beyond those of self-determination or self-rule per se" (174–75). Here we cannot retreat to the idea of an organic ethnic or cultural identity, for the reasons that lead us to reject Walzer's communitarian endorsement of white Australia. Nor must we fall back on the idea that there is simply an inherent right of sovereign members to exclude outsiders from joining the polity. Hence a doctrine of human rights beckons, offering two grounds for participation in democratic process with bearing on the question of membership and immigration: (1) the right of persons affected by political decisions to have an equal opportunity to influence the making of those decisions, and (2) the right of persons to codetermine the direction of common or joint activity. The former *all-affected* criterion is institutionally feasible and morally compelling, argues Gould, if it is circumscribed as follows: "People at a distance are to be regarded as affected by a decision if their human rights are affected," including most broadly the right to freedom as self-development (178). The latter *common activity* criterion applies where *persons* (not citizens) are objectively engaged in joint activity, each having a right to participate "in the common decisions that bind all the members of the group" (176). On either of these grounds a person's right to democratic participation arises from the universal right of individuals as agents to "control the conditions of their own activity" and not to be passively under the control of others (175). In this light, democratic participation is a corollary of an individual right to "equal agency or equal (positive) freedom" (176.) Both principles provide the independent basis for inclusion needed to avoid having to explain why existing members of a democracy should have an unqualified moral right to select who will become new members without regard for the welfare of those they wish to exclude.

Under conditions that clearly prevail in the world today Gould's position does not leave wealthy democracies with the authority to deny entry, or even citizenship, to impoverished nonmembers who wish to join: "The exercise of democracy deserves to remain ineffective when its outcome is such that it violates the very rights and liberties for the sake of which democracy itself has been instituted. For if democracy is required by equal rights to self-development, the decisions made should not be allowed to undercut democracy's own ground" (197).

This thesis justifies open borders from two angles. Most directly, says Gould, a policy of closed borders will deny the neediest segment of humanity access to resources necessary for "self-development or self-transformation as a process over time" (32–33). A border is in this case clearly a denial of positive freedom. Secondly, as we know, the economic and military policies of wealthy states often do great harm to peoples in distant countries. With Gould's rendition of the all-affected principle we can support the right of the latter to immigrate to the states that determine their fate. In a world where differing racial, ethnic, and cultural identities correspond to great inequality in access to resources, and where these inequalities are both created and compounded by economic and political actions of powerful states in whose councils the poor of other lands have entirely no say, advocates of human rights should support the entrance of downtrodden immigrant populations into the wealthier communities and the creation of multiethnic, multicultural, and multiracial nationalities. Scrambling people up will make it easier to represent the interests of all humanity in the policy-making forums where their fate is effectively determined, and thus make it politically more difficult for the privileged to prey upon the weak in faraway lands. It will be a practical advance, says Gould, toward the goal that political communities "be opened to democratic participation by those widely affected by their decisions" (1).

Now despite the differences in their theoretical starting points, I think Gould is mistaken that she and Habermas differ in their conclusions about democratic exclusion and human rights. Indeed, in his principal work on this topic, Habermas takes pains to emphasize the conceptual ties between human rights and democratic sovereignty in a way that sets a moral and legal limitation on the latter. He is unequivocal on this point: "The principle of democracy can only appear at the heart of a *system* of rights. The logical genesis of these rights comprises a circular process in which the legal code, or legal form . . . and hence the democratic principle, are *co-originally* constituted" (1998, 121–22). Thus in a discussion directly on the issue of immigration and the legal status of aliens and stateless persons Habermas rebukes the "anti-Polish sentiments" of Germans who "forget that the rights of citizen guarantee liberty because they contain universal human rights" (1998, 508–9). There is, then, he says, a clear "human rights component of citizenship" independent of international agreements, which when "strengthened through supranational rights . . . might even affect the core opportunities for exercising political influence" (1998, 509).

It is beyond the scope of this chapter to determine which philosopher's theory of human rights passes the final test of consistency and coherence. Suffice it to say that both theories move strongly toward an open borders position, and to both theories liberal nationalists will object that millions of impoverished people with unfamiliar languages and a distinct national identity will weaken the solidarity needed for social justice within the affluent states to which they have immigrated. It is on this practical thesis that the argument turns. I will now consider a salient counterexample to the liberal nationalist objection. I will argue that while a permissive border policy with Mexico and other Hispanic states may very well weaken the sense of nation now prevalent in the United States, such a policy actually increases the prospects for social justice. If this is correct, then we have a significant exception to the generalization assumed in the liberal nationalist argument that a strong national identity is the key to social solidarity.

3. Race, Immigration, and the American Exception

Liberal nationalists gain support for their position from the widely held belief that a universalist human rights approach is beyond the capability of human nature, or at least beyond the moral and cultural resources available in the modern world. This is a serious challenge to those who like Habermas and Gould hope to institutionalize human rights principles in a way that effectively guides the conduct of states. Indeed, Gould pledges to avoid "purely utopian projections" and to make "proposals for reform and transformation ... grounded on an understanding of empirical possibilities" (180). She proposes a "concrete universalist approach"—"concrete" because it recognizes the "requirement that abstract moral, political and legal norm ... be put in the context of actual social conditions to understand critically why they have not been realized" (114). With this in mind, "philosophical approaches have to be closely linked with social critique and developed with an eye to the emerging possibilities of practical change" (5).

In my view there is currently little prospect of reforming global political institutions that obstruct the realization of a human right to positive freedom. There may, however, be another approach to these practical aspirations. It will help to begin by interpreting a most puzzling counterexample to the liberal nationalist thesis on immigration. The striking exception is the United States, a country with a vivid sense of nationhood but unable to sustain political support for redistributive policies such as those found in Canada and European social democracies.

In his defense of liberal nationalism Miller directly addresses the American anomaly. As we saw, he claims that members of a nation affirm the good of their national community as a personal goal, and this is what moves them to sacrifice for the benefit of fellow citizens in need. Why, then, has nationalism failed to yield these results in the United States, where "national identity is strong," unlike Canada, where social solidarity is strong even though national identity and unity appear to be weaker? Miller's answer is that national identity is generally necessary for solidarity, but not sufficient: "It is not only the *strength* of national identity ... but also the *character* of national identity that matters from the point of view of social justice ... in particular the extent to which the nation conceives itself along solidaristic or individualistic lines. ... When explaining welfare policy and so forth, this may sufficiently account for the case of the United States, whose public culture is by common consent unusually individualistic" (94).

Miller's explanation is not supported by the most careful empirical studies of American political culture. A substantial body of research shows that the ethos of individualism is *not* the driving force behind opposition to liberal welfare policies. In their seminal study of race, policy preferences, and party identification in the United States, Donald Kinder and Lynn Sanders established that since the antipoverty programs of the 1960s the primary cause of resistance to liberal welfare policies has been antiblack hostility among a majority of white Americans. The Kinder-Sanders finding is based on national election study data that provide a comprehensive longitudinal sampling of the voting age population at every national election from 1952 to 1992. From the set of questions testing attitudes about race, we know that in the eyes of roughly 60 percent of white voters black people generally do not try hard enough to overcome adversity and squander socially provided assistance they have not earned. These "resentful" white voters are hostile specifically to African Americans perceived as a group unworthy of the nation's help (Kinder and Sanders 1996, 116–19, 148; see also Schuman et al. 1997; Gilens 1999; and Sears, Henry, and Kosterman 2000). In the view of these voters, write Kinder and Sanders, African American moral failure explains why forty years after the 1960s civil rights reforms many have not yet achieved the American dream (106–15). While the hostility of these voters is typically *expressed through* the individualistic ethos of hard work and personal responsibility, variations among individuals in their commitment to individualism in the abstract do not explain why many white Americans favor this value over equality on issues related to race. On the contrary, whether white Americans are guided in their political choices by a collective commitment to social equality or to the so-called American creed of hard work and individual responsibility depends more than anything else on a very specific judgment about the connection between race and good character, that is, between blacks and "a threat . . . to civic virtue" (108). Divisions created by race, not by moral or political principle, explain the divergence between American politics and European social democracy.

We should be interested in the political implications of these findings, as well as their theoretical bearing on the assumption that nationality is the indispensible foundation for social solidarity. Given this assumption the problem is that white Americans continue to tie national identity to racial categories that exclude the descendants of slaves. The solution then is to separate American nationality from race, that is, to make what it means to be American more race neutral. This means transforming what Walzer calls the "national self-understanding" or what Miller sees in the American "public culture."

But how will this be done? The history of progress toward racial equality in the United States leaves little hope that we can succeed by these means, certainly if we must envision an enduring great awakening on the white side of the racial divide. Since the founding of the Republic there have been only three, very special periods in which forward movement toward racial equality has occurred, and they have all required the solvent of military emergency—the Revolutionary War itself, the Civil War, and World War II and the Cold War. Only when the idea of racial equality was necessary to the defeat a powerful foe (the British, the Confederacy, Nazi Germany, and the Soviet Union) have black Americans been able to challenge the institutions of white supremacy. Moreover, the gains made in these periods have been difficult to secure. Whenever the period of military emergency has passed, there has followed a lengthy period of retreat in which the old racial hierarchy has been partially restored. There is good reason to believe that the United States has been in such a period of reaction for the past forty years (Klinker and Smith 1999).

There is a further problem with proposals that start with the reform of culture or national identity. They fail to see the *contemporary* causes that reinforce white racial resentment. White antiblack resentment is not simply the outcome of a racist political culture passed on as an idea or bad habit from one generation to the next. It is ever rejuvenated in white perceptions of *present-day* racial inequality, which appear to confirm the assumption of black cultural failure. Racial inequality—especially high rates of poverty and imprisonment—stimulates white racism. White racism manifested in antiblack discrimination and political reaction in turn reinforces racial inequality. It seems that we are caught in a cycle of self-reinforcing evils that will be undone only by the intervention of some *external force*. It is therefore hard to see how a change in the "self-understanding" of the "nation" can come about as a way to move the United States beyond this impasse.

Let us consider another strategy. The disruptive force we need could be the forty-three million Latino and Latina people living in the United States, now 14 percent of the total population and increasing at a rate of 3.3 percent per year. Although nearly half of all Latinos and Latinas live in Texas and California, significant numbers of them are creating new communities throughout the country. Thirteen states now have more than half a million Latino and Latina residents each: Arizona, California, Colorado, Florida, Georgia, Illinois, Nevada, New Jersey, New Mexico, New York, North Carolina, Texas, and Washington (U.S. Bureau of the Census 2006). From now until mid-century Latinos and Latinas are expected to account for two-thirds of total U.S. population growth. Their numbers may have achieved a size and geographical reach sufficient to challenge the traditional assimilationist model that integrated European immigrant groups into the main current of Anglo society. Both in the Southwest and in the major metropolitan centers there is developing "a forceful variegated alternative to mainstream North American culture" (Davis 2001, 23).[1] The new Latino metropolis is "remaking urban space in novel ways that cannot be assimilated to the earlier experiences of either African-Americans or European immigrants" (49). In the central metropolitan districts, Spanish is now the primary language, the "idiom of daily life" combining "cultural unity and blue-collar solidarity" that is revitalizing American cities "on an epic scale" (59, 62–67).

Davis notes a "fundamental structural characteristic" of the emergent Latino metropolis: the basic building blocks of Spanish-speaking urban neighborhoods are not transient individuals, or even transient house-holds, but "entire transnationalized communities" whose close relation-ship with their home villages in Mexico, the Dominican Republic, El Salvador, and so on, is crucial to a "communal survival strategy" made necessary by xenophobic border militias and martial law repression

---

[1] Quoting Juan Flores, *Divided Border: Essays in Puerto Rican Identity* (Houston: Arte Público Press, 1993), 184.

justified by the war on drugs and the war on terror (98). To meet subsistence needs, residents of these villages have sent out groups that form a conduit between the home base and the urban centers to the north. "Unable to secure a full livelihood either in Mexico or in the United States," writes Davis, "migrants must extend their families and their households across the border, thus creating transnational households and a transnational community" (97). Travel and communication between these communities continue, and would become more common if the current draconian travel restrictions were abandoned. We may ask whether these developments augur a new *postnational identity*, not only combining the "physical and cultural continuity of Mexico in the US southwest" but also reaching to the growing Latino metropolis in Chicago, New York, and Boston (19). Moreover, we should hope that maintaining a non-Anglo or panethnic identity will distance Latinos and Latinas from white antiblack racial resentment that is deeply ingrained in the political mainstream. In this light the growing Latino and Latina population could be the sleeping dragon of U.S. politics—that disruptive force we need to overturn the long period of reaction that has isolated urban African Americans and immobilized left-wing solidarity politics since the 1960s (Guinier and Torres 2002, 11–22; Alcoff 2007, 179–82).

To summarize, in order to defend the importance of national identity, liberal nationalist theorists must explain why in the United States nationalism and solidarity are strikingly disconnected. Miller's account—that American social unity is weakened by a libertarian public culture—is empirically wrong. The failure to finish the struggle for racial justice is the reason why there is so little solidarity and social democracy in America. As I have argued, Latino and Latina immigration could well contribute the missing political will needed to advance toward this goal. The millions entering from Mexico, Central America, South America, and the Caribbean islands can strengthen an antiracist political force capable of making the United States a significantly more egalitarian society.

In making this case, one of my aims has been to focus a human rights position, as Gould proposes, on "the context of actual social conditions" and "emerging possibilities of practical change" (5). Immigration from the south into North America gives us a salient example of a *nonutopian on-the-ground force for a more just human community*. Its potential political impact in the United States was evident in the spring of 2006 when millions of Latinos and Latinas in cities across the country organized to protest reactionary anti-immigrant legislation brewing in Washington, and in many major cities carried out what effectively amounted to a general strike. Whether acting through community organizations, labor unions, cross-border coalitions, or university classrooms and academic research, the historic flow of population from south to north in the Americas gives intellectuals and activists an opportunity to bring theory and practice together on the side of human rights principles.

Achieving a more solidaristic nation will require an oppositional social movement determined to challenge the racial status quo. The growing Latino population, joined with African Americans, might become that force, one so politically strong that the majority population will simply have to deal with it. In that case, letting in Latino and Latina immigrants is more likely to foster a redistributive ethic than keeping them out. If the conceptions of human rights we find in Habermas and Gould foster sympathy and support for these developments, then they are both on that score a cogent interpretation of liberal values.

4. Wider Applications?

A theory of global justice is nonutopian if it can be joined to the urgent needs of an active mass of humanity united to a political strategy for realizing its key principles. The American experience with Latino and Latina immigration suggests a model for how theory and practice can be joined in this sense. But can this template be transferred to the migrations affecting the European Union? Certainly the same desperation drives people to violate border restrictions on both continents, the same resentments against alien intruders arise, and the same tragedies result (Government Accounting Office 2006; see also Haski 2007 and Albahari 2006). Habermas has noted, latent in this turmoil, the same political possibilities in the European Union that I have here noted in the United States: "Immigration from Eastern Europe and the poverty-stricken regions of the Third World will heighten the multicultural diversity of society. This will no doubt give rise to social tensions. But if those tensions are dealt with productively, they can foster a political mobilization that will give additional impetus to the new endogenous social movements already emergent within nation-states—I am thinking of the peace, environmental and women's movements" (1998, 506). It is politically significant, however, that a high proportion of immigrants into the European Union are from the Middle East and other Muslim lands. For Europeans this fact makes clash-of-civilization concerns much more powerful and immediate than they are in North America. One hopes that European left-wing parties and human rights and democracy advocates will resist these anxieties and strongly support Muslim immigrants seeking entry into and citizenship in the European Union countries in which they wish to reside.

My point is that the all-affected principle of democratic participation may be more effectively realized on the ground, through the migration of oppressed peoples into the countries of privilege, than through the representational reform of global institutions. U.S. and E.U. sanction policies and military interventions, from the Gulf War to the present, have had a devastating impact on Palestinians, Iraqis, Lebanese, Afghanis, Somalians, and Islamic peoples throughout Africa and the

Middle East. We may propose that the marginalized majority of humanity whose human rights are put at risk by actions and policies of powerful states be represented in the chambers of multinational or transnational institutions where world-regulating decisions decide their fate. But there seems little prospect of this at the present time. Here is an alternative strategy that liberals and progressives in the United States and Europe may find worthy of support: represent these interests in the public discussions and democratic processes of the Western countries where many of these violations of human rights are authorized. Would it make a difference if substantial numbers from the countries or regions who suffer these injustices became confident and mobilized residents or citizens of states where these policies are debated, financed, and directed? Could U.S. and European neocolonial policies be challenged if Islamic immigrants in Europe become a critical mass capable of strikes and protests in the streets of London, Paris, Berlin, and Copenhagen? So far, support for Muslim immigrants from European left parties has been tepid at best (Brun and Hersh 2008). Nevertheless, solidarity for a development of this kind seems warranted by the thesis that human rights have priority over the authority of citizens to determine who will become members of the nation.

References

Albahari, Maurizio. 2006. "Death and the Modern State: Making Borders and Sovereignty at the Southern Edges of Europe." Center for Comparative Immigration Studies Working Paper 137 (May).

Alcoff, Linda. 2007. "Comparative Race, Comparative Racisms." In *Race or Ethnicity? On Black and Latino Identity*, edited by Jorge J.E. Gracia, 170–88. Ithaca, N.Y.: Cornell University Press.

Brun, Ellen, and Jacques Hersh. 2008. "The Danish Disease: A Political Culture of Islamophobia." *Monthly Review* 60, no. 2 (June): 11–22.

Cole, Phillip. 2001. *Philosophies of Exclusion: Liberal Political Theory and Immigration*. Edinburgh: Edinburgh University Press.

Davis, Mike. 2001. *Magical Urbanism: Latinos Reinvent the U.S. City*. New York: Verso Press.

Gilens, Martin. 1999. *Why Americans Hate Welfare: Race, Media and Politics and Antipoverty Policy*. Chicago: University of Chicago Press.

Gould, Carol C. 2004. *Globalizing Democracy and Human Rights*. Cambridge: Cambridge University Press.

Guinier, Lani, and Gerald Torres. 2002. *The Miner's Canary: Enlisting Race, Resisting Power, Transforming Democracy*. Cambridge, Mass.: Harvard University Press.

Habermas, Jürgen. 1998. *Between Facts and Norms*. Cambridge, Mass.: MIT Press.

———. 2001. "The Postnational Constellation and the Future of Democracy." In *The Postnational Constellation: Political Essays*, edited by Max Pensky, 58–112. Cambridge: Polity Press.

Haski, Pierre. 2007. "Illegal Aliens: Crocodile Tears, Then Indifference." *Rue 89*, April 6.

Kinder, Donald R., and Lynn M. Sanders. 1996. *Divided by Color: Racial Politics and Democratic Ideals*. Chicago: University of Chicago Press.

Klinker, Philip A., and Rogers M. Smith. 1999. *Unsteady March: The Rise and Decline of Racial Equality in America*. Chicago: University of Chicago Press.

Kymlicka, Will. 2002. *Contemporary Political Philosophy: An Introduction*. New York: Oxford University Press.

Miller, David.*On Nationality*. 1995. New York: Oxford University Press.

Schuman, Howard, Charlotte Steeh, Lawrence Bobo, and Maria Krysan. 1997. *Racial Attitudes in America: Trends and Interpretations*. Cambridge, Mass.: Harvard University Press.

Sears, David O., P. J. Henry, and Rick Kosterman. 2000. "Egalitarian Values and Contemporary Racial Politics." In *Racialized Politics: The Debate About Racism in America*, edited by David O. Sears, Jim Sidanius, and Lawrence Bobo, 75–117. Chicago: University of Chicago Press.

United States Bureau of the Census. 2006. Sept. 5. Available at http://www.census.gov/Press-release/www/releases/archives/facts_for_features_special_editions/007173.html

United States Government Accounting Office. 2006. "Illegal Immigration: Border-Crossing Deaths Have Doubled Since 1995." GAO-06-770.

Walzer, Michael. 1983. *Spheres of Justice: A Defense of Pluralism and Equality*. New York: Basic Books.

INDEX